Woman in Front of A Hut and Tree *(Ink and pastel on paper)*

The English Writings of Rabindranath Tagore

The English Writings of Rabindranath Tagore

Volume Seven

Lectures Addresses

Introduction by

Mohit K. Ray

ATLANTIC
PUBLISHERS & DISTRIBUTORS (P) LTD

Published by
ATLANTIC
PUBLISHERS & DISTRIBUTORS (P) LTD
B-2, Vishal Enclave, Opp. Rajouri Garden,
New Delhi-110027
Phones : 25413460, 25429987, 25466842

Sales Office
7/22, Ansari Road, Darya Ganj,
New Delhi-110002
Phones : 23273880, 23275880, 23280451
Fax : 91-11-23285873
web : www.atlanticbooks.com
e-mail : info@atlanticbooks.com

ISBN 81-269-0760-6 (Vol. VII)
ISBN 81-269-0666-9 (Set)

Printed in India
at Syndicate Binders, NOIDA (U.P.)

CONTENTS

PREFACE

One distinctive feature of the Volumes V-VIII—a feature that marks them out from the previous volumes—is that these volumes include many writings, speeches and utterances of persons other than Tagore. The exigency of the situation and the special character of these volumes make it obligatory to use others' writings, particularly when publishing conversations, interviews, etc.

The volumes offer a wide spectrum of Tagore's English prose pieces—lectures, essays, letters, speeches, tributes, and conversations and interviews. In range and depth these writings show how myriad-minded Tagore was, and how true is Aldous Huxley's assessment that 'he was at once a great idealist and a practical man of actions'. He was a poet with a soaring imagination reaching unimaginable heights, a thinker of the highest order who could also be equally concerned with the miserable condition of the village farmers and engaged in co-operative movement and rural reconstruction. A lover of children, he would write poems for children, write textbooks for them, and would also make a fine analysis of the crisis of civilization. A man of remarkable courage of conviction, he would not hesitate to renounce his knighthood and yet would have his own views about nationalism and would be critical about it. It may not immediately concern us here but the fact remains that the same man started painting when he was around seventy and left us a legacy of some two thousand doodles and paintings which have been praised highly by connoisseurs. A few specimens used in these volumes will justify the accolades. A singer himself, he has left us a collection of, again, some two thousand songs. These facts do not immediately concern us here but they are relevant in giving us an idea of the mighty stature of Tagore about whom we can always say what Arnold said about

Shakespeare: "Others abide our questions; Thou art free./ We ask and ask, thou smilest and art still, outtopping knowledge." And, unlike Shakespeare who remained confined only to drama and poetry, Tagore traversed all the fields of literary universe and whatever he touched turned into gold. He was not only a 'world poet', 'a great sentinel' or 'a universal man' but also an artist of the highest order.

We begin this set of volumes with the speech that Tagore delivered at Stockholm in 1921. Since Tagore could not attend the Nobel Award Ceremony at Stockholm in 1913, this speech may be regarded as 'the Nobel Prize Acceptance Speech'. The speech very succinctly describes 'the growth of a poet's mind'. We learn about his early exposure to Nature, how he 'used to live in utmost seclusion in the solitude of an obscure Bengal village by the river Ganges in a boat house', his growing love for the children, his translation of the *Gitanjali* 'without having any desire to have them published, being diffident of my mastery of that language', his enthusiastic reception in the West, his faith in the cultural heritage of India, for all its splendours and wisdom and wealth, his identification of the spirit of India as 'the ideal of unity' which he considers as 'the highest aim of our spiritual exertion to be able to penetrate all things with one soul, to comprehend all things as they are, and not to keep out anything in the whole universe—to comprehend all things with sympathy and love'. The speech, in brief, gives us an idea, though in an embryonic form, of the quality and substance of Tagore's vision of man and India. All his writings can be seen as elaborate manifestations of this vision in diverse forms.

ESSAYS

Thoughts from Rabindranath Tagore was first published by Macmillan, New York, in 1921 under the title *Thought Relic,* with 103 pages. The next edition edited by C.F. Andrews came out in 1929 under the title *Thoughts from Tagore* divided into three parts and containing 192 passages. The passages are meditative in nature.

The first edition of *The Religion of Man,* originally delivered as Hibbert Lectures at Manchester College, Oxford, in May

1930, was published by Allen and Unwin in 1930. Tagore made many major corrections in the edition and Macmillan, New York, brought out the second edition, incorporating all these changes, in 1931. The text reproduced here is the second edition. It should, however, be borne in mind, that these lectures are different from Kamala lectures delivered in Calcutta, published as *Mānuṣer Dharma* (Religion of Man) in Bengali, though there is a marked affinity in tone and temper.

Man was originally delivered as a course of three lectures, at Andhra University, in 1933.

Letters to a Friend, a revised and enlarged edition of *Letters from Abroad* (1922), was published by George Allen and Unwin, London, in 1928. The Preface and the first two essays are written by Charles Freer Andrews (1871–1940). These are also reproduced for a proper understanding of the letters. It is for the same reason that Andrews has presented the letters in several chapters with introductory notes. The letter dated 21 April was actually written not to Andrews but to Rothenstein with a copy to Andrews who by mistake included it in the volume.

Mahatmaji and the Depressed Humanity was published by the Visva-Bharati Bookshop, Calcutta, in 1932. The book contains lectures, essays, telegrams, etc., occasioned by Gandhi's decision to 'fast unto death' in protest 'against the communal award by Prime Minister Ramsay MacDonald'.

East and West, containing the letters exchanged between Gilbert Murray (1866–1957) and Tagore, was first published in Paris in 1935. Murray, because of his Greek scholarship and love of liberal values, was a great admirer of the poetry of Tagore.

LECTURES AND ADDRESSES

Race Conflict, originally an address delivered at the Congress of the National Federation of Religious Liberals held at Rochester, New York, in 1912, was published in *The Modern Review* in 1913.

The Spirit of Japan, originally a lecture delivered in Japan in 1915, was first published in *The Modern Review* in June 1917.

The Meeting of the East and the West, a critique of the contemporary political situation in India and originally published in the *Manchester Guardian,* was reprinted in *The Modern Review* in June 1918.

At the Cross Roads, also an essay on the political situation in India, was published in *The Modern Review* in July 1918.

The Message of the Forest, originally a lecture delivered in Bangalore on the occasion of the Festival of Fine Arts in January 1919, was published in its revised and enlarged version in May 1919.

Construction Versus Creation, originally an address delivered at the Gujarat Literary Conference, Ahmedabad, on 2 April 1920, was included in *Letters and Addresses,* edited by Anthony X. Soares and published in 1920.

A Cry for Peace was first published in *The Modern Review* in May 1919.

The Call of Truth, a criticism of Gandhi's non-cooperation movement, was published in *The Modern Review* in October 1921.

The Union of Cultures was published in *The Modern Review* in November 1921. The idea contained in the essay later crystallized in the form of Visva-Bharati, an international university.

A Vision of India's History was first published in *Visva-Bharati Quarterly* in 1923.

The Way to Unity was published in *Visva-Bharati Quarterly* in July 1923.

International Relations, originally a lecture delivered in Japan, was first published in *Visva-Bharati Quarterly* in 1924.

The Indo-Iranians was first published in *Visva-Bharati Quarterly*, Vol. 1, No. 3, October 1922.

Notes and Comments was first published in *Visva-Bharati Quarterly* in January 1924.

The Fourfold Way of India was first published in *The Modern Review* in August 1924.

The Schoolmaster was published in *The Modern Review* in October 1924.

City and Village, originally a lecture delivered in Turin, Italy, was published in *Visva-Bharati Quarterly* in October 1924.

The Voice of Humanity, originally a lecture delivered at Milan, during his first visit to Italy under Mussolini, was published in *Lectures and Addresses* in 1928.

The Indian Ideal of Marriage, based on the Bengali essay *Bhāratīya Bibāher Ādarśa* was published in *Visva-Bharati Quarterly* in July 1925.

The Cult of the Charka was published in *The Modern Review* in September 1995.

Judgment was published in *Visva-Bharati Quarterly* in October 1925.

The Philosophy of Our People, originally delivered as the Presidential Address at the First Indian Philosophical Congress in 1925, was published in *Visva-Bharati Quarterly* in January 1926.

The Rule of the Giant, originally a lecture delivered at Dhaka University, was published in *Visva-Bharati Quarterly* in July 1926.

The Meaning of Art, originally a lecture delivered at Dhaka University, was published in *Visva-Bharati Quarterly* in April 1926.

Notes and Comments, originally published in *Atlantic Monthly*, was reprinted in *Visva-Bharati Quarterly* in April 1927.

The Principle of Literature was first published in *Visva-Bharati Quarterly* in July 1927.

The Function of a Library was published in *Visva-Bharati Bulletin* in January 1929.

On Oriental Culture and Japan's Mission, originally a lecture delivered in Tokyo on 15 May 1929, was published by Indo-Japanese Association, Tokyo.

Ideals of Education, originally an address delivered in Tokyo in 1929, was published in *Visva-Bharati Quarterly* in April-July 1929.

The Philosophy of Leisure, originally an address delivered in Canada, was published in *Visva-Bharati Quarterly* in April-July 1929.

India and Europe was published in *Visva-Bhàrati Quarterly* in April-July 1929.

Wealth and Welfare was published in *The Modern Review* in February 1930.

The Educational Mission of the Visva-Bharati, originally a lecture broadcast by Radio New York, was published in *The Modern Review* in June 1931.

Meeting of the East and the West, originally an address delivered at a reception in New York in 1930, was published in *Visva-Bharati Quarterly,* Vol. 8, Part-3, 1930-31.

My Pictures was first published in *The Modern Review* in December 1930.

The First and the Last Prophets of Persia, a summary of a speech delivered at New History Society, New York in 1930, was published in *Visva-Bharati Quarterly*, Vol. 8, Part-4, 1931-32.

My School was first published in *The Modern Review* in January 1931.

International Goodwill is a summary of the speech at the All Peoples' Association, London, on 8th January 1931.

Lectures in Iran and Iraq are lectures that Tagore delivered during his visits to Iran and Iraq in 1932.

Asia's Response to the Call of the New Age, originally an address delivered in Teheran, was published in *The Modern Review*, October 1932.

Can Science be Humanised? was published in *Visva-Bharati News,* August 1934.

Rammohun Roy, originally the Presidential Address at Rammohun Roy Death Centenary, was published in *The Modern Review* in March 1933.

To the Youth of Hyderabad, originally a lecture delivered in Hyderabad in 1933, was published in 1963 (with a brief note by Padmaja Naidu).

Women's Place in the World is originally an address delivered at the All-India Women's Conference, Calcutta, in 1933-34 (24 Dec-2 Jan).

Reply to the Madras Corporation Address was first published in *Visva-Bharati News* in November 1934.

The Religion of an Artist was first published in *Visva-Bharati Quarterly* in April 1926 under the title "Meaning of Art", and later a revised version was published in *Contemporary Indian Philosophy* in 1936. It was also published in book form by Visva-Bharati in 1953.

To the Citizens of Delhi was first published in *Visva-Bharati News*, May-June 1936.

The Communal Award, originally the Presidential Address at a Conference held in Calcutta in 1936 to discuss the Communal Award, was first published by Dr Radhakumud Mukherjee.

Address at the Parliament of Religions, originally the Presidential Address at the Sri Ramakrishna Centenary Parliament of Religions, Calcutta, in March 1937, was published in *Visva-Bharati Quarterly* in May 1937.

China and India, originally an address delivered on the occasion of opening the 'Cheena Bhavan' at Santiniketan on 14 April 1937, was published by Prabhat Kumar Mukherjee.

To Subhas Chandra Bose is a translation by Tagore himself of his original Bengali address entitled *Deśañayak* written in May 1939.

Convocation Address at Gurukula Kangri, convocation address to the graduates of Gurukula Kangri, is available in typescript at Rabindra Bhavan, Santiniketan.

Crisis in Civilisation, Tagore's last public address, delivered on 14 April 1941, was published in *Visva-Bharati News*, Vol. 9, No. 2 and in *The Modern Review* in May 1941.

MISCELLANEOUS WRITINGS

A. Open Letters, Speeches, Tributes, etc.

The letter *The Problem of India* was first published in *The Modern Review* August 1910.

The letter *Spiritual Civilisation* was first published in *Visva-Bharati News* in October-November 1933.

National Language of India, Part 1 & 2 were published on 21 January 1918 and 26 March 1937, respectively.

The Object and Subject of a Story was first published in *The Modern Review* in September 1918.

The letter *Vernaculars for the M.A. Degree* was published in *The Modern Review* in November 1918.

The letter *Hindu Intercaste Marriage Validating Bill*, originally sent to the Editor of *Bharat Sevak*, was reprinted in *The Modern Review* in February 1919.

This Youth which Lies Hidden in My Heart was published in *The Modern Review* in February 1919.

On Some Educational Questions, first published in *The Mysore Economic Journal* under the title "Sir Rabindranath Tagore's Views on Some Educational Questions", was reprinted in *The Modern Review* in April 1919.

Poet's Contribution to Your Noble Work is Tagore's response to Gandhi's letter requesting him for a message on the occasion of launching 'Satyagraha' against the 'Rowlatt Act'.

The letter *When Badges of Honour Make Our Shame Glaring* evinces Tagore's reaction to the Jallianwallabagh Massacre.

A Great Crime ... in the Name of Law is Tagore's message to the first memorial meeting of the Jallianwallabagh Massacre, held in Bombay on 13 April 1923.

On British Mentality in Relation to India was published in *The Modern Review* in April 1921.

The Efficacy of Ahimsa was published in *The Bengalee* on 3 February 1922.

Message to the Young was published in *Visva-Bharati News* in July 1934.

Introducing Elmherst appeared on the occasion of Elmherst's arrival at Santiniketan in 1921.

Farewell to Dr. M. Winternitz was reprinted in *Visva-Bharati Quarterly,* October 1923.

To My Ceylon Audience was published in *Visva-Bharati Quarterly* in January 1924.

The *Letter to Lord Lytton* was written on 22 August 1924 in reaction to Lord Lytton's comment on Indian women.

The letter *Birth Control Movement* written on 30 September 1925 to Margaret Sanger, Editor, *Birth Control Review,* was published in *Amrita Bazar Patrika* on 5 January 1926.

Knighthood was published in *The Modern Review* in February 1926.

Deshbandhu Chittaranjan Das is Tagore's message of condolence on the death of Chittaranjan Das on 16 June 1925.

Romain Rolland was written in 1925 and included in *Rolland and Tagore* (1945), edited by Alex Aronson.

Farewell Address to Carlo Formichi was originally delivered in 1925. Later it was published in *Visva-Bharati Quarterly* in 1926.

Philosophy of Fascism was published in *Manchester Guardian* on 5 August 1926.

Fascism Denounced, a rejoinder to Formichi's letter (*Manchester Guardian,* 25 August 1926), was published in *Manchester Guardian* on 15 September 1926.

Protest against the Policy of Repression was published on 3 February 1927.

Henry Barbusse's Appeal: Tagore's Response was published in *Visva-Bharati Bulletin* in July 1927.

Freedom, a letter to J.T. Sunderland (who was writing a book on Indian struggle for independence) was written in February 1927.

Mother India, the first letter registering Tagore's protest against Catherine Mayo's *Mother India*, was first published in *Manchester Guardian* in October 1927; the second letter was addressed to the editor, *Nation*, New York, on 9 December 1927.

Colour Prejudice, a letter—Tagore's protest against colour prejudice—was published in *The Modern Review* in April 1928.

To the World League for Peace was written on 3 September 1928.

At the Immigration Office, originally published in *The Japan Adviser*, Tokyo, was reprinted in *Visva-Bharati Quarterly* in November 1929.

East is East was published in *Visva-Bharati Quarterly* in April-July 1929.

Protest Against the Arrest of Mahatma Gandhi was published in *Manchester Guardian* on 16 May 1930.

India: An Appeal to Idealism was published in *Spectator* on 7 June 1930.

Race and Colour Prejudice was published in *The Friend* on 13 June 1930.

Faith in British Justice was published in *Spectator*, London, on 30 August 1930.

Message to the Quaker Society of Friends was published in *Visva-Bharati Quarterly*, Vol. 8, Part-4.

I am Proud of My People was published in *Natal Witness* on 20 September 1930.

Statement Contradicted was published in *The New York Times* on 10 October 1930.

The Women's International League, originally published in *Pax International*, was reprinted in *The Modern Review* in November 1930.

The Colour Bar was published in *Spectator* on 17 April 1931.

Takagaki: Professor Nokuzo Takagaki was a Japanese expert in *Jujitsu*, and came to Santiniketan in 1929, and stayed for about two years.

India and Britain was published in *The Times* on 16 May 1931, and later in *The Modern Review* in July 1931.

On Proselytism was published in *Indian Social Reformer,* Bombay on 11 July 1931.

Sarnath is the text of the message sent by Tagore on the inauguration of the reconstructed *Vihar* at Sarnath.

Imprisonment of Gandhi is the cable sent by Tagore in protest against government repression.

Message to Iraq Air Force was sent to the Priest of the Iraq Air-Force on 13 April 1932.

The World's Children was published in *The World's Children* in September 1932.

Appeal to America was published in *Dharma,* New York in July-December 1932.

Welcome Address to Professor Davoud is the text of the formal welcome speech of Tagore on 9 January 1933.

On the Centenary of Wilberforce is the text of the message sent to the Centenary Celebration Meeting at Hull in honour of William Wilberforce.

Deshapriya J.M. Sengupta was published in *Visva-Bharati News* in August 1933.

Homage to Islam is the message on Sirat un Nabi that was published in *Forward* on 27 November 1933. The other message was published in *The Peshwa,* Delhi, in February 1936.

Bihar Earthquake and the Mahatma is Tagore's reaction to Mahatma's observations on the calamity on 15 January 1934.

The letter *Protest Against the Nazis* was published in *Israel's Messenger* on 3 August 1934.

My Ideals with regard to the Sreebhavana was published in *Visva-Bharati News* in August 1934.

Communal Award: To Madan Mohan Malviya is statements recording Tagore's position in regard to the Communal Award made by Ramsay McDonald.

Farewell to Abdul Ghafar Khan: Abdul Ghafar Khan came to visit Santiniketan to meet his son who was then a student at Kalabhavan.

My Young Friends was published in *Visva-Bharati News* in December 1934.

A Letter to an English Friend was published in *Visva-Bharati News* in December 1935.

Ishopanishat was published in *Visva-Bharati News* in April 1935.

Ramchandra Sharma Undertakes Fast: Tagore's Appeal was occasioned by Ramchandra Sharma's fast to stop animal sacrifice in the Kalighat temple in September 1935.

A Message of Condolence to Maharajkumari Vidyavati Devi of Kasmunda on the occasion of her personal bereavement.

To Indian National Congress was published in *Visva-Bharati News* in January 1936.

The Rice We Eat was published in *Visva-Bharati News* in January 1936.

Message to World Peace Congress was sent to Brussels on 5 September 1936.

New Education Fellowship was published in *Visva-Bharati News* in February 1936.

The English in India was published in *Manchester Guardian* on 2 October 1936.

Spanish Civil War was published in a pamphlet entitled *Spain* (Calcutta) in March 1937.

Appeal to the United Party of Sind was published in *The Hindu* on 25 April 1937.

In Defence of the Workers on Strike was published in *The Hindu* on 30 April 1937.

On India was published in *Visva-Bharati News* in July 1937.

Appeal for Andaman Prisoners was occasioned by the demand of the release of the Andaman prisoners in August 1937.

In Response to Rasbehari Bose's Appeal was Tagore's response to Rashbehari Bose's cable on the issue of Indo-Japanese friendship.

Vande Mataram was written in response to Jawaharlal Nehru's request to dispel confusions regarding the song.

Appeal to Journalists was published in *The Amrita Bazar Patrika* on 25 December 1937.

Jagadish Chandra Bose was published in *Visva-Bharati News* in December 1937.

The British Constitution in India was published in *Manchester Guardian* on 10 March 1938 and reprinted in *Visva-Bharati News* in April 1938.

To the People of China: Section 1 was published in *Visva-Bharati News* in July 1938 and Section 2 was published in *The Amrita Bazar Patrika* on 26 December 1939.

'Fascism' of the State of Travancore was published in *The Amrita Bazar Patrika* on 6 October 1938.

Letters to Czechoslovakia records Tagore's sympathy for the suffering Czechoslovakians.

Tagore and Noguchi was published in *Visva-Bharati Quarterly* in November 1938 under the title "Poet to Poet".

W.B. Yeats was published in *Hindusthan Standard* on 1 January 1939.

Bihar Cooperative Federation: 21st Conference was published in *Hindusthan Standard* on 22 August 1939.

A Tribute to Mahatma Gandhi was published in the Commemoration Volume, edited by Dr S. Radhakrishnan, on the occasion of the 70th birthday of Mahatma Gandhi in 1939.

European Order and World Order was published in *The Modern Review* in February 1940.

Freedom of Mind was first published in different newspapers on 4 February 1940, and reprinted in *Visva-Bharati News* in February 1940.

Telegram to Roosevelt is Tagore's telegram to Roosevelt on the occasion of the fall of Paris in June 1940.

Bengal's Great Inheritance records Tagore's reaction to the Secondary Education Bill (December 1940).

Man's Lost Heritage was published in *Visva-Bharati News* in November 1940.

Welcome to Xu Beihong was published in *Visva-Bharati News* in February 1940.

Message to 'Forward' was published in *The Modern Review* in February 1941.

Reply to Miss Rathbone records Tagore's reaction to Miss Rathbone's 'Open Letter to Indian', published in June 1941.

B. On Books

Thirty Songs from the Punjab and Kashmir is Tagore's Foreword to the book that was published in February 1913.

To the Nation is an Introduction to the English translation of Paul Richard's book, published in New York in 1917.

The Web of Indian Life is an Introduction to Sister Nivedita's book *The Web of Indian Life*, written on 21 October 1917.

A Great Channel for Communication is a Foreword to the Bengali Book of English Verse, published by Longman's Greene & Co., Bombay, 1918.

The Robbery of the Soil is an Introduction to L.K. Elmherst's book *The Robbery of the Soil.* It was read as lecture on 28 July 1922.

Zoroastrian Hymns is an Introduction, originally published by Macmillan, New York, in 1924.

The Case for India was published in *The Modern Review,* March 1931.

Voiceless India is Foreword to the book published in 1930 from America.

Christ was published in *Visva-Bharati News,* March 1933.

Rebel India is Tagore's review of the book, published in *The Modern Review* in January 1933.

Preface to 'Deliverance' is Preface to Sarat Chandra Chatterjee's *Niskriti* translated by Dilip K. Roy, and published in 1944.

When Peacocks Called is Foreword to Hilde Seligman's *When Peacocks Call* (1940).

CONVERSATIONS AND INTERVIEWS

Marguerite Wilkinson and Tagore was published in *The Touchstone,* New York, in February 1921.

Benedetto Croce and Tagore was published in *Visva-Bharati Quarterly,* October 1936.

Romain Rolland and Tagore was published in *Rolland and Tagore* (Visva-Bharati, 1945).

Salvadori and Tagore was published in *Visva-Bharati Quarterly,* October 1926.

Angelica Balban and Tagore was printed in *My Life as a Rebel,* published in New York (1965).

Interview with F.L. Minigerode was published in *The Weekly Press*, New Zealand, 2 December 1926.

H.G. Wells and Tagore was published in *A Tagore Reader* [Ed. Amiya Chakrabarty], Boston, 1961.

Einstein and Tagore was published in *The New York Times* on 10 August 1930.

Conversations in Russia was published in *The Modern Review* in November-December 1930.

Interview with the 'Jewish Standard': On the Palestinian Problem was published on 28 November 1930 (reprinted in *Rabindra-Bhavana,* autumn, 1990).

Interviews in Persia was originally published in *Parasya-Yatri* in 1933.

Tagore on Films was published in *The Observer,* London, on 8 August 1925.

MOHIT K. RAY

LECTURES AND ADDRESSES

International Relations

When I was about to start for my tour in China and Japan there was an enthusiastic meeting in Calcutta, where my countrymen came together to express their joy at my taking this journey to the great Eastern countries. I felt with a sense of delight that the consciousness of kinship was waxing stronger among our people and that its growth might lead to a great future for Asia.

My friends who came to wish me happy times on these shores, asked me also to convey to your country their feelings of love and respect for you. They also requested me to ask you to rise above circumstances, favourable or unfavourable, and to prove the dignity of Eastern mind. They are all waiting to see a great Renaissance in Asia through Japan, where life is at its floodtide, and they wish she would wake up to the great responsibility she has, not only to her own people, but to the great continent to which she belongs.

At the same time, they wanted me to offer to your people their heartfelt sympathy for the disaster[1] which has so suddenly overtaken your country. I am sure that the calamities over which you have no hand came to prove your manhood, and are in themselves an opportunity. Disasters only become absolutely disastrous when we know not how to deal with them.

Now that I have come to Japan, I realize with what courage you have accepted your tribulation. I see no sign of despair in your faces; I see that you have within yourselves that indomitable resourcefulness which will help you to make good the loss. I do not mean that they will merely make your position stronger even than before; but the fact that you are able to face misfortune of such an overwhelming nature in the right spirit will gain for you greater prestige among other nations, and give you a firmer confidence in your own power.

1. The great earthquake of 1923.

All great civilizations are built upon numberless ruins—the toppled-down towers of victory and wealth. It is only human beings in this world of life who have found their greatness through the desperate urgings of unfavourable circumstances. Humanity has never been pampered, petted and spoilt by Nature, but rather respected by being given constant opportunity to overcome the obstacles of failures and losses. I believe that what has now happened to you, and has brought your gathered resources of years to the dust in a moment, will inspire you to make a better beginning for a more vigorous experiment. You will realize that the people's life, like a waterfall, finds its full force of movement through courageous leaps from peak to peak of new trials.

This earthquake has only been the cause of physical upset for you, but unfortunately, closely following this, you have also received lately a rude moral shock in your national relations with another people, and this has deeply hurt your people, even more than the former which was only physical, because it has come with deliberate purpose from human hands. And yet what I expect to see among your people at this time of crisis is the same dignity of calm and patient fortitude.

You are on your trial to-day. The eyes of all nations are upon you in this calamity. Great tribulations in our history should never fail to give us the occasion to bring out the best resources of our life, so as not only to reveal them to the outer world, but—and this is more valuable—to reveal them to ourselves. If to-day you can discover some hidden source of magnanimity with which to face the insult and injury, if you can keep the majesty of your mind unimpaired, then you will be happy, and future generations will be thankful to you.

You have discovered one thing, that this earthquake, though but physical, and therefore causing you only material loss, has yet a great similarity to the disturbance of your relations with a Western country;[1] for, the latter is also external, having in it no acknowledgment of moral law. Any relationship which had a

1. America: the reference is to the anti-Japanese emigration laws of the United States.

moral value would have been stronger than before at this time of suffering. But your relationship, as it was, was precarious. Any little event would have proved its hollowness. This was inevitable because it was not based upon the comradeship of human hearts. It had for its basis a sense of mere expediency, that lacked the frankness of youth and had the calculating spirit of senility. It was a treacherously shifting base upon which you could never have built your best hopes.

It is unfortunate that such disillusionment always gives rise to our baser passions. We feel angry and vengeful and eager to retaliate. Only then it becomes a complete defeat. Is it right that you, along with your political defeat, should accept moral defeat? I hope that your people, through your spiritual generosity, through your true pride of civilization and through that sense of hospitality which has been your birthright for centuries, will exercise your mind that has been trained and gifted with a wonderful self-control.

I should deplore very deeply the appearance of any sign of decay in these great traits of character that you possess. This is the time when you can bring out of your store all the wealth of moral heroism that you have inherited from your forefathers. This is the time to put to shame those others who have treated you in this unchivalrous manner, showing that their profession of friendship was all the while waiting for your weak moment, shamelessly to contradict itself. I do not think that any symptom of political hysteria on your part is at all seemly at this time, or in accordance with your national tradition.

If we find you indulging just now in vulgar boisterousness, we shall know that it is weakness, which you have borrowed through those importers of moral drugs from abroad. We have been schooled in the West, where they have become hypnotized by the sight of open and public expressions of vengefulness, the modern version of the naked war-dance of the savage. I hope that you will be saved from this. Real suicide it would be, if you were to forget your own true character and the fact that there is a kind of death far worse than physical death itself.

In the East, we have had the courage to have faith even in impossible ideals. You all know that it was a prophet of the East who could say, 'Love your enemies.' You know, too, of another prophet of the East who could say, 'Conquer anger by non-anger and evil by goodness.' There are those in the West who have accepted these teachings in their churches and yet who feel extremely nervous when they are reminded of them, when they find that such teaching is commercially unprofitable and politically inconvenient. Some of our friends here, who have studied Indian history, will tell you how these ideals have been pursued and believed in, and how men went to extreme lengths of non-killing, of non-violence, and of non-anger.

You have perhaps also learnt from the newspapers how a prophet[1] has arisen in India, who has likewise proclaimed that you have to conquer violence by non-violence. He speaks like a prophet of the East and insists that what has been translated into the Bible of the West must not only be pursued in the personal lives of individuals but must be given the best possible expression in our national lives.

Perhaps most of you will not accept this teaching—you will not be able to apply it to your national life. I understand your misgivings and sympathize with you in your want of faith. But let us discuss this point.

There was a time when our lives were simpler, when the spirit of the people was hospitable. This spirit has been overcome by the spirit of the Nation, with its intense consciousness of self-interest concentrated in political organization. Such an unlimited cultivation of over-consciousness of self by the whole people must inevitably produce its harvest of suspicion, hatred and inhospitable exclusiveness. And, therefore, if you have been rudely treated by a nation, and abruptly hustled out whenever it has been safe for it to disclose its moral crudity, there is no cause for surprise. It is of no use to be angry either against the earthquake, or against such eruptions of moral catastrophe, which are inevitable when this phenomenon that we term the Nation is rampant.

---

1. Mahatma Gandhi.

To be just and fair, you have to acknowledge that you also have been unjust and grasping where your nation has had a safe opportunity to manifest its evil aspect. I have a deep love and respect for you as a people, but when as a nation you also can be deceptive, cruel and efficient in handling those methods in which the Western nations show such mastery. You must not plume yourselves that when you are suffering from smallpox your skin and temperature behave better than those of other people who have the same malady.

Let us consider how this demoniacal power of the Nation has arisen. The nature of the people depends for its manifestation upon its creative personality. It has religion, arts, literature, traditions of social responsibility and cooperation. Its wealth to maintain itself and power of defence are secondary; they are not the ultimate ends for the people. But the Nation manifests itself in its property. The people represent life, the nation materials; when they are in harmony, that is to say, when material possessions keep to their own limits and the creative life is unhampered in its spontaneous activity, then civilization is hospitable and generous. This being the case in the olden times it was possible for India to find her home in the heart of China and Japan, and your administrators did not busy themselves to find out if some groups of idealists, freed from barriers of passport offices, were finding access to the heart of your country, instead of into its goals with police spies at their heels.

But when material possessions become too vast for a people, or when in competition with others the desire for material wealth rouses its ambition, then all its time and mind are occupied with very little else. The man who is a 'millionaire' is dragged by the very weight of his millions to the path of the multitude of millions. Then he has no time for culture, or for the poetry of life; he strictly barricades himself against visitors whom he cannot but suspect to be self-seekers, being selfish in his own outlook upon life. In other words he becomes professional, and the human in him is banished into the shade.

Since Nature's storehouse of power and wealth has been opened by the help of science, some people who know how to take advantage of it have suddenly grown enormously rich and others are incited to follow their example. The people who were human, who were creative and social in their self-expression, have become professional, enormously self-centred and anti-social in their tendency of mind. Material wealth and power, with their very bulk, have occupied the greater part of the space, time and mind of the people, necessitating a tremendous expense of thought and resources for ensuring their safety.

Material possessions create the worst divisions in human society when they are disproportionately big and naturally unmindful of moral responsibility. Therefore the Nation, the presiding genius of the material department of the people, cannot but be hard and exclusive. And in the modern age this department has become the most proudly domineering of all other manifestations of human society. It has made the craving for money universal and has given the name of Progress to the raising of the material standard of living.

We all know how those who are immoderately rich suffer from a sense of class distinction; how money, which is a dead thing, acts as an impenetrable wall around their self-imprisonment. Within this dungeon of illusion they are proud of their segregation. This process is going on not only with individuals, but with the prosperous nations. And it is just these prosperous nations which become most suspicious of idealism, which barricade their doors with spies, police and prohibitions in order to safeguard their citadel of wealth, where the human spirit languishes and where there is no touch of life.

Such nations are doomed and they carry the curse of God in their money-bags. They will die in the very enclosures which they have built for themselves—enclosures of wealth, of high walls of national distinction impenetrable for others. Yet these are the people who once professed faith in a man, and even accepted him to be their God, who said it was easier for a camel to pass through the needle's eye than for the rich to find access to the Kingdom of Heaven.

The Kingdom of Heaven is here on this earth. It is there, where we realize our best relations with our fellow-beings, where there is no mutual suspicion and misunderstanding—

there is the Kingdom of Heaven, in the spirit of comradeship and love. Christ was right when He said that the path to such a Kingdom is closed for him who thinks more of his money than of his soul, more of his soul, more of his personal right than of his human responsibility. Now that the whole human world has surrendered itself to the lure of money and power, the severance of human relationship is everywhere becoming evident and the fight between classes is spreading wide.

If you must have peace you will have to fight the spirit of this demon, the Nation. You may think it hopeless, but do you not realize that its first appearance was not so long ago, not more than two centuries; that it has not the sign of immortality upon it, that already it is tottering towards its downfall? You must know that if we cling to this sinking ship we also shall be drowned.

Let me appeal to your imagination. If we could go back into the distant past, we would know of facts that are not in histories. We would know that groups of men grew into great peoples through overcoming a feeling of distrust and cultivating sympathy for each other. It was not at all easy; for our passions are individualistic, our selfishness immensely strong. And yet the impossible has been attained in some societies. A system of discipline has been established, the sentiments of sympathy cultivated, and the ferocious savage has been tamed on a wholesale scale. We must also know that those who went on indulging in their selfish isolation perished.

Suppose that the idealists had been there in those days, and that they had had the courage to speak to those who still believed in robbery and muscular brutality and to warn them that they would never form great nations, do you think that they would have been listened to? They would promptly have been eaten up!

In the early history of life in this world, with its display of stupendous bodily bulk and strength, when puny man first appeared on this earth, could his final victory have been predicated by the logic of appearances? In the same manner, it is apparently unbelievable today that only those who can overcome the egoistic sense of nationalism, who can develop the understanding of sympathy that pierces through barriers of race differences, who have the enduring strength of meekness, will inherit the earth; and not those who are imagined to be born rulers of men.

Often have my Western friends almost sneeringly said to me that we in the East have no faith in Democracy, and thereupon they have asserted the superiority of their own mind over ours. Not being combative, I did not want to argue the matter and contradict them in their deep-rooted illusion. I know that in our part of the world we have some people who, as being of noble descent, are considered aristocrats, and enjoy special rights. My Western friends believe that they have no such anomalies in their part of the world.

Be that as it may, one thing they must admit, that because our aristocracy is restricted to a narrow circle, the rest of the people have the true democratic spirit, which is the spirit of the community. About one thing there can be no difference of opinion, that we never had an aristocracy of the whole people, like this monstrous aristocracy so proud of its European blood, which has no pity for others who are darker in colour, for those Asiatics and Africans who can be exploited with impunity, as the common people used to be exploited in France before the revolution broke out.

These monster aristocrats consider us to be plebeian because we are of another continent. While loudly protesting their democracy, they extort false evidence from a make-believe science to prove their race superiority and their right to inherit the earth. These aristocrats of monstrous girth and open jaws are out to feast upon the life-blood of peoples whom they have dubbed ignoble, who are expected to feel grateful for providing comfort to the Nordic race with their own extinction. They assert their race aristocracy, not merely through their home-made science, but through the coercion of darker continents to slavery by the shattering argument of bombs. Today, they are almost openly ready to drop their pretensions to moral culture; but nevertheless they cling to their two illusions, the one of the Nordic race, and the other of Democracy.

We, who do not profess democracy, acknowledge our human obligations and have faith in our code of honour. But are you also going to allow yourselves to be tempted by the contagion of this belief in your own hungry right of inborn superiority, bearing the false name of democracy? Leave the unreality of these professions; hold up to us something which is your very own and not mere imitation. Do you not see how this malady of imitation is rapidly spreading from shore to shore, from nation to nation? It has the same monotony of features, in its offices, barracks, dress and manners, its attitude of mind. Every people in this world is vying with its neighbour to copy it, because being non-living it is easy to copy indefinitely. It is a mask that can be precisely similar in its multiplication, not a face which has spontaneous variety of self-expression.

But the mask can easily smother the living individuality of the face. That is what is happening everywhere in the world—the monotony of the nation killing the individuality of the people. The stone pavement, which can be made in the same stereotyped plan everywhere, deprives the soil of its unique personality of flowers and harvest. Through this deadening influence even your arts and crafts, all the delicate idioms of expression in your life and surroundings, are fast losing their own living character and stiffening into the standardized convention made in a foreign world. The Nation makes this mould, which may be useful; but we cannot afford to pay its cost with the inspiration of creative life, which is inherent in living peoples.

It is the people in the Western countries that have produced its literature, its art, its music and dance; it is the spirit of the people that spoke through the voice of the great dramatists and artists of Greece, through the voice of Dante, Shakespeare and Goethe; it is the soul of your people which reigns in your homes, giving them a profound quiet of beauty, in the dignified self-control of your behaviour, in the combination of usefulness and grace in all things that you produce, in your inimitable paintings and dramatic performances.

But what are these products of the Nation—the machinery of destruction and profit-making, the double-dealings of diplomacy—in the face of which moral obligation lies defeated and the spirit of human brotherhood destroyed? You have been tempted, or perhaps almost compelled, to accept them; and we in India are envying you, ready for ourselves to accept as much of them as comes our way. The cruelty and meanness of lies and exaggeration and the greed of self-seeking are creeping up over that soil on which were born those great sages who preached *maitri* and self-emancipation.

Whenever the spirit of the Nation has come it has destroyed sympathy and beauty, and driven out the generous obligations of human relationship from the hearts of men. It has spread the ugliness of its cities and its markets into the minds and enthroned the demon of deformity in the hearts of men. Though today it dominates the spirit of man everywhere in the world, it will die like the worm which lies in the heart of the fruit that it has devoured. It will die; but unfortunately it may meanwhile destroy things of unrivalled worth, the products of centuries of self-control and spiritual training.

I have come to warn you in Japan—the country where I wrote my first lectures against Nationalism at a time when people laughed my ideas to scorn. They thought that I did not know the meaning of the word, and accused me of having confused the word Nation with State. But I stuck to my conviction, and now after the war do you not hear everywhere the denunciation of this spirit of the Nation, this collective egoism of the people, which is universally hardening their hearts?

I have come once again to remind you. I hope to be able to meet individuals in this country who have the courage of faith needed to bring about a great future. Let Japan find her own true mind, which will not merely accept lessons from others, but will create a world of her own, which will be generous of its gifts to all humanity. Make all other peoples of Asia proud in their acknowledgment of your greatness, which is not based upon the enslavement of victims, upon the accumulation of material wealth exclusively for your own enjoyment—wealth which is not accepted by man for all time and is rejected by God.

1924

The Indo-Iranians

Pods burst, and winged seeds are borne away by the winds to distant soils where, in combination with new environments, variations are produced, and nature, full of creative curiosity, is given opportunity for making new experiments. In the history of man, such experiments have been made with races, driven by some ethnic storm, who reached lands far away from their original habitation, different in climate and surroundings.

The Indo-Iranian people, like a great river, started on their nomad career from their now-forgotten land of birth, in some obscure dawn of history. At last the current of emigration divided into two streams, one finding its destination in the west of the Hindukush, and the other pouring into the plains of India through some gap in its mountain barrier. There are vague records of a conflict of creeds in the Aryan race even before it had bifurcated into its Iranian and Indian branches. And both these communities carried away with them the seeds of that conflict which afterwards had their different stages of development in their respective soils.

The two people, though racially one, were placed in environments which were greatly different. The Iranians had for their neighbours the western races of Asia, who, in the main, were their equals both in physical features and mental gifts; and so they were never faced with the multifarious moral and spiritual problems resulting from colour distinction and from conflicting contact with races most of whom were inferior to them in culture. But such were the conditions which their destiny imposed upon the Aryans who came to India. There is also another fact, which distinguishes the Indian Aryans from all other branches of this race; it is that they were the one people who evolved a civilization of a high order in a country which is tropical in climate.

That such difference of circumstances and surroundings should produce different characteristics in brother communities, separated for long centuries, is only what can be expected. There are scholars, who have taken up the task of comparing these two peoples, dwelling only on the contrast which they present in their ideals. But certainly it is of equal if not greater importance to trace some underlying strand of unity in their development of mind, owing to their common race. That their growth of life should take opposite directions reaching to absolute contradiction, cannot be natural; and history, as far as it can be accurately traced, does not point in that direction.

The most important of all outstanding facts of Iranian history is the religious reform brought about by Zarathushtra. There can be hardly any question, that he was the first man we know who gave a definitely moral character and direction to religion, and at the same time preached the doctrine of monotheism which offered an eternal foundation of reality to goodness as an ideal of perfection. All the religions of the primitive type try to keep men bound with regulations of external observances. These, no doubt, have the hypnotic effect of vaguely suggesting a realm of right and wrong, but the dimness of light produces phantasms, leaving men to aberrations. Zarathushtra was the greatest of all the pioneer prophets who showed the path of freedom to man, the freedom of moral choice, the freedom from the blind obedience to unmeaning injunctions, freedom from the multiplicity of shrines which distract our worship from the single-minded chastity of devotion.

To most of us, it sounds like a truism to-day when we are told that the moral goodness of a deed comes from the goodness of intention. But it is a truth which once came to man like a revelation of light in the darkness, and has not yet reached all the obscure corners of humanity. We still see around us men who fearfully follow, hoping thereby to gain merit, the path of blind formalism, which has no living moral source in the mind. This will make us understand the greatness of Zarathushtra. Though surrounded by believers in magical rites, he proclaimed in those dark days of unreason that religion has its truth in its moral significance, not in external practices of imaginary value; that its value is in upholding man in his life of good thoughts, good words and good deeds.

'That prophet,' say Dr. Geiger, 'qualifies his religion as "unheard of words" (Yasna 31.1) or as a 'mystery' (Y. 48.3) because he himself regards it as a religion quite distinct from the belief of the people hitherto. The revelation he announces, is to him no longer a matter of sentiment, no longer a merely undefined presentiment and conception of the Godhead, but a matter of intellect, of spiritual perception and knowledge. This is of great importance; for there are probably not many religions of so high antiquity in which this fundamental doctrine, that religion is a knowledge or learning, a science of what is true, is so precisely declared as in the tenets of the Gathas. It is the unbelieving that are unknowing; on the contrary, the believing are learned, because they have penetrated into this knowledge.' (Y. 30.3)

We may incidentally mention here, as showing the parallel to this in the development of Indian religious thought, that all through the Upanishad, spiritual truth is termed with a repeated emphasis—*vidyā,* knowledge, which has for its opposite—*avidyā,* acceptance of error, born of unreason.

The outer expression of truth reaches its white light of simplicity through its inner realization. True simplicity is the physiognomy of perfection. In the primitive stage of spiritual growth, when man is dimly aware of the mystery of the infinite in his life and the world, when he does not fully know the inward character of his relationship with this truth, his first feeling is either of dread, or of greed of gain. This drives him into wild exaggeration in worship, frenzied convulsions of ceremonialism. But in Zarathushtra's teachings, which are best reflected in his Gathas, we have hardly any mention of the ritualism of worship. Conduct and its moral motives, such as *Vohumano, Asha* and *Aramaiti,* have there received almost the sole attention.

The orthodox Persian form of worship in ancient Iran included animal sacrifices and offering of *haoma* to the *daevas.* That all these should be discountenanced by Zarathushtra, not only shows his courage, but the strength of his realization of the Supreme Being as spirit. We are told that it has been mentioned by Plutarch, that 'Zarathushtra taught the Persians to sacrifice to Ahura Mazda "vows and thanks-giving".' The distance between faith in the efficacy of the bloodstained magical rites, and cultivation of the moral and spiritual ideals as the true form of worship, is immense. It is amazing to see how Zarathushtra was the first among men who crossed this distance with a certainty of realization which imparted such a fervour of faith to his life and his words. The truth which filled his mind was not a thing which he borrowed from books, or received from teachers; he did not come to it by following a prescribed path of tradition, but it came to him as an illumination of his entire life, almost like a communication to his personal self, and he proclaimed this utmost immediacy of his knowledge when he said:

When I conceived of Thee, O Mazda, as the very First and the Last, as the most Adorable One, as the Father of Good Thought, as the Creator of Truth and Right, as the Lord Judge of our actions in life, then I made a place for Thee in my very eyes. (Yasna 31.8) (Translation D.J. Irani)

It was the direct stirring of his soul which made him say:

Thus do I announce the Greatest of all! I weave my songs of praise for him through Truth, helpful and beneficent of all that live. Let Ahura Mazda listen to them with His Holy Spirit, for the Good Mind instructed me to adore Him; by his Wisdom let Him teach me about what is best. (Yasna 45.6) (D.J. Iran.)

The truth, which is not reached through the analytical process of reasoning, and does not depend for proof on some corroboration of outward facts or the prevalent faith and practice of the people,—the truth, which comes like an inspiration, out of context with its surroundings, brings with it an assurance that it has been sent from a divine source of wisdom, that the individual who has received it is specially chosen and therefore has his responsibility as the messenger of God. Zarathushtra felt this sacredness of his mission and believed himself to be the direct medium of communication of Divine Truth.

So long as man deals with his God as the dispenser of benefits only to those of His worshippers who know the secret of propitiating Him, he tries to keep Him for his own self or for the tribe to which he belongs. But directly the moral or spiritual nature of God is apprehended, this knowledge is thrown open to all humanity; and then the idea of God, which first gives unity only to a special people, transcends limitations of race, and gathers together all human beings within one spiritual circle of union. Zarathushtra was the first prophet who emancipated religion from the exclusive narrowness of the tribal God, the God of a chosen people, and offered it to the universal man. This is a great fact in the history of religion. The Master said, when the enlightenment came to him:

Verily, I believed Thee, O Ahura Mazda, to be the Supreme Benevolent Providence, when Sraosha came to me with the Good Mind, when first I received and became wise with Thy words! And though the task be difficult, though woe may come to me, I shall proclaim to all mankind Thy message, which Thou declarest to be the best. (Y. 43.11) (D.J. Irani)

He prays to Mazda:

This I ask Thee, tell me truly, O Ahura, the religion that is best for all mankind, the religion, which based on truth, should prosper all that is ours, the religion which establishes our actions in order and justice by the Divine songs of Perfect Piety, which has for its intelligent desire of desires, the desire for Thee, O Mazda! (Y. 444.10) (D.J. Irani)

With the undoubted assurance and hope of one who has got a direct vision of Truth he speaks to the world:

Harken unto me, Ye, who come from near and from far! Listen, for I shall speak forth now; ponder well over all things weigh my words with care and clear thought. Never shall the false teacher destroy this world for a second time, for his tongue stands mute, his creed exposed. (Y. 45.1) (D.J. Irani)

I think it can be said without doubt that such a high conception of religion, uttered in such a clear note of affirmation, with a sure conviction that it is a truth of the ultimate ideal of perfection which must be revealed to all humanity, even at the cost of martyrdom, is unique in the history of any religion belonging to such a remote dawn of civilization.

There was a time when, along with other Aryan peoples, the Persians also worshipped the elemental gods of nature, whose favour was not to be won by any moral duty performed, or service of love. That, in fact, was the crude beginning of the scientific spirit trying to unlock the hidden sources of power in nature. But through it all there must have been some current of deeper desire, which constantly contradicted the cult of power and indicated a world of inner good, infinitely more precious than material gain. Its voice was not strong at first, nor was it heeded by the majority of the people, but its influence, like the life within the seed, was silently working.

Then comes the great teacher; and in his life and mind the hidden fire of truth suddenly bursts out into flame. The best in the people works for long obscure ages in hints and whispers, till it finds its voice which can never again be silenced. For that voice becomes the voice of man, no longer confined to a particular time or people. It works across intervals of silence and oblivion, depression and defeat, and comes out again and again with its conquering call. It is a call to the fighter, the fighter against untruth, against all that lures away man's spirit from its high mission of freedom into the meshes of materialism.

Zarathushtra's voice is still a living voice,—not alone a matter of academic interest for historical scholars who deal with the dead facts of the past; nor merely the guide of a small community of men in the daily details of their life. Rather, of all Teachers, Zarathushtra was the first who addressed his words to all humanity, regardless of distance of space or time. He was not like a cave-dweller who, by some chance of friction had lighted a lamp, and, fearing lest it could not be shared with all, secured it with a miser's care for his own domestic use. But he was the Watcher in the night, who stood on the lonely peak facing the East and broke out singing the poems of light to the sleeping world when the sun came out on the brim of the horizon. The Sun of Truth is for all, he declared,—its light is to unite the far and the near. Such a message always arouses the antagonism of those whose habits have become nocturnal, whose vested interest is in the darkness. And there was a bitter fight in the lifetime of the prophet between his followers and the others who were addicted to the ceremonies that had tradition on their side, and not truth.

I have said, in the beginning of this paper, that there are indications of a conflict of creed in the Indo-Iranian race, whose seeds were carried away by the two sections into which it was divided. It is a remarkable fact that the Indian Aryans had, among their nature gods, some who represented the moral ideals of man. I can do nothing better than quote from a discussion on the subject by Professor Carnoy of Louvain University. He says:

The religious situation in the other branch of the Aryans, as it is described in the Vedas, shows striking similarities to the Iranian one. There the cult of the Indo-European elemental deities is at the basis of Vedic religion, where the power of the gods and their continuous action in the thorough natural phenomena provide us with an exuberant mythology, but, among the deities the group of the *Aditya* occupies a very special position and stands eminently for the maintenance of the moral law, reproducing to a great extent the characteristics of Ahura Mazda.

Here also there is a triad. Instead of Mazda, Mithra and Anahita, we find Varuna, Mitra and Aryaman. The last member of the triad is different; instead of a goddess of fertilising waters we have a beneficent and healing deity, essentially helpful to man, and invoked at times as the dispenser of beneficent waters. The identity of the first two members on the other hand, is hardly questionable. In India as well as in Iran the eye of Mitra is the sun, with which he is watching over human tribes. His activity is expressed by the verb *vat,* which is also used for the payment of debts (in Rigveda, II.ii. 4, he and Varuna are mentioned as the gods who make men pay their debts). He is the god of contracts and pledges. Those who do not abide by their pledged word are sinning against him, like the *Mithro-druj*, 'breaker of contract', in Iran.

The original identity between Varuna and Mazda is generally accepted. Varuna is the most exalted deity of the Veda. As it was the will of Mazda that had made Darius a King, it is

Varuna's will or command that rules the world. He is the *dhritavrata,* he whose commands are firm and immutable. His will often identified with *rita,* the *asha* or *arta* of the Iranians, which is the great law of the world, moral and material, the principle of all order, causing the sun to rise, rain to fall, rivers to flow, fire to come out of the rubbed sticks *(ritajan agni)* and imposing on man the moral obligations of justice, truth and piety. If man be guilty of rebellion against the *rita,* he becomes loaded with the chains of Varuna and has to pray him to be released from his fetters and obtain the freedom of innocence *(aditi).*

Here the author quotes from the Rigveda the prayer of Sunahshepa to Varuna. 'Sunahshepa bound to three pillars, invokes thee, O Aditya, O Varuna, O King, release him.... May our prayer and our sacrifice release us from thy wrath, of thee who are the King, wise Asura, release us from the chains of the sins which we have committed. May Varuna make loose my chain.... May we then follow thy path and go to Aditi.'

It has been said that the great Asura, Varuna, like an evening star, attained his place in the Vedic worship at an early time, and then losing his distinction disappeared in the nebulae of the Indian nature deities. In the Rigveda we find prayers directly addressed to him asking to be forgiven for transgressions:

However we break thy laws from day to day, men as we are, O God Varuna, do not deliver us unto death, nor to the blow of the furious, nor to the anger of the spiteful.

But we also find the worshipper afraid of Varuna's immutable law of retribution asking Indra to stand between his wrath and the sinner:

On the days when evil men do penance for their sin, on these days be gracious to us, O Indra; the sins which Varuna the wise god, sees in us, from their guilt may Indra deliver us.

There is a curious passage in Chāndogya Upanishat in which the different sound qualities of the hymns associated with different gods are mentioned with appreciation, excepting that of Varuna which is described as ill-sounding, giving, as it were, a hint to the people that the hymn to Varuna must be shunned.

It seems from this that the worshippers of the *Devas,* like a band of light-hearted school children, in their awe of the mysterious idea of sin, tried to play the truant by altogether ignoring Varuna in their rituals.

Then came the time when Indra, representing wealth and power, attained the predominant position in the Vedic Pantheon and Varuna, representing the ideal of righteousness, occupied a subordinate place. In our epics there is no mention of Varuna's having any guiding influence in human affairs, while Indra appears as constantly active in modifying events of history and destinies of individuals. His activities had hardly any moral meaning; they were mostly capricious, and often immoral, like those of his prototype in the Greek mythology.

While admitting all this, I cannot think that the moral principle which was once enthroned in the Indian ideal of Divinity could vanish altogether without even a struggle. There can be no doubt that all through the development of ancient Indian Religion the conflict between the two opposing principles remained active. The history of this struggle remains vague and contradictory, because the later Indian chroniclers represent an age of priestly supremacy in Indian society. As we find in all historical writings obsessed by some political or religious propaganda, the later compilation of legends and historical records in India affords evident traces of suppression and distortion of facts, slurring over of important events and putting wrong emphasis on others. There is no doubt, that we in India had our own special Publicity Department, which had its usual function of selecting and arranging facts according to its particular purpose, thus muddling the memory of the people and inscribing on it impressions that are incorrect. Yet, through all such obscuration of truth and lapses of racial remembrance, glimpses are seen which show that there were deadly combats between the representatives of two different ideals, such as we find in Iran in the time of Zarathushtra.

We are told that 'Zarathushtra was descended from a kingly family' and also that the first converts to his doctrine were of the ruling caste. But the priesthood, 'the Kavis, and the Karapans, often succeeded in bringing the rulers over to their side'. So we find that, in this fight, the princes of the land divided themselves into two opposite parties as we find in India in the Kurukshetra War. 'With the princes have the Kavis and the Karapans united,' —so complains the holy singer (Yasna 46.II)—'in order to corrupt man by their evil deeds'. Among the princes that stood against Zarathushtra as his enemies, the mighty Bendva is to be included, who is mentioned in Yasna 49.1-2. From the context of the passages we can of course conclude that he stood on the side of the infidels. A family or a race of princely blood were probably the Gremma (Y. 32. 12-14). Regarding them it is said that 'they, allied with the Kavis and the Karapans, have established their power in order to overpower the prophet and his partisans'. In fact, the opposition between the pious and the impious, the believers and the unbelievers, seems very often to have led to open combat. The prophet prays to Ahura that he may grant victory to his own, when both the armies rush together in combat, whereby they can cause defeat among the wicked, and procure for them grief and trouble.

There is evidence in our legends that in ancient India there also have been fights between the representatives of the orthodox faith and the Kshatriyas, who owing to their own special vocation, had a comparative freedom of mind about the religion of external observances. The proofs are strong enough to lead us to believe that the monotheistic religious movement had its origin and principal support in the kingly caste of those days, though a great number of them also fought to oppose it.

I have discussed at length in another paper the growth in ancient India of the moral and spiritual element in her religion, which had accompanied the Indian Aryan people from the time of the Indo-Iranian age, showing how the struggle with its antagonistic force has continued all through the history of India. I have shown how the revolution which accompanied the teachings of Zarathushtra, breaking out into severe fights, had its close analogy in the religious revolution in India whose ideals are still preserved in the Bhagavadgita.

It has been a matter of supreme satisfaction to me to realize, that the Iranian and the Indian Aryans, who sprang from the same parent source, are not contradictory in their natures like light and darkness. Both of them were faced by the same great problem, the distraction of unrelated heterogeneity, which so deeply hurts our spiritual nature; both of them have undergone the struggle to attain simplicity of devotion, the infinity of the One. The purification of faith which was the mission of the great teachers in both communities followed a similar line. We have already seen how Zarathushtra spiritualised the meaning of sacrifice, which in former days consisted in external ritualism entailing bloodshed. The same thing we find in the Gita, in which the meaning of the word *Yajña* has been translated into a higher significance than it had in its crude form.

According to the Gita, the deeds that are done solely for the sake of self fetter our soul; the disinterested action, performed for the sake of the giving up of self, is the true sacrifice. For creation itself comes of the self-sacrifice of Brahma, which has no other purpose; and therefore, in our performance of the duty which is self-sacrificing, we realize the spirit of Brahma.

It is interesting to note that the growth of the same ideal in the same race in different geographical situations has produced results, that, in spite of their unity, have certain aspects of difference. The Iranian monotheism is more ethical, while the Indian is more metaphysical, in character. Such a difference in their respective spiritual developments was owing, no doubt, to the active vigour of will in the old Persians and the contemplative quietude of mind in the Indians. This distinction in the latter arises out of the climatic conditions of the country, the easy fertility of the 'soil and the great stretch of plains in Northern India which offered no constant physical obstacles to be daily overcome by man'.

The Zoroastrian ideal has accepted the challenge of the principle of evil, which is the negative pole of existence, and has enlisted itself in the fight on the side of Ahura Mazda, the great, the good, the wise. In India, although the ethical side is not absent, the emphasis has been more strongly laid on subjective realization through a stoical suppression of desire, and the attainment of a perfect equanimity of mind by cultivating indifference to all causes of joy and sorrow. Here the idea, over which the minds of men brooded for ages in an introspective intensity of silence, was that man as a spiritual being has to realize his truth by breaking through his sheath of self. All the desires and the feelings that limit his being are keeping him shut in from the region of spiritual freedom. In man, the spirit of creation is waiting to find its ultimate release in an ineffable illumination of Truth.

The aspiration of India is for attaining the infinite in the spirit of man. On the other hand, as we have seen, the ideal of Zoroastrian Persia is distinctly ethical. It sends its call to men to work together with the Eternal Spirit of Good in spreading and maintaining *Kshathra,* the kingdom of righteousness, against all attacks of evil. This ideal gives us our place as collaborators with God in distributing his blessings over the world.

> Clear is this to the man of wisdom as to the man who carefully thinks:
> He who upholds Truth with all the might of his power,
> He who upholds Truth the utmost in his word and deed
> He, indeed, is thy most valued helper, O Mazda Ahura!
>
> Y. 31.22 (D.J. Irani)

It is a fact of supreme moment to us, that the human world is in an incessant state of war between that which will save us and that which will drag us into the abyss of disaster. Our one hope lies in the fact, that Ahura Mazda is on our side if we choose the right course. The law of warfare is severe in its character; it allows no compromise. 'None of you,' says Zarathushtra, 'shall mind the doctrine and precepts of the wicked; because thereby he will bring grief and death in his house and village, in his land and people! No, grip your sword and cut them down!' (Y. 31. 18)

Such relentless attitude of fight reminds us of the Old Testament spirit. The active heroic aspect of this religion reflects the character of the people themselves, who later on spread their conquests far and wide and built up great empires by the might of their sword. They accepted this world in all seriousness. They had their zest in life and confidence in their own strength. They belonged to the western half of Asia and their great influence travelled through the neighbouring civilization of Judea towards the Western Continent. Their ideal was the ideal of the fighter. By force of will and deeds of sacrifice they were to conquer *haurvatat*—welfare in this world, and *ameratat*—immortality in the other. This is the best ideal of the West, the great truth of fight. For paradise has to be gained through conquest. That sacred task is for the heroes, who are to take the right side in the battle, and the right weapons.

There was a heroic period in Indian history, when this holy spirit of fight was invoked by the greatest poet of the Sanskrit Literature. It is not to be wondered at that his ideal of fight was similar to the ideal that Zarathushtra preached. The problem with which his poem starts is that paradise has to be rescued by the hero from its invasion by the evil beings. This is the eternal problem of man. The evil spirit is exultant and paradise is lost when *Sati,* the Spirit of *Sat* (Reality), is disunited from *Siva,* the Spirit of Goodness. The Real and the Good must meet in wedlock if the hero is to take his birth in order to save all that is true and beautiful. When the union was attempted through the agency of passion, the anger of God was aroused and the result was a tragedy of disappointment. At last, by purification through penance, the wedding was effected, the hero was born who fought against the forces of evil and paradise was regained. This is a poem of the ideal of the moral fight, whose first great prophet was Zarathushtra.

We must admit that this ideal has taken a stronger hold upon the life of man in the West, than in India,—the West, where the vigour of life receives its fullest support from Nature and the excess of energy finds its delight in ceaseless activities. But everywhere in the world, the unrealized ideal is a force of disaster. It gathers its strength in secret even in the heart of prosperity, kills the soul first and then drives men to their utter ruin. When the aggressive activity of will, which naturally accompanies physical vigour, fails to accept the responsibility of its ideal, it breeds unappeasable greed for material gain, leads to unmeaning slavery of things, till amidst a raging conflagration of clashing interests the tower of ambition topples down to the dust.

And for this, the prophetic voice of Zarathushtra reminds us that all human activities must have an ideal goal, which is an end to itself, and therefore is peace, is immortality. It is the House of Songs, the realization of love, which comes through strenuous service of goodness.

All the joys of life which thou holdest, O Mazda, the joys that were, the joys that are, and the joys that shall be, Thou dost apportion all in Thy love for us.

We, on the other hand, in the tropical East, who have no surplus of physical energy inevitably overflowing in outer activities, also have our own ideal given to us. Our course is, not so much through the constant readiness to fight in the battle of the good and evil, as through the inner concentration of mind, through pacifying the turbulence of desire, to reach that serenity of the infinite in our being which leads to the harmony with the all. Here, likewise, the unrealized ideal pursues us with its malediction. As the activities of a vigorous vitality may become unmeaning, and thereupon smother the soul with a mere multiplicity of material, so the peace of the extinguished desire may become the peace of death; and the inner world, in which we would dwell, become a world of incoherent dreams.

The river whose current is checked, is choked by its own accumulation. The negative process of curbing desire and controlling passion is only for saving our energy from dissipation and directing it into its proper channel. If the path of the channel we have chosen runs withinwards, it also must have its expression in action, not for any ulterior reward, but for the proving of its own truth. If the test of action is removed, if our realization grows purely subjective, then it may become like travelling in a desert in the night, going round and round the same circle, imagining all the while that we are following the straight path of progress.

This is why the prophet of the Gita, in the first place, says:

Whoso forsaketh all desires and goeth onwards free from yearnings, selfless and without egoism, he goeth to peace.

But he does not stop here, he adds:

Surrendering all actions to Me, with thy thoughts resting on the Supreme Self, from hope and egoism freed, and of mental fever cured, engage in battle.

Action there must be, fight we must have,—not the fight of passion and desire, of arrogant self-assertion, but of duty done in the presence of the Eternal, the disinterested fight of the serene soul that helps us in our union with the Supreme Being.

In this, the teaching of Zarathushtra, his sacred gospel of fight, finds its unity. The end of the fight he preaches is in the House of Songs; in the symphony of spiritual union. He sings:

Ye, who wish to be allied to the Good Mind, to be friend with Truth, Ye, who desire to sustain the Holy Cause, down with all anger and violence, away with all ill-will and strife! Such benevolent men, O Mazda, I shall take to the House of Songs!

In concluding my paper I have to confess that I am not a scholar; the detailed facts of history, which are the battleground of the learned, are not my province. I am a singer myself, and I am ever attracted by the strains that come forth from the House of Songs. When the streams of ideals that flow from the East and from the West mingle their murmur in some profound harmony of meaning it delights my soul.

In the realm of material property men are jealously proud of their possessions and their exclusive rights. Unfortunately there are quarrelsome men who bring that pride of acquisition, the worldliness of sectarianism, even into the region of spiritual truth. Would it be sane, if the man in China should lay claim to ownership of the sun because he can prove the earlier sunrise in his own country?

For myself, I feel proud whenever I find that the truth which dwells in the best thoughts of India has also been uttered in a different language, in a different part of the world. The best in the world have their fundamental agreement because they are pure in truth. And therefore it is their function to unite; and dissuade the small from bristling up, like prickly shrubs, in the pride of the minute points of their differences, only to hurt one another.

It rejoices my heart to know, that the peoples who once had nourished their seeds of civilization together and blended their voices in an original mother tongue which belonged to them both, should, even after their long period of separation, have kept some primal similarity of expression in the growth of their respective histories. For we find that both of these peoples have carried in the depth of their nature the quest of the spiritual unity in religion.

Zarathushtra arose as the herald of that mission in Western Asia. He revealed to his people the idea of the One in the midst of the chaos of formal worship. It is the same genius of race in Persia which gave birth to the great Sufi poets who sang of the nearness of God in a language of intimacy, defiantly giving a shock to the dignity of distance upheld by the orthodox creed of Godhead. That this spiritual quest in that people is not dead, is proved by the later rise of Bahaism, crowned with martyrdom, which preaches the federation of man in the Kingdom of Supreme Truth. It is needless to describe in detail how in India also the same quest has been running its course through the wilderness of obstacles which the heterogeneity of race and creed offers to her.

In India, the disunited kinsmen have met over and over again. The Persian monarchs extended their kingdom to the Western Provinces of India, and the dim recollection of their blood relationship came to the Indian mind when in the Purāṇas they were recognized as the Kshatriyas who had fallen off from their orthodox rites. For nearly two centuries a part of North-Western India was a Persian Province. That Iran and India had a very early connection can be guessed by some Greek allusion to the custom of the dead being left to be devoured by vultures in the locality of Taxila, at the time of Alexander the Great.

It was not merely an extension of kingdom; the proofs are numerous that the Persians had also extended their influence over the Indian arts. The scholars agree that in the later development of the Mahāyāna Buddhism the Zoroastrian influence is unquestionable. It has to be noted that it was a Persian King who accepted Buddhism for his religion and was the first to take this religion to China, translating Buddhist scriptures into Chinese. That the Persian influence affected Hinduism also has been discussed by Sir Charles Eliot, in his book named 'Hinduism and Buddhism', from which I quote the following:

> The Brihatsamhitā says, that the Magas,—that is the Magi,—are the priests of the sun, and the proper persons to superintend the consecration of temples and images dedicated to that deity, but the clearest statements about this foreign cult are to be found in the Bhavishya Purāṇa, as to its introduction obviously based upon history. By the advice of Gurmukha, priest of King Ugrasena, he imported some Magas from Sakadvipa. That this refers to the importation of Zoroastrian priests from the country of the Sakas (Persia, or the Oxus region) is made clear by the account of their customs,—such as the wearing of a girdle called Avyanga (the Aivyaonghen of the Avesta)—given by the Purāṇa. It also says that they were descended from a child of the sun, called Jarasabda, or Jarasasta, which no doubt represents Zarathushtra.

At last, in a later age, the disciples of Zarathushtra took their shelter in India, the meeting ground of races and cultures in the East. They have brought with them a new store of energy and adventurous spirit into this land, giving, in spite of the smallness of their number, a strong impetus to our national life, opening up the industrial resources of this country, bravely standing up for its rights, and generously helping in the cause of its welfare. This courage of fight, this cheerful spirit of work and active benevolence, they owe to the teaching of their great prophet, whose benediction rings in these words (D.J. Irani):

> Happiness be the lot of him, who works
> for others' happiness.
> May the Supreme Lord give him the powers
> of health and strength!
> For the struggle to uphold Truth, I beseech
> these gifts from Thee, O Lord.

1923

Notes and Comments

It struck my heart with dismay, when I visited Ceylon, to find that the people there have lost the consciousness of their unity with their Indian kinsmen. Not having in their mind a continental background for their culture and aspiration, they have permitted their intellectual and spiritual individuality to miss its shelter, and easily to drift into the vagabondage of imitation.

They seem to have forgotten that political division is merely a division of property through which we can change our residence, but not our brotherhood.

When the mouth of the branch of a great river is choked up, the branch becomes reduced to a stagnant pool; the pulsation of the ocean heart no longer reaches it, nor the living message that flows from the hoary height of the inaccessible. A community, cut off from its parent stem by disastrous oblivion, is sure to forget the great meaning of its own personality, and thus to fall a prey to the force of other personalities and be bent and clipped and hammered by them to their purposes. A tree grows in its own shape and finds its fulfilment, but when cut off from its root it is, as timber, at the mercy of the dealers who turn it into toys of their fancy.

Life is original; it is adventurous; it seeks itself in endless experiments, the outcome of its spontaneous creative impulse. The people, who passively lend themselves to imitation, prove that life has lost its best claim on their hearts. It is the temptation of *Māra,* the evil spirit of Untruth, which whispers to us that we can be better than we are by seeming to be something else.

Thus we yield ourselves to being slowly robbed of the best gift given to us by God,—the dignity of our individual existence with its infinite possibilities of creation. We must never allow this to happen on either side of the water that divides this island of Ceylon from India.

Our subconscious self has the accumulation of ages of creative memory, wherein has grown in secret the racial genius which creates. The whole current of a people's history generates its own special energy of guidance in this region lying beneath the surface-consciousness of our mind. This is why, when we try to imitate some other people's history, we remain so pathetically unaware of the absurdities that are produced.

There can be no doubt that Ceylon's subconscious mind, its racial mind, has unbroken connection with that of India; the language which she speaks has all the subtle modulations, her physical organism all the characteristic gestures, that belong to it. When her conscious self tries to ignore this, and attaches itself to some alien mentality, then its progress, like that of a three-legged race in which legs belonging to different individuals are tied together, takes on a gait which is neither efficient, nor graceful.

All our efforts which are unmixed imitations are lame, for in them our conscious will ignores the co-operation of its great partner, our fundamental personality, which nevertheless goes on working in the subsoil of our consciousness. History, properly studied, saves us from these unrhythmic strivings which go contrary to the direction of our inmost nature; and Ceylon, if she would do herself justice, must acknowledge that her intellectual and spiritual history runs in one stream with the cultural history of India.

The great religion of the Buddha had once spread its living spirit of Unity over the greater part of Asia. It drew races together and turned their hope and faith away from the turmoil of self-seeking.

True, the modern facilities of science have also established human communication across geographical barriers; but in this, man has only utilised physical forces to overcome physical obstructions. Buddhism was the first spiritual force, known to us in history, which drew close together such a large number of races separated by most difficult barriers of distance, by differences of language and custom, by various degrees and divergent types of civilization. It had its motive power, neither in international commerce, nor in empire-building, nor in scientific curiosity, nor in a migratory impulse to occupy fresh territory. It was a purely disinterested effort to help mankind forward to its final goal.

The religion, which flowed from the comprehensive mind of Buddha, has its negative aspect,—the control of passion and renunciation of self,—for purifying spiritual ideas and religious phraseology from all narrowness, anthropomorphic, or egotistic; it is the path of discipline through elimination. But this cannot be the whole of it; and that this has not been all, is amply proved by the direction and form which Buddhism has naturally taken in the greater part of the Buddhistic world.

A seed has, as a portion of its body, the sheath which is hard, which is for its protection; but it also has its kernel which grows, which takes it out of its obscurity and spreads its branches wide. The special aspect of Buddhism, that has grown and spread its branching life far away from its mother soil, that has subdued the savage in the races which were primitive, and inspired in them art and literature, must have been its religious nucleus, carrying in itself the vital principle of Buddha's teaching. This life force, which is the positive element in Buddhism, has neither been lost in India herself; it is still working in the heart of even her lattermost religions in various shapes.

I have lately been reading a book about Buddhism, written by one who professes this religion. Our Buddhist author has tried to prove, that though Buddhism had its origin in geographical India, neither did its seed come from the Indian culture, nor did its root draw sap from the Indian mind. In other words, he would make out that it was an accident, which had no previous history, no natural genesis in a continued line of ancestors. In his zeal, the author is acrimoniously violent in the assertion that Buddhism as a religion is absolutely contrary to whatever preceded it in the religious history of India.

The child in the very process of birth manifests an apparent antagonism to the mother. All the same, the birth can never be a repudiation of the parent. There can be no question that Buddhism was one of the great products of the mother-heart of India.

We are free to admit that after centuries of its domination there was, outwardly a violent reaction against it. But when the history of that period is thoroughly investigated, I have no doubt that it will be found that what was forcibly thrown out was no part of the original idea of Buddhism, but a medley of miscellaneous aberrations, interpolated mostly from the dense tangle of non-Aryan superstitions.

That which I value most in my religion or my aspiration, I seek to find corroborated, in its fundamental unity, in other great religions, or in the hopes expressed in the history of other peoples. Each great movement of thought and endeavour in any part of the world may have something unique in its expression, but the truth underlying any of them never has the meretricious cheapness of utter novelty about it. The great Ganges must not hesitate to declare its essential similarity to the Nile of Egypt, or to the Yangtse-Kiang of China. Only a water-spout displays a sudden arrogance of singularity and vanishes in the void, leaving mother Nature ashamed of so monstrous a production!

Whenever we find, in the immensity of the human mind the prototype of something which we hold most precious in ourselves, we should rejoice. The pride of special possession can cling only to those results of pot culture, which have merely market value. But great truths, like great monarchs of the forest, disdain to exhibit any extravagant speciality, which may offer temptation to those who are jealous of their proprietary right in rareness. The great is never alone; it has its aristocracy of the sublime, its common kinship of the immortal.

This is why, because I consider Buddhism to be one of the greatest religious achievements of man, I find a delight in discovering some of its essential similarities, not only to the spiritual thought of ancient India, but to that of other great religions as well. Is it right that we should have pride merely in some special production of man, but not in Man himself? Only those, who have no respect for humanity as a whole, can believe that Truth, in its supreme aspect, has been reached only once by one chosen people, leaving no alternative to others but to borrow from it, or else to live in utter spiritual destitution.

I cannot accept from anybody the statement, that Buddhism was a freak of human nature, and that as a religion, utterly unlike any other religion in the world, it is not only unrelated, but contradictory to its spiritual surroundings; that it is the science and art of self-extinction referring to a world where there is no true principle of unity anywhere, within man, or outside him.

Once again I assert that no religion whatsoever can for a moment stand on the basis of negation. It must have some great truth in its heart which is positive and eternal, and for whose sake Man can offer all that he has, and be glad. And, in this, Buddhism must have its inherent relation and resemblance to that spiritual endeavour in ancient India which led men to leave aside their material possessions and seek the fulfillment of their life.

And what is this truth which the Buddha preached, which is eternal? It is Dharma, difficult to be rendered in English, Perhaps it may be translated as the 'highest ideal of perfection'. Certainly it is not a logical abstraction, nothing which is merely subjective. It is a reality which has to be reached, and according to the degree of our relationship with it, we attain the fulfilment of life. So this Dharma and the Brahma of our Upanishads are essentially the same, in regard to that which is supreme Reality.

The Buddhist Dharma does not consist in mere reason, blind and dark. It comprises within itself the highest spiritual enlightenment; it is eternally true for all beings; its laws are not restricted to any boundary of outward circumstances. Therefore, it has the principle of reality, wisdom, and infinity. Likewise it has been said in the Upanishad: Satyam, Jnanam, Anantam Brahma, *Brahma is truth, wisdom, and eternity*. Then again, Dharma has not merely its reality, like the universal force of gravitation; it has its moral value, it leads us to peace, goodness and love. Similarly the Brahma of the Upanishad, who is Satyam, is also Santam, Sivam, Advaitam, which means that in Brahma is peace, goodness and union.

Dharma in Buddhism, or *Dharma Kāyā,* as it has been termed in some of the Buddhist scriptures, is an eternal reality of

Peace, Goodness and Love, for which man can offer up the homage of his highest loyalty, his life itself. This Dharma can inspire man with almost superhuman power of renunciation, and through the abnegation of self, lead him to the supreme object of his existence, a state that cannot be compared to anything we know in this world; and yet of which we can at least have a dim idea, when we know that it is only to be reached, not through the path of annihilation, but through immeasurable love. Thus, to dwell in the constant consciousness of unbounded love is named by Lord Buddha: Brahma-Vihara,—*moving in Brahma.*

However, let me not dwell too long on my own idea about the essential points of resemblance between the truths of Buddhism and the truths inculcated in the Upanishads. Those who want to indulge their sectarian pride by believing that they only are the fortunate people in the world, in possession of a religion absolutely solitary in its singularity, I shall leave to their exultation. But I cannot allow the historical link of Buddhism with India's mind to be ignored, and I must assert that the truest relationship among human beings is that of ideals; a relationship more real indeed than even the kinship of blood.

What is this Visva-Bharati, this international institution—I was asked to explain. It may not be out of place to reproduce in our journal the explanation which I gave of the Visva-Bharati ideal to my Ceylon audience.

The word 'international' may sound too indefinite,—its meaning appearing large only because of its vagueness, like water acquiring volume by turning into vapour. I do not believe in an internationalism which is amorphous, whose features are broadened into flatness. The internationalism of Visva-Bharati must be the internationalism of India, with its own distinct character.

The true universal finds its manifestation in the individuality which is true. Beauty is universal, and a rose reveals it because, as a rose, it is individually beautiful. By making a decoction of a rose, jasmine and lotus, you do not get to a realization of some larger beauty which is interfloral. The true universalism is not the breaking down of the walls of one's own house, but the offering of hospitality to one's guests and neighbours.

Like the position of the earth in the course of its diurnal and annual motions, man's life, at any moment, must be the reconciliation of its two movements, one round the centre of its own personality, and another whose centre is in a luminous ideal comprehending the whole human world. The international endeavour of a people must carry the movement of the people's own personality round the great spirit of man. The inspiration must be its own, which is to help it in its aspiration towards fulfilment. Otherwise, mere cosmopolitanism but drifts on the waves, buffeted by wind from all quarters, in an imbecility of movement which has no progress.

One of the objects of Visva-Bharati is concerned with the personality of the people she represents,—to rescue this personality from the dimness of ignorance. As a people we must be fully conscious of what we are. It is a truism to say that the consciousness of the unity of a people implies a knowledge of its parts as well as of its whole. But, we not only have no such knowledge of India, we do not even have an eager desire to cultivate it.

By asserting our national unity with vehemence in our patriotic propaganda, we assure ourselves that we possess it, and thus continue to live in a make-believe world of political day-dreams. The greater part of Bengal's knowledge of the Punjab consists in its relative position upon the maps of India,—a mere outline of information of a dead kind. How many Bengalis are there, who have studied the message of Nanak that has come to us through the Sikhs? And are there students in the Punjab, who have tried to understand the Vaishnavism of Chaitanya, and what place it occupies in the religious culture of India? India is the one place in the world, where the science of Ethnology can be studied with the full advantage; and yet it has never aroused any enthusiasm in our students.

The fact is, we have a very feeble human interest in our own country. We love to talk about politics and economics; we are ready to soar into the thin air of academic abstractions, or to roam in the dusk of pedantic wildernesses; but we never care to cross our social boundaries and come to the door of our neighbouring communities, personally to inquire how they think and feel and express themselves, and how they fashion their lives.

The love of man has its own hunger for knowing. Even if we lack this concerning our fellow-beings in India, except in our political protestations, at least love of knowledge for its own sake could have brought us close to each other. But there also we have failed and have suffered. For weakness of knowledge is the foundation of weakness of power. Until India becomes fully distinct in our mind, we can never gain her in truth; and where truth is imperfect, love can never have its full sway. 'Know thyself,' for the giving of self is waiting for that knowledge. One of the endeavours of Visva-Bharati is to help us to *know* ourselves; and then along with it, her other mission will be fulfilled which is to inspire us to *give* ourselves.

What has given such enormous intellectual power to Europe is her concentration of mind. She has evolved a means by which all the countries of that continent can think together. Such a great concert of ideas, by its own pressure of movement, naturally wears away all her individual aberrations of thought and extravagances of unreason. It keeps her flights of fancy close to the limits of reticence. All her different thought-rays have been focused in one common culture, which finds its complete expression in all the great European universities.

The mind of India, on the other hand, is divided and scattered; there is no one common pathway along which we can reach it. Upto the present, in all our patriotic endeavours, our effort has been to establish our unity on the basis of our common interest in the political or economic situation. It is like gathering coals for our railway journey, while the locomotive is nowhere to be found!

So I must guard myself against the least chance of my audience carrying away the belief that Visva-Bharati bases its ideal upon any ulterior expectation, political or otherwise. Its one object is to help each student to realize his personality, as an individual representing his people, in such a broad spirit, in such an unobstructed sunshine of spiritual expansion of consciousness, that he may know how it is the most important fact of his life for him to have been born to the great world of man.

1924

The Fourfold Way of India

An artist carefully selects his lines and colours and harmonises them in such a manner that they no longer remain a sum total of lines and colours. They transcend themselves to form a picture in which the artist's ideal of perfection finds its release in a final attainment. Similarly, India in pursuit of her ideals of liberation, a liberation in the bosom of the Perfect, tried to train and manipulate life's forces towards a deliberate end. Life, according to her, must not only grow within itself but outgrow itself into a higher meaning which is beyond it, as the flower outgrows itself into the fruit. Lines through their discipline of limits lead the form to the region of beauty which is the expression of the Limitless. India's aim has been to guide life's current through its boundaries of banks towards an unbounded sea of freedom. The object of this paper is to discuss the principles and method of such an art of living which once India taught her children to follow.

The flesh is impure, the world is vanity, therefore renunciation in the shape of self-mortification is necessary for salvation,—this was the ideal of spiritual life held forth in mediaeval Europe. Modern Europe, however, considers it unwholesome to acknowledge an overlasting feud between the human world of natural desires and social aims on the one hand, and the spiritual life with its discipline and aspiration on the other. According to her, we enfeeble the moral purpose of our existence if we put too much stress on the illusoriness of this world. To drop down dead in the race course of life, while running at full speed, is acclaimed by her to be the most glorious death.

It is true that Europe has gained a certain strength by pinning its faith on the world, by refusing to dwell on its evanescence, on the certainty of death,—condemning the opposite frame of mind as morbid. Her children are, perhaps, thereby trained to be more efficient in competition, to gain victory in the struggle which, in their view, represents the whole of life. But, whatever may be the practical effect of leading this life as if its connection with us were interminable, that is not a fact.

Doubtless Nature, for its own biological purposes, has created in us a strong faith in life, by keeping us unmindful of death. Nevertheless, not only our physical existence, but also the environment which it builds up around itself, desert us in the moment of triumph. The greatest prosperity comes to its end, dissolving into emptiness; the mightiest empire is overtaken by stupor amidst the flicker of its festival lights. All this is none the less true because the truism bores us to be reminded of it. Therefore all our works which make for the composition of our life have to be judged according to their harmony with their background, the background which is death.

And yet, it is equally true that, though all our mortal relationships have their end, we cannot ignore them with impunity while they last. If we behave as if they do not exist, merely because they will not persist, they will all the same exact their dues, with a great deal over by, way of penalty. We cannot claim exemption from payment of fare because the railway train has not the permanence of the dwelling house. Trying to ignore bonds that are real, albeit temporary, only strengthens and prolongs their bondage.

That is why the spirit of attachment and that of detachment have to be reconciled in harmony, and then only will they lead us to fulfillment. Attachment is the force which draws us to the truth in its finite aspect, the aspect of what is, while detachment leads us to freedom in the infinity of truth which is the ideal aspect. In the act of walking, attachment is in the step that the foot takes when it touches the earth; detachment is in the movement of the other foot when it raises itself. The harmony of bondage and freedom is the dance of creation. According to the symbolism of Indian thought, the god Siva, the male principle of Truth, represents freedom which is of the spirit, while the goddess Sivani, its female principle, represents the bonds, which are of the real. In their union dwells the ideal of perfection.

In order to achieve the reconciliation of these opposites, we must first come to a true understanding of man; that is to say, we must not cut him down to the requirement of any particular duty. To look on trees only as firewood, is not to know the tree in its completeness. Similarly, to look on man merely as the protector of his country, or the producer of its wealth, is to reduce him to soldier or merchant or diplomat, to make his efficiency as such the measure of his manhood. Not only is such a view limited, it is destructive. And those whom we would thus glorify are but assisted to a rocket-like descent.

How India once looked on man as greater than any purpose he could serve, is shown by the well-known couplet of a Sanskrit poet which may be translated thus: For the family, sacrifice the individual; for the community, the family; for the country, the community; for the soul, all the world.

A question will be asked: 'What is this soul?' Let us first try to answer a much simpler question: 'What is life?' Certainly life is not merely the facts of life that are evident to us, the breathing, digesting and various other functions of the body; not even the principle of unity which comprehends them. In a mysterious manner it contains within it a future which continually brings itself out from the envelopment of its present, dealing with unforeseen circumstances, experimenting with new variations. If its presence, with dead materials, chokes the path of its ever-unfolding future, then it is a traitor that betrays its trust. The soul, which is our spiritual life, contains our infinity within it. It has an impulse that urges our consciousness to break through the dimly lighted walls of animal life where our turbulent passions fight and scream to find their throne within that narrow enclosure. Though, like animals, man is dominated by his self, he has an instinct that fights against it, like the rebel life within a seed that breaks through the dark prison bringing out its flag of freedom in the realm of light. Our sages in the East have always maintained that self-emancipation is the highest form of freedom for man,—because it is his fulfilment in the heart of the Eternal, and not merely some reward achieved through some process of what is called salvation.

That was what had been preached and practised in India. Our sages saw no end to the dignity of the human spirit which found its consummation in the Supreme Spirit itself. Any limited view of man would therefore be a false view. He could not be merely Citizen or Patriot, for neither city nor country, nor, for the matter of that, the bubble called the world, could contain his infinity.

A poet of classical India, who was once a King, has said: *What if you have secured the fountain-head of all desires; what if you have put your foot on the neck of your enemy, or by good fortune gathered friends around you; that, even, if you have succeeded in keeping mortal bodies alive for ages, what then?*

The realm of our desires is for the creature who is imprisoned within his self. These desires not having their perspective of the eternal have some fanciful value for which the prisoners scramble in the dark and bred each other's skulls. You can only direct man's life towards its perfection if you remind him that there is something for him which is ultimate and those who stop of that can never find the answer to the question: What then?

Europe is incessantly singing paeans to Freedom, which to her means freedom to acquire, freedom to enjoy, freedom to wish freedom is by no means a small thing, and much toil and care are required to maintain it in this world.

In the process of attaining freedom a man must bind his will in order to save its forces from distraction and wastage, so as to gain be it the velocity which comes from the bondage itself. Those who seek liberty in a political plane must constantly curtail it and reduce their freedom of thought and to that narrow limit which is necessary to making political liberty secure, very often at the cost of liberty of conscience. Are the soldiers of England free men, or are they of merely living guns? And what of the others in her mines and factories—mere bondage of the machines they work,—who assist with their life's blood to paint red the map of England's Empire. How few are the Englishmen who really participate in this political freedom of theirs? Europe may have preached and striven for the rights of the individual, but where else in the world is the individual so much of a slave?

The only reply to this is the paradox to which I have already referred. Freedom can only be attained through bonds of discipline, through sacrifice of personal inclination. Freedom is a profit which can only be gained if you lay out a commensurate capital of self-restriction.

Individualism was also the object of India's quest,—not of this narrow kind, however, for it stretched up towards self-emancipation,—so it tried to gain this larger individual freedom through every detail of life, every relation of family and society. And as in Europe her ideal of freedom has manifested itself in the full rigour of mechanical and military bonds, so the ideal of India found its expression in the strict regulation of the most intimate details of the daily life. If we fail to see the ideal behind and focus our view on its external manifestations which are of the present age, then indeed in India individual liberty appears most thoroughly fettered. It has happened over and over again in the history of man when the means have got the better of the end. It occurs either when some passion like greed lures away our mind from the ideal end to the material means itself, making us blind to their relative value, or when through lassitude of spirit our endeavour falls short of its aim and takes pride in conforming to regulations that no longer have their meaning, that exact our sacrifices without giving us anything in return.

That is what has happened in our country. We still submit to the bondage of all kinds of social restrictions, but the emancipation which was the object is no longer in our view. So that if now the looker-on should come to the conclusion that the social system of India is only a device for keeping down its people by unmeaning prohibitions, we may get angry, but we shall find it difficult to give an effective contradiction.

It is not my object to lament our downfall. What I wish to point out is that India had originally accepted the bonds of her social system in order to transcend society, as the rider puts reins on his horse and stirrups on his own feet in order to ensure greater speed towards his goal. India knew that society was not the ultimate end of man, but through the mutual help and collective endeavour of individuals it was the best means of training him for and leading him to liberation. And her bonds were even more severe than those which Europe has imposed on herself. That was because an even greater freedom was in contemplation. Her present plight only shows that the deeper the lake, the more cavernous is its hollow when it has dried up.

The reconciliation of these opposite aspects of bondage and freedom, of the means and the end, is thus referred to in one of our sacred scriptures:

'In darkness are they who worship only the world, but in greater darkness they who worship the Infinite alone. He who accepts both, saves himself from death by the knowledge of the former, and by that of the latter attains immortality.'

That is to say, we must first have our fulness of worldly life before we can attain the Infinite. Desire must be yoked to work for the purpose of transcending both desire and work, and then only can union with the Supreme be thought of. The mere renunciation of the world does not entitle to immortality.

The same scripture says:

'Performing work in this world, must thou desire to live a hundred years. O man, no other way is open to thee. His work never absolutely attaches itself to man.'

A full life with full work can alone fulfil the destiny of man. When his worldly life is thus perfected, it comes to its natural end, and the fetters of work are loosened and drop off.

In Europe we see only two divisions of man's worldly life—the period of training and that of work. It is like prolonging a straight line till, wearied, you drop off your brush. Such elongation of a straight line can never produce a picture; it can have no design; so it is unmeaning. Work is a process and cannot really be the end of anything; it must have some gain, some achievement, as its object. And yet Europe has omitted to put before man any definite goal in which its work may find its natural termination and gain its rest. To acquisition, whether of material or of knowledge, there is no limit. And European civilization puts all its emphasis on the progress of this cumulative acquisition forgetting that the best contribution which each individual can make to the progressive life of humanity is in the perfection of his own life. So their end comes in the middle of things; there is no game, but only the chase.

We, also, say that the desire is not exhausted, but rather increases, with the getting. How then is one to come to the end of work? The reply that India of old gave was, that there is an exception to this general rule, that there *is* a plane wherein getting does arrive at its terminus, whereto if we strive to attain, our work shall come to an end, and rest be ours. The Universe cannot be so madly conceived that desire should be an interminable singing with no song to which it can be completed.

India has not advised us to come to a sudden stop while work is in full swing. It is true that the unending procession of the world has gone on, through its ups and downs, from the beginning of creation till to-day; but it is equally obvious that each individual's connection therewith *does* get finished. Must he necessarily quit it without any sense of fulfilment? Had that been so, he would have been unfortunate indeed.

On the one hand, I represent in me an endless current of generations; with my life I add to its flow, I contribute as much as I can to its store of ever increasing experience of knowledge and possibilities of power. On the other hand, I represent the individual whose life has a beginning and end in itself and therefore who must find some ideal of perfection in that limited period of time. The unending stream can have no idea of completeness, its nature is movement. To remain for a moment its part and then to vanish means struggle and no realization. Those who say that the world is a humming top of absurdity which only hums and whirls for no reason whatever, should not preach their gospel of work and help this madness of movements. As in the heart of all things there is the impulse of unending progress, so there must also be the ideal of fulfilment which only gives meaning to all movements. Who is to realize it if not the individual? The movement which is in the finite has its claims from him, but the fulfilment which is in the infinite has also its call to him. When we respond to that call, then death does not come as an abrupt interruption to our world or reality. Directly we know the truth which is ultimate, we enter the realm of the everlasting yes.

In the division of man's world-life which we had in India, work came in the middle, the freedom at the end. As the day is divided into morning, noon, afternoon and evening, so India has divided man's life into four parts, following the indication of his nature. The day has the waxing and waning of its light, so has man of his bodily powers; and acknowledging this, India gave a connected meaning to his life from start to finish.

First came *Brahmacharya,* the period of education; then *garhasthya,* that of the world's work; then *vanaprasthya,* the retreat for the loosening of bonds; and finally, *pravrajya,* the expectant awaiting of freedom through death.

Nowadays we have come to look upon life as a conflict with death,—the intruding enemy, not the natural ending,—in impotent quarrel with which we spend every stage of it. When the time comes for youth to depart, we would hold it back by main force. When the fervour of desire slackens, we would revive it with fresh fuel of our own devising. When our sense organs weaken, we urge them to keep up their efforts. Even when our grip has relaxed, we are reluctant to give up possession. We fain would ignore all the rest of our life except only its morning and noon. And when at last the growing dusk compels us to acknowledge its afternoon and evening, we are either in a rebellious or in a despairing frame of mind, and so unable to make due use of them. We are not trained to recognise the inevitable as natural, and so cannot give up gracefully that which has to go, but needs must wait till it is snatched from us. The truth comes as conqueror only because we have lost the art of receiving it as guest.

The stem of the ripening fruit becomes loose, its pulp soft, but its seed hardens with provision for the next life. Our outward losses, due to age, likewise have corresponding inward gains. But, in man's inner life, his will plays a dominant part, so that these gains depend on his own disciplined striving; that is why, in the case of undisciplined man, it is so often seen that his muscles slacken, the legs totter, and yet his stern hold on life refuses to let go its grip, so much so that he is anxious to exercise his will in regard to worldly details even after his death. This kind of tenacity is coming to be regarded, even in our country, as something to be proud of but what is there so glorious in it?

Renounce we must, and through association gain,—that is the truth of the inner world.

Man leaves the refuge of the womb in order to achieve the further growth of body and mind in which consists the whole of the child life; next, he has to leave the self-nurtured security of this narrow world and enter the fuller which has varied relations with the multitude; lastly comes the decline of the body, and enriched with his experiences, man should now leave the narrower life for the universal life, to which he must dedicate his accumulated wisdom on the one hand and, on the other, should himself enter into relations with the Life Eternal; so that, when finally the decaying body has come to the very end of its tether, the soul views it breaking away quite simply and without regret, in the expectation of its own rebirth into the infinite.

From individual body to community, from community, to universe, from universe to Infinity,—this is the soul's normal progress.

Our sages, therefore, keeping in mind the goal of this progress, did not, in life's first stage of education, prescribe merely the learning of books or things, but *brahmacharya,* the living in discipline, whereby both enjoyment and its renunciation would come equally easy to the strengthened character. Life being a pilgrimage, with liberation in the Supreme Being as its object, the living of it was a spiritual exercise to be carried through its different stages, humbly, reverently and vigilantly. And the pupil, from his very initiation, has this final consummation kept in his view.

The series of adjustments between within and without which constitute the physical life, have become automatic; but in the case of man, his mind comes in as a disturbing factor which is still in the stage of conscious experimentation and which therefore may involve him in endless trouble before its activities can be attuned to universal law. For instance, the body may have come to the end of its requirement of food for the time, whereas the mind will not have it so, but, seeking to prolong the enjoyment of its satisfaction, even beyond actual need, spurs on the tongue and the stomach to greater efforts, thus upsetting age-long adjustments and creating widely ramified trouble in the process of the superficial effort required for procuring needless material.

Once the mind refuses to be bound by actual requirements, there ceases to be any reason why it should cry halt at any particular limit, and so, like trying to extinguish fire with oil, its acquisitions only make its desires blaze up all the fiercer. That is why it is so essential to habituate the mind, from the very beginning, to be conscious of, and desirous of keeping within, the natural limits, in other words, to attune itself to the universal nature, so that, with every liberty to play its varied tunes, it may learn to avoid discord with the Good and the True.

After the period of such education comes the period of worldly life. Our law-giver Manu tells us that,

'It is not possible to discipline ourselves so effectively if out of touch with the world, as while pursuing the world-life with wisdom.'

That is to say, wisdom does not attain completeness except through the living of life; and discipline divorced from wisdom is not true discipline, but merely the meaningless following of custom, which is only a veil for ignorance.

Work becomes true, only when desire has learnt to control itself. Then alone does the householder's state become a centre of welfare for the society, and instead of being an obstacle helps on the final liberation. When all his work is true, having the detachment of unselfishness, its obligations cannot curtail the freedom of his spirit.

When the second stage of life has thus been spent, when the crops that were raised on the field of youth have been harvested and garnered and done with, life's evening comes, the time to leave the enclosure of labour for the open road; to set out for home where peace awaits us. Have we not been toiling through the live-long day for this very home,—the Home which is fulfilment itself?

After the infant leaves the womb, it still has to remain close to its mother for a time, remaining attached in spite of its deliverance, until it can adapt itself to its new freedom. Such is the case in the third stage of life, when man, though aloof from the world, remains in touch with it. He still gives to the world of his store of wisdom, as the ripe fruit dropped from its stem, gives food to the world before its seed finds soil for its further life. His wisdom comes to the world like a shower of rain which is for all, because it is taken up in the upper air of disinterested detachment.

Then at last comes a day when even such free relations have their end, the emancipated spirit steps out of all bonds to face the Supreme Spirit. Just as a good housewife, while dealing with diverse men and things in the course of her duties, is after all doing the work of her husband's household all the time, openly and tacitly acknowledging at every step her relationship with him, yet at the end of the day she puts aside all her work and betakes herself with her husband to the solitude of their union, so does the soul, whose world-work is done, put away all finite matters and come all alone to its communion with the Eternal.

Only in this way can man's world-life be truly lived from one end of it to the other, without being engaged at every step in trying conclusions with death and without being overcome when death arrives in due course, as by a conquering enemy.

This fourfold way of India attunes the life of man to the sublime harmony of the universe, leaving no room for untrained desires to forget their simple relations therewith and to pursue their destructive career unchecked, but leading them on to their final relations with the Supreme.

I feel that the doubt may arise here: how far is it possible so to mould the whole people of any country? To which I would reply that when the wick is ablaze at its tip, the whole lamp is said to be alight. Whatever may be the ideal of the righteous life, it finds luminous expression only in the top-most few. If in any country even a small number of its people succeed in realizing an ideal, that is a gain for the whole of it.

However dire may be the outward degeneration which has overtaken us in India, there is an inmost core still alive within us, which refuses to acknowledge anything less than the Supreme as the highest gain. Even now when any great soul strikes a higher note, our whole being responds, and no lesser consideration of worldliness can stop it from so doing.

Now-a-days, on occasions of festivity in our country, we have acquired the habit of adding a foreign brass band to the usual set of our own festive pipes, thereby creating a terrible confusion of sound. Nevertheless, the plaintive Indian note of our real yearning may be discerned by the sensitive ear, through all its clash and clang. But while, in the public part of our homes, the foreign big drum and blatant trumpet proclaim the pride of wealth and the emulation of fashion, those who are in touch with the privacy of our inner life, know that this deafening din does not penetrate there.

We were not always this kind of a market crowd, jostling and elbowing one another so vulgarly, quarrelling over privileges and titles, advertising our own worth in unashamed exaggeration. The whole thing is sheer imitation and mostly sham. It has no redeeming feature of courtesy or gracefulness. But, before this age of make-believe overtook us, we had an inherent dignity of our own, which was not impaired by plain living or poverty. This was for us like a congenital armour which used to protect us against all the insults and trials of our material vicissitudes. But this natural protection has been wheedled away from us, driving us to take our stand behind bluster and bluff. Dignity has now become an outside thing which we must bolster up by outward show. As we no longer reckon inward satisfaction to be the fulness of wealth, we have to hunt for its paraphernalia in foreign shops, and never can gather together enough.

But, in spite of all this, I say that it has not worked its way into the core of our being. It is yet of the outside and therefore, perhaps, so excessively obvious. Just because we have *not* become really used to our new acquisitions, do we make so much of a turmoil about them, like the boisterous movements of the inexpert swimmer.

Moreover, I cannot at all admit that there can be anything in man's higher life which is only good in a particular geographical latitude. It is never true that we must take refuge in meekness because we are weak, or that we want righteousness only as a convenient cloak for hiding our indigence. Ideals preached by great personalities of the world need for their acceptance more steady courage, perfect training, power of sacrifice, than those which are needed to make good our school-learnt lessons on the profits of insensate competition and the duplicity and carnage of a hungry nationalism thriving on human flesh.

To prepare, in a spirit of reverence and by a life of discipline, for the world-life in which the soul is to attain maturity amidst her daily work of self-dedication and find at the serene end of her physical existence her own perfect revelation in a world of ineffable light and life,—is the only way through which a human being can attain to existency and fulness of meaning.

If we believe this, then we must also recognize that each and every people must strive to realize it, overcoming their respective obstacles, in their own way. If they would live in truth, then everything else,—the luxury of individual riches, the might of nations,—must be counted as subordinate. The spirit of man must triumph and liberate itself, if man's incessant endeavour during all these ages is to attain its fulfilment.

If that is not to be, and yet if by the help of some magic wand of progress men find an inexhaustible source of incessant profit, some weapon that in a second can kill millions of enemies, some potion that can keep their mortal bodies alive for ages,—what then?

1924

The Schoolmaster

If fifty years ago some prophet had come and told me that I was to be invited to a meeting of the teachers of Japan to discuss my ideas of education, it would have startled even the imagination of a poet. For, I suppose, some of you at least know that, once I was thirteen, I have hardly ever been inside an educational institution until literally when I have my reputation as a poet and am invited to lecture.

Thus, when I felt it my duty to start a school for the children, I had hardly any experience of education. This was possibly an advantage for me. Not being tied down by cut and dried doctrines of education, I had to find my own experience through experiment and failure. I was made intensely conscious, when I was young of what was wrong in education. It drove me away from school, and it was that which made me decide, when quite old, to found an institution where some of these mistakes should not be made, mistakes from, which I had suffered as a boy.

When, at about the age of five, I was forced to attend school, my whole heart rose in rebellion against an arrangement where there was no tinge of colour, no play of life, where the lessons had no context with their surroundings, and where I was banished from that paradise, to which I had been born, where Nature dwells full of beauty,—and this for no crime but that of being born ignorant. I was banished into a cage where education was provided from outside as birds are fed. My whole heart felt the dignity of treatment, even though I was so young.

Our system of education refuses to admit that children are children. Children are punished because they fail to behave like grown-up people and have the impertinence to be noisily childish. Their educators do not know, or they refuse to acknowledge that this childishness is Nature's own provision and that the child through its restless mind and movements should always come into touch with new facts and stumble upon new information. Thus the child becomes the battle-ground for a fight between the schoolmaster and mother Nature herself.

The schoolmaster is of opinion that the best means of educating a child is by concentration of mind, but Mother Nature knows that the best way is by dispersion of mind. When we were children, we came to gather facts by such scattering of mental energy, through unexpected surprises. The surprise gave us that shock which was needed to make us intensely conscious of the facts of life, of the world. Facts must come fresh to children to startle their minds into full activity. But such activity itself was held to be intolerable by the schoolmaster who reigned in the class I was compelled to attend. The master insisted that I should have to be passive and my mind rebelled every moment; for Mother Nature encouraged me never to accept this tyranny from that man.

It is the utter want of purpose in child life which is important. In adult age, having made our life a bundle of a few definite purposes, we exclude all facts outside their boundaries. Our purpose wants to occupy all the mind's attention for itself, obstructing the full view of most of the things around us; it cuts a narrow bed for our deliberate mind which seeks its end through a restricted passage. The child, because it has no conscious object of life beyond living, can see all things around it, can hear every sound with a perfect freedom of attention, not having to exercise choice in the collection of information. It gives full rein to its restlessness which leads its mind into knocking against knowledge. Like a stream going over pebbles, its hurls itself against obstructions, and through them finds more and more velocity.

But the schoolmaster, as I have said, has his own purpose. He wants to mould the child's mind according to his ready-made doctrines and therefore wants to rid the child's world of everything that he thinks will go against his purpose. He excludes the whole world of colour, of movement, of life, from his education scheme, and snatching the helpless creature from the mother heart of Nature, shuts it in his prison-house, feeling sure that imprisonment is the surest method of improving the child mind. This happens only because he himself is a grown-up person who, when he wants to educate himself has to take the deliberate course of choosing his own subject and material. Therefore he naturally thinks that in educating children that kind of choice is good which is exclusive, that children should attain special facts and that they should have a special manner of acquiring facts. He does not understand that the adult mind in many respects not only differs from, but is contrary to the child mind.

It is like forcing upon the flower the mission of the fruit. The flower has to wait for its chances. It has to keep its heart open to the sunlight and to the breeze, to wait its opportunity for some insect to come seeking honey. The flower lives in a world of surprises, but the fruit must close its heart in order to ripen its seed. It must take a different course altogether. For the flower the chance coming of an insect is a great event, but for the fruit its intrusion means an injury. The adult mind is a fruit mind and it has no sympathy for the flower mind. It thinks that by closing up the child mind from outside, from the heart of Nature and from the world of surprise it can enable it to attain true maturity. It is through this tyranny of the adult mind that the children are everywhere suffering, and when I was about forty I thought I must save some of them, so far as lay in my power, from these mistakes made by prudent people of adult age.

There is no room for surprises in the schoolroom, only the perfect symmetry which can be of non-life. Every morning, exactly on the stroke of the clock, the pupil must attend school, must come to a particular class to hear the same subject taught by the same teacher of forbidding aspect. Exactly at a particular hour he finds his freedom. The holidays are all on the calendar long beforehand and everything is mechanically accurate and perfect.

This is all right for grown-up people. It is profitable for a businessman to be steady and punctual in his work, in his routine. It is even enjoyable when he has a prevision of the profit at the end of the month; he is rewarded when he finds something at its value.

But the child has no such reward of expectation. From day to day, from month to month he goes on through the routine, not knowing what he is to get from his unmeaning sufferings. At the end of the year he comes to the terrible trial of examinations. Then come injustice, for boys who work hard, but to get full marks, are deprived of the reward of their labour, the consolation of the priest. This is a cruel slavery in which to drill the child mind. It is demoralizing. It perfect obedience at the cost of individual responsibility and initiative of mind.

Has it any great or real value? We are saved from trouble when the children, who have their restless wings given them by Nature are at last put into this cage. But we kill that spirit of liberty in their mind, the spirit of adventure, which we all bring with us into the world, the spirit that every day seeks for new experiences. This freedom is absolutely necessary for the intelligent growth of the mind, as well as for the sweet nature of children.

Eventually the whole scheme goes wrong, the police have to come and take the place of conscience. We are raising prisoners for our prison-houses, inmates for our lunatic asylums: we are limiting the mind of the children by crushing their inherent power of gathering facts for themselves, by generalization and analysis, through breaking things and being naughty. The spirit of naughtiness is the greatest gift the child of man brings with him.

When I started my school, I was fortunate in having almost all the naughty boys of the neighbourhood and even from different parts of the country. Because our parents were not used to sending their boys to boarding-schools, only the most intractable boys came so that I had an interesting gathering of just those children who are most preached against in the Sunday-school books.

Who were these naughty boys? Those who had a special gift of energy which the whole spirit of discipline prevailing in respectable society could not wholly still into absolute passivity. Therefore they were considered troublesome and therefore the parents often asked me to punish them,—even when they did nothing wrong. They believed in the code of punishment itself as though it were some bitter medicine for the liver, a regular dose of which was good for the moral health of wicked boys.

But you must know that vigour and energy are Nature's best gifts to children, and there is always a fight between this vigour and the code of respectability in our civilized homes. Through this eternal conflict have been born all kinds of aberration and real wickedness, through an unnatural repression of what is natural and good in itself.

I never used any coercion or punishment against my unruly boys. Most of us think that in order to punish boys who are wicked, a restraint of their freedom is necessary. But restriction itself is the cause of Nature going wrong. When mind and life are given full freedom they achieve health. I adopted the system of freedom cure, if I can give it the name. The boys were allowed to run about, to climb difficult trees, and often to come to grief in their falls. They would get drenched out in the rain, they would swim in the pond. Through Nature's own method a cure came to these boys who were considered wholly bad and when they returned home, their parents were surprised to find the immense change effected.

Freedom is not merely in unrestricted space and movement. There is such a thing as unrestricted human relationship which is also necessary for the children. They have this freedom of relationship with their mother, though she is much older in age,—in fact through her human love, she feels no obstruction in their communion of hearts, and the mother almost becomes a comrade to her children. This gift of love which Nature has given the mother is absolutely necessary for children because this love is freedom, and so I felt, in this Institution, that our young pupils who come away from their mothers, should have their freedom of relationship with their teachers.

I became the playmate of my students and shared their life completely. When I had a few, I was almost the only teacher they had, and yet they were not frightened at the disparity of age between them and myself. They felt the spirit of home in this place. What is the spirit of the home? It is the natural kinship of a boy with his brothers, his family, and the resulting atmosphere in which the heart finds its full amount of space.

Most teachers do not know that in order to teach boys they have to be boys. Unfortunately schoolmasters are obsessed with the consciousness of their dignity as grown-up persons and as learned men, and therefore they always try to burden the children with their grown-up manners and their learned manners, and that hurts the mind of the students unnecessarily.

I try to let them realize that though we have our difference of age, yet, like wayfarers, we are travelling the same path together—old and young, we are working for the same goal. It is not that we, the teachers, have reached that goal and they the pupils, are immensely away from us. This immensity of difference is a frightful thing. It should never be allowed to work on the minds of children.

There is a lack of living growth in our educational institutions. These institutions are things completed. They are made with iron bars and skilfully built for the accommodation of children within them. But I wanted to let the boys feel that it was not their cage but their nest—that is to say, they also had to take part in building it themselves. The edifice of education should be our common creation, not only the teachers', not only the organizers', but also the students'. The boys must give part of their life to build it up and feel that they are living in a world which is their very own and that is the best freedom which man can have.

If we live in an arrangement which is not our own, but which is made by somebody else, however wise he may be, it is no real world of freedom for us. For our creative mind craves expression for itself in building its own world. I wanted to give that satisfaction to my students, and to give them freedom to manage their own affairs as much as was possible. I always urged them to realize that this school was not mine, but theirs; that the school was not completed—that it waited for its completion through their co-operation; that they have come to learn, by collaborating with their teacher. And I think that students in my institution understood my idea and, because they understood it, they developed an intense love for this institution which they always take occasion to visit whenever they find time and opportunity after they have left it.

I had to consider these significant facts: The birds and animals and men are born with an active mind which seeks its freedom. This activity which they bring with them seeks its world of freedom for its self-education. Then it also has its activity of heart, which seeks for its freedom in the natural relationship of sympathy. Then also it has its activity of soul which seeks its opportunity to create the world for itself—a world of freedom. All these we have to keep in mind in our effort to educate children.

This active mind of theirs must not be thwarted by constant imposition from outside; and their active heart must not be restricted through the unsympathetic obstruction of artificial relationship; and the active creative will must not be allowed to dwindle away into utter passivity through want of opportunity. So in my institution I try to make provision for these three aspects of freedom—freedom of mind, freedom of heart and freedom of will.

I have a deep-rooted conviction that only through freedom can man attain his fulness of growth, and when we restrict that freedom it means that we have some purpose of our own which we impose on the children, and we have not in mind Nature's own purpose of giving the child its fulness of growth. When we want to have more leaves from a tree, we try to train it in such a manner as to suppress its energy of producing flowers and fruit and then all its energy can be utilized in producing leaves, but that does not really give completeness of life for the tree.

If we have some purpose expressed through our educational institutions—that children should be producing patriots, practical men, soldiers, bankers, then it may be necessary that we have to put them through the mechanical drill of obedience and discipline! but that is not the fulness of life, not the fulness of humanity. He who knows that Nature's own purpose is to make the boy a full man when he grows up—full in all directions, mentally and mainly spiritually—he who realizes this, brings up the child in the atmosphere of freedom. Unfortunately we have our human weakness, and we have our love of power, and some teachers—most schoolmasters—have that inherent love of power in them, and they find this field ready-made for its exercise upon these helpless children.

I have noticed this fact, that those teachers who pride themselves on being disciplinarians are really born tyrants, as so many men are, and in order to give outlet to their inherent lust for tyranny, they make use of these helpless children and impose on them their own code of behaviour. They try to crush their minds with tasks which are lifeless, which are mechanical, which kill the intellectual mind, the fresh mind. They impose all kinds of torture because these tyrants take pleasure at the very sight of it, and such a great opportunity for such enjoyment they can never hope to attain outside their school premises.

This is not only torture and misery for the pupils, but it causes the greatest mischief possible in the human world,—this choice of the schoolmaster's profession by people who ought to have for their vocation that of executioner or prison-warder or something of that kind. An immense amount of sympathy and understanding and imagination are needed to bring up human children. They are not produced and trained for some purposes of display, they are not dancing bears or monkeys. They are human beings, with the treasure of their mind and their spirit. And that work should never be left to the care of those who have no imagination, no real sympathy for children, who cannot be a child. He who has lost the child in himself is absolutely unfit for this great work of educating human children.

Unfortunately for me the language I am using is not yours nor mine, and it is taking a long time. I cannot go fully into details about my system and manner of education owing to this obstruction. But I have given you the general principles of the education which I believe to be true, and it is this—that as God himself finds his own freedom is his own creation and then his nature is fulfilled, human beings have to create their own world and then they can have their freedom! And for that they must be trained, not to be soldiers, not to be clerks in a bank, not to be merchants, but to be the makers of their own world and their own destiny. And for that they must have all their faculties fully developed in the atmosphere of freedom.

We, who only believe in book education, distort the minds of those boys who have their natural gift of teaching themselves through their work, through their direct observation. We force them to accept book lessons, and by doing it we kill for good their power to create their own world. This is happening in most of the human boys. We impose upon them our ideas and also those which are secondhand ideas for us.

That to create our own world has been the purpose of God, we see when we find that, even as children we had our one and only pleasure in that play where, with trifling materials, we gave expression to our imagination. That is more valuable to us as children than gold or bank-notes or anything else. The same thing is true with regard to every human individual. We forget this value of the individual creative power because our minds become obsessed with the artificial value which is made prevalent in society by other peoples' valuation of a particular manner of living, a particular style of respectability. We force ourselves to accept that imposition and we kill the most precious gift that God has given us, the gift of creation, which comes from His own nature.

God is creator, and as His children we, men and women, also have to be creators. But that goes against the purposes of the tyrant, of the schoolmaster, of the educational administration, of most of the governments, each of whom want the children to grow up according to the pattern which they have set for themselves.

1924

City and Village

The standard of living in modern civilization has been raised far higher than the average level of our necessity. The strain, which such rise of standard makes us exert, increases in the beginning our physical and mental alertness. The claim upon our energy, again, accelerates its growth; and this, in its turn, produces activity that expresses itself by the raising of life's standard still higher.

When this standard attains a degree a great deal above the normal, it encourages the passion of greed. The temptation of inordinately high living, normally confined to a negligibly small section of the community, becomes widespread. This evergrowing burden is sure to prove fatal to any civilization, that puts no restraint on the emulation of self-indulgence.

In the geography of our economic world, the ups and downs produced by the inequality of fortune are healthy only within a moderate range. In a country divided by the constant interruption of steep mountains no great civilization is possible, because therein the natural flow of communication becomes difficult. Large fortunes and luxurious living, like the mountains, form high walls of segregation; they produce worse divisions in society than any physical barriers.

There are some who believe that in the eradication of the idea of property the solution is to be found, for then, and then only, will the communal spirit find its full freedom. But we must know that the urging which has given rise to property, is something fundamental in human nature. If you have the power, you may tyrannically do violence to all that constitutes property; but you cannot change the constitution of mind itself.

Property is a medium for the expression of our personality. If we look at the negative aspect of this personality, we see in it the limits which separate one person from another. And when, in some men, this sense of separateness takes on an intense emphasis, we call them selfish. But its positive aspect reveals the truth, that it is the only medium through which men can communicate with one another. Therefore, all through the course of human history, men have tried to cultivate the sentiments that give our personality its greatest significance, thereby enabling it to bring us close together in bonds of sympathy.

If we kill our individuality because it is apt to be selfish, then human communion itself loses its meaning. But if we allow it to remain and develop, then being creative by nature, it must fashion its own world. Most often and for most men, property is the only frame that can give a foundation for such creation of a personal world. It is not merely money, not merely furniture; it does not represent merely acquisitiveness, but is an objective manifestation of our taste, our imagination, our constructive faculties, our desire for self-sacrifice.

Through this creative limitation which is our personality, we receive, we give, we express. Our highest social training is to make our property the richest expression of the best in us, of that which is universal, of our individuality whose greatest illumination is love. As individuals are the units that build the community, so property is the unit of wealth that makes for communal prosperity, when it is alive to its function. Our wisdom lies not in destroying separateness of units, but in maintaining the spirit of unity in its full strength.

When life is simple, wealth does not become too exclusive, and individual property finds no great difficulty in acknowledging its communal responsibility, rather, it becomes its vehicle. In former days, in India, public opinion levied heavy taxes upon wealth and most of the public works of the country were voluntarily supported by the rich. The water-supply, medical help, education and amusement were naturally maintained by men of property through a spontaneous adjustment of mutual obligation. This was made possible, because the limits set to the individual right of self-indulgence were narrow, and surplus wealth easily followed the channel of social responsibility. In such a society, property was the pillar that supported its civilization, and wealth gave opportunity to the fortunate for self-sacrifice.

But with the rise of the standard of living, property changes its aspect. It shuts the gate of hospitality, which is the best means of social intercommunication. It displays its wealth in an extravagance which is self-centred. It begets envy and irreconcilable class division. In short, property becomes anti-social. Because, with what is called material progress, property has become intensely individualistic, the method of gaining it has become a matter of science and not of social ethics. It breaks social bonds; it drains the life sap of the community. Its unscrupulousness plays havoc all over the world, generating forces that can coax or coerce peoples to deeds of injustice and wholesale horror.

The forest-fire feeds upon the living world, from which it springs, till it is completely exhausted along with the fuel. When a passion, like greed, breaks loose from the barrier of social control, it acts in like manner, feeding upon the life of society, and the end is annihilation. It had ever been the object of the spiritual training of man to fight those passions that are anti-social and keep them chained. But lately some abnormal temptation has set them free and they are fiercely devouring all that is affording them shelter.

There are always insects in our harvest field which, in spite of their robbery, leave a sufficient surplus for the tillers of the soil, and it does not pay to try to exterminate them. But when some pest, that has enormous powers of self-multiplication, attacks our food crop, it has to be dealt with as a calamity. In human society, in normal circumstances, there are a number of causes that make for wastage, yet it does not cost us too much to ignore them. But to-day the blight, that has fallen on our social life and its resources, is disastrous, because it is not restricted to limited regions. It is an epidemic of voracity that has infected the total area of civilization.

We all now-a-days claim our right of freedom to be extravagant in our enjoyment, to the extent that we can afford it. Not to be able to waste as much upon individual gratification, as my rich neighbour does, merely proves a poverty of which I am ashamed, and against which my womenfolk and my parasites are permitted to cherish their grievance. Ours has become a society in which, through its tyrannical standard of respectability, all the members are goading one another to spoil themselves to the uttermost limit.

There is a continual screwing up of the ideal of convenience and comfort, the results of which, however, inevitably fall short of the energy spent by reason of the wastage involved. The very shriek of advertisement itself, which must constantly accompany the progress of production, means the squandering of an immense quantity of material and life force, and merely helps to swell the sweepings of time.

Civilization to-day has turned into a vast catering establishment. It maintains constant feasts for a whole population of gluttons. The intemperance, which could safely have been tolerated in a few, has spread its contagion to the multitude. The universal greed, produced as a consequence, is the cause of the meanness, cruelty and lies, in politics and commerce, that vitiate the whole human atmosphere. A civilization with such an unnatural appetite must depend for its existence upon numberless victims, and these are being sought in those parts of the world where human flesh is cheap. In Asia and Africa a bartering goes on, whereby the future hope and happiness of entire peoples are sold for the sake of providing fastidious fashion with an endless train of respectable rubbish.

The consequence of such material and moral drain is more evident when one studies the conditions manifested in the fatness of the cities and the physical and mental anaemia of the villages, almost everywhere in the world. For cities have become inevitably important. They represent energy and materials concentrated for the satisfaction of that exaggerated appetite, which is the characteristic symptom of modern civilization. Such abnormal devouring process cannot be carried on, unless certain parts of the social body conspire and organize to feed upon the whole. This is suicidal; but, before its progressive degeneracy ends in death, the disproportionate enlargement of the particular section looks formidably great, and conceals the starved pallor of the entire body,—the sacrifice of the great maintaining the small in its enormity, and creating for the time being an illusion of wealth.

The living relationship, in a physical or social body, is the sympathetic mutuality of help among its members and organs, whereby a perfect balance of communication between them is maintained, so that the consciousness of unity is not obstructed. The resulting health and wealth are of secondary importance,—the unity is ultimate in itself. The perfect rhythm of reciprocity which generates and maintains this unity is disturbed whenever some ambition of power establishes its dominance in life's republic.

What in the West is called democracy can never be true in a society where greed grows, uncontrolled, encouraged, even admired by the populace. In such an atmosphere, a constant struggle goes on among individuals to capture public organizations for the satisfaction of their own personal ambition, and democracy becomes like an elephant whose one purpose in life is to give joy rides to the clever and the rich.

In this kind of Body politic, the organs of information and expression, through which opinions are manufactured, together with the machinery of administration, are all openly or secretly manipulated by those prosperous few, who have been compared of old to the camel, which can never pass through a needle's eye,—the gate that leads to the kingdom of ideals. Such a society necessarily becomes inhospitable and suspicious, and callously cruel against those who preach their faith in spiritual freedom. In such a society, people are intoxicated through the constant stimulation of what they call progress, a progress which they are willing to buy at the cost of civilization itself, like the man for whom wine has more attraction than food.

Villages are like women. In their keeping is the cradle of the race. They are nearer to nature than towns; and are therefore in closer touch with the fountain of life. They have the atmosphere which possesses a natural power of healing. It is the function of the village, like that of woman, to provide people with their elemental needs, with food and joy, with the simple poetry of life, and with those ceremonies of beauty which the village spontaneously produces and in which she finds delight. But when constant strain is put upon her through the extortionate claim of ambition; when her resources are exploited through the excessive stimulus of temptation, then she becomes poor in life, her mind becomes dull and uncreative; and from her time-honoured position of the wedded partner of the city, she is degraded to that of maid-servant. While, in its turn, the city, in its intense egotism and pride, remains unconscious of the devastation it constantly works upon the very source of its life and health and joy.

Those who are familiar with the Hindu Pantheon know that in our mythology there is a demi-god named Kuvera, similar in character to Mammon. He represents the multiplication of money whose motive force is greed. His figure is ugly and gross with its protuberant belly, comic in its vulgarity of self-exaggeration. He is the genius of property that knows no moral responsibility. But the goddess, Lakshmi, who is the Deity of Prosperity, is beautiful. For prosperity is for all. It dwells in that property which, though belonging to the individual, generously owns its obligation to the community. Lakshmi is seated on a lotus, the lotus which is the symbol of the universal heart. It signifies that she presides over that wealth which means happiness for all men, which is hospitable.

By some ill-luck, Lakshmi has been deprived of her lotus throne in the present age, and Kuvera is worshipped in her place. Modern cities represent his protuberant stomach, and ugliness reigns unashamed. About one thing we have to be reminded, that there is no cause for rejoicing in the fact that this ugliness has an enormous power of growth and that it is prolific of its progeny. Its growth is not true progress; it is a disease which keeps the body swelling while it is being killed.

The sunshine that is diffuse maintains life in a whole forest of trees; and the sunshine of wealth is symbolised in Lakshmi. The sunshine, when it is focussed through a burning glass on a narrow spot, can reduce the same forest of trees to ashes; this hungry fire of concentrated wealth is symbolised in Kuvera, and he is the presiding deity of our modern cities.

Modern cities are continually growing bigger only because no central spirit of Unity exercises vital control over their growth of dimension. There can be no end to their addition of hugeness, because their object is not to modulate human relationships into some beauty of truth, but to gain convenience.

When in the Sanskrit poem, *Meghaduta,* we follow the path of the cloud messenger and in imagination pass over the old-world towns mentioned in it, with their beautiful names, we feel that the poet in reciting them was giving voice to his hungering delight of some remembrance; we instinctively know that these towns expressed more than anything else the love and hope of man, treasuring some of the splendour of his soul in their houses and temples with their auspicious decoration daily accomplished by women, and even in the picturesque bartering that went on in their market places.

We can imagine what Delhi and Agra must have been in the time to which they belonged. They manifested in their development some creatively human aspect of a great empire. Whatever might have been its character, these cities even in their decay still retain in their magnificence the true product of the self-respect of man. But modern cities merely give opportunities, not ideals.

Cities there must be in man's civilization, just as in higher organisms there must be organized centres of life, such as the brain, heart, or stomach. These never overwhelm the living wholeness of the body; on the contrary, by a perfect federation of their functions, they maintain its richness. But a tumour round which the blood is congested, is the enemy of the whole body upon which it feeds as it swells. Our modern cities, in the same way feed upon the whole social organism that runs through the villages; they continually drain away the life stuff of the community, and slough off a huge amount of dead matter, while assuming a lurid counterfeit of prosperity.

Thus, unlike a living heart, these cities imprison and kill the blood and create poison centres filled with the accumulation of death. When a very large body of men comes together for the sake of some material purpose, then it is as a congestion and not a congregation. When men are close together and yet develop no intimate bond of human relationship, there ensues moral putrefaction. Wherever in the world, this modern civilization is spreading its dominion, the life principle of society, which is the principle of personal relationship, is injured at the root.

All this is the result of an almost complete substitution of true civilization by what the West calls Progress. I am never against progress, but when, for its sake, civilization is ready to sell its soul, then I choose to remain primitive in my material possessions, hoping to achieve my civilization in the realm of the spirit.

People, as a whole, do and must live in the village, for it is their natural habitation. But the professions depend upon their special appliances and environment, and therefore barricade themselves with particular purposes, shutting out the greater part of universal nature, which is the cradle of life. The city, in all civilizations, represents this professionalism,—some concentrated purpose of the people. That is to say, people have their home in the village and their offices in the city.

We all know that the office is for serving and enriching the home, and not for banishing it into insignificance. But we also know that when goaded by greed, the gambling spirit gets hold of a man, he is willing to rob his home of all its life and joy and to pour them into the hungry jaws of the office. For a time such a man may prosper, but his prosperity is gained at the cost of happiness. His wife may shine in a blaze of jewelry, rousing envy along the path of her economic triumph, but her spirit withers in secret, thirsting for love and the simple delights of life.

Society encourages the professions only because they are of service to the people at large. They find their truth when they belong to the people. But the professions, because they get all power into their hands, begin to believe that people live to maintain them. Thus we often see that a lawyer thrives by taking advantage of the weaknesses of his clients, their helpless dread of loss, their dishonest love of gain. The proportion between the help rendered and its reward demanded, loses its legitimate limit, when it is not guided by any standard of social ethics.

Such a moral perversion has come to its extreme length to-day in the relationship of the city and the village. The city, which is the professional aspect of society, has gradually come to believe that the village is its legitimate field for exploitation, that the village must at the cost of its own life maintain the city in all its brilliance of luxuries and excesses; that its wealth must be magnified even though that should involve the bankruptcy of happiness.

True happiness is not at all expensive, because it depends upon that natural spring of beauty and life which is harmony of relationship. Ambition pursues its path of self-seeking by breaking this bond of harmony, cutting gaps, creating dissensions. It feels no hesitation in trampling under foot the harvest field, which is for all, in order to snatch away in haste the object of its craving. To-day this ambition, wasteful and therefore disruptive of social life, the greatest enemy of civilization, has usurped the helm of society.

In India we had our family system, large and complex, each family a miniature society in itself. I do not wish to discuss the question of its desirability. But its rapid decay in the present day clearly points out the nature and process of the principle of destruction which is at work in modern civilization. When life was simple and its needs normal, when selfish passions were under control, such a domestic system was perfectly natural and fully productive of happiness. The family resources were sufficient for all and the claims on them were never excessive on the part of one or more of its individual members. But such a group can never survive, if the personal ambition of a single member begins separately to clamour for a great deal more than is necessary for him. When emulation in augmenting private possession, and the enjoyment of exclusive advantage runs ahead of the common good and general happiness, the bond of harmony, which is the bond of sustenance, must give way and brothers must separate, nay, even become enemies.

The passion that rages in the heart of modern civilization is, like a volcanic flame, constantly struggling to throw up eruptions of individual bloatedness. The stream of production, which thereupon gushes forth, may give one the impression of a huge, indefinite, gain. But such interruption needs must disturb man's creative mind. We forget that it is only the spirit of creation evolving out of its own inner abundance, that adds to our true wealth; and that the spirit of production but consumes our resources in the process of building and filling it storehouses. Therefore our needs which stimulate production must observe the limits of the normal. If we go on poking them into a bigger and bigger flame, the conflagration will no doubt dazzle our sight, but its splendour will leave on its debit side a black heap of charred remains.

When our wants are moderate, the rations we claim do not exhaust the common store of nature and the pace of their restoration does not hopelessly fall behind that our consumption of them. This moderation, moreover, leaves us leisure to cultivate happiness, the happiness which is the artist soul of the human world, creating beauty of form and rhythm of life. But man to-day forgets that the divinity in him is revealed by the halo of his happiness.

The Germany of the period of Goethe was considered to be poor by the Germany of the period of Bismarck. Possibly the standard of civilization, illumined by the mind of Plato, or by the life of the Emperor Asoka, is underrated by the proud children of modern times who compare it with the present age of progress, an age dominated by millionaires, diplomats and war-lords. Many things that are of common use to-day were absolutely lacking in those days. But are those who lived then to be pitied by the young boys of our time, who have more of the printing press, but less of the mind?

I often imagine that the moon, being smaller in size than the earth, begat life on her soil earlier than was possible on that of her companion. Once, she too had her constant festival of colour, music, movement; her storehouse was perpetually replenished with food for her children who were already there and who were to come. Then in course of time, some race was born to her, gifted with a furious energy of intelligence, which began greedily to devour its surroundings. It produced beings, who, because of the excess of their animal spirit coupled with intellect lacked the imagination to realize that the mere process of addition did not create fulfilment; that acquisition because of its bigness did not produce happiness; that movement did not constitute progress merely because of its velocity; that progress could have meaning only in relation to some ideal of completeness. Through machinery of tremendous power, they made such an addition to their natural capacity for gathering and holding, that their career of plunder outstripped nature's power of recuperation. Their profit-makers created wants which were unnatural and dug big holes in the stored capital of nature, forcibly to extract provision for them. When they had reduced the limited store of material, they waged furious wars among their different sections for the special allotment of the lion's share. In their scramble for the right of self-indulgence they laughed at moral law and took it to be a sign of racial superiority to be ruthless in the satisfaction of their desires. They exhausted the water, cut down the trees, reduced the surface of the planet into a desert riddled with pits. They made its interior a rifled pocket, emptied of its valuables. At last one day, like a fruit whose pulp has been completely eaten by insects which it sheltered, the moon became a lifeless shell, a universal grave for the voracious creatures who had consumed the world to which they were born.

My imaginary selenites behaved exactly in the way that human beings are behaving on this earth, fast exhausting the stores of sustenance not because they must live their normal life, but because they strain their capacity of life to a pitch of monstrous excess. Mother Earth has enough for the healthy appetite of her children and something extra for rare cases of abnormality. But she has not nearly enough for the sudden growth of a whole world of spoilt and pampered children.

Man has been digging holes into the very foundations, not only of his livelihood, but also of his life; he is feeding upon his own body. The reckless wastage of humanity which ambition produces, is best seen in the villages, where the light of life is being dimmed, the joy of existence dulled, the natural threads of social communion snapped every day. It should be our mission to restore the full circulation of life's blood into these maltreated limbs of society; to bring to the villages health and knowledge;

wealth of space in which to live; wealth of time in which to work and to rest and to enjoy; respect which will give them dignity; sympathy which will make them realize their kinship with the world of men, and not merely their survient position.

Streams, lakes and oceans are there on this earth. They exist not for the hoarding of water exclusively within their own areas. They send up the vapour which forms into clouds and helps towards a wider distribution of water. Cities have their functions of maintaining wealth and knowledge in concentrated forms of opulence, but this also, should not be for their own sake; they should be centres of irrigation; they should gather in order to distribute; they should not magnify themselves, but should enrich the entire commonwealth. They should be like lamp-posts, and the light they support must transcend their own limits.

Such a relationship of mutual benefit between the city and the village can remain strong only so long as the spirit of co-operation and self-sacrifice is a living ideal in society. When some universal temptation overcomes this ideal, when some selfish passion gains ascendancy, then a gulf is formed and goes on widening between them; then the mutual relationship of city and village becomes that of exploiter and victim. This is a form of perversity whereby the body-politic becomes its own enemy and whose termination is death.

We have started in India, in connection with our Visva-bharati, work of village reconstruction, the mission of which is to retard this process of race suicide. If I try to give you the details of our work, they will look small. But we are not afraid of this appearance of smallness, for we have confidence in life. We know that if as a seed it represents the truth that is in us, it will overcome opposition and conquer space and time. According to us, the poverty problem is not the most important, the problem of unhappiness is the great problem. Wealth, which is the synonym for the production and collection of things, men can make use of ruthlessly. They can crush life out of the earth and flourish. But, happiness, which may not compete with wealth in its list of materials, is final, it is creative; therefore it has its source of riches within itself.

Our object is to try to flood the choked bed of village life with the stream of happiness. For this the scholars, the poets, the musicians, the artists, have to collaborate, to offer their contributions. Otherwise they must live like parasites, sucking life from the people and giving nothing back to them. Such exploitation gradually exhausts the soil of life, which needs constant replenishing, by the return to it of life, through the completion of the cycle of receiving and giving back.

Most of us, who try to deal with the poverty problem, think of nothing but a greater intensive effort to production, forgetting that this only means a greater exhaustion of materials as well as of humanity. This only means giving exaggerated opportunity for profit to a few, at the cost of the many. It is food which nourishes, not money; it is fulness of life which makes one happy, not fulness of purse. Multiplying materials intensifies the inequality between those who have and those who have not, and this deals a fatal wound to the social system, through which the whole body is eventually bled to death.

1924

The Voice of Humanity

My friends, I have been waiting for this moment. When Prof. Formichi asked me to tell him what would be my subject this evening, I said I did not know; for you must understand that I am not a speaker. I am nothing better than a poet. When I speak, I speak *with* my surroundings and not *to* my surroundings. Now that I see your kind faces, your silent voice has reached my heart, and my voice will blend with it. When the heart wishes to pay its debt, it must have some coin with the stamp of its own realm upon it—and that is our mother tongue. But I do not know your beautiful language, neither do you know mine. Since, therefore, that medium cannot be used for the commerce of thought and sentiment between you and myself, I have reluctantly to use the English language, which is neither yours nor mine. Therefore at the outset I ask you to forgive me—those of you who do not know this language, as also those of you who do—because my English is a foreigner's English.

Now I know what I am going to speak to you about. It will be in answer to the question as to what was the urging that brought me to you across the sea. Some time in 1921 I felt a great desire to make my pilgrimage to the shrine of humanity, where the human mind was fully awake, with all its lamps lighted, there to meet face to face the Eternal in man. It had occurred to me that this present age was dominated by the European mind only because that mind was fully awake. You all know how the spirit of great Asia is going through an age-long slumber in the depth of night, with only few lonely watchers to read the stars and wait for the sign of the rising sun across the darkness. So I had this longing to come to Europe and see the human spirit in the full blaze of its power and beauty. Then it was that I took that voyage—my voyage of pilgrimage to Europe—leaving for the moment my own work at Shanti-Niketan and the children I loved.

But this was not my first visit to Europe. In the year 1878, when I was a boy, barely seventeen, I was brought over by my brother to these shores. It will be difficult for you to realize what visions we had in the East, in those days, of this great continent of Europe. Though I was young, and though my knowledge of English was very insufficient, yet I had heard of her great poets and her heroes, of the ideal Europe of literature, so full of the love of freedom and of humanity.

Italy was my first introduction to Europe. In those days the steamers stopped at Brindisi, and I still remember, when we reached the port, it was midnight under a full moon. I came rushing up on deck from my bed, and shall never forget that marvellous scene, enveloped in the silent mystery of the moonlight—the sight of Europe asleep, like a maiden dreaming of beauty and peace.

It was fortunate for me that Brindisi was a small town, a quiet place, not so aggressively different from the scenes to which I had been accustomed from my childhood. I felt sure that its heart was open to me, to welcome the boy poet, who though young was even in those days a dreamer. I was greatly elated as I left the steamer to pass the night in what I suppose in these days of progress would be termed a third-rate hotel, having no electric light or other conveniences. I felt that I was in the arms of this great mother Europe and my heart seemed to feel the warmth of her breast.

The next day I woke and, with my brother and an Indian friend, wandered into an orchard close by, a garden of paradise which threatened no punishment against trespassers. Ah, what delight I had that morning in the limpid sunlight, in the hospitality of leaf and fruit and flower! There was an Italian girl there, who reminded me of our Indian maidens, with eyes dark like bees, which have the power to explore the secret honey-cells of love in the lotus of our hearts. (You know, with us the lotus is the emblem of the heart.) She was a simple girl with a coloured kerchief round her head and a complexion not too white. That is, it was not a pallid lack of complexion. (I wish to be forgiven when I say that the complexion of whiteness is the complexion of the desert, not the complexion of life.) Hers was like that of a bunch of grapes caressed by the warm kisses of the sun, the sun which had modulated the beauty of her face, giving it a tender bloom.

I need not dwell at length upon the feelings I experienced; it is enough to say that I was of the impressionable age of seventeen. I felt that I had come to a land of beauty, of repose and joy, which even at that time inspired my mind with the idea that one day I should claim its welcome for me.

With me it was a case of love at first sight; but for my companions it was but a fleeting moment, so that I was not free to stay, but had to continue the journey with my brother, who wanted me to hasten to my lessons in English. Being a truant by nature, I had always refused to attend my classes, and thus having become a problem to my elders, they had decided to send me to England to learn under compulsion the language which, according to their notion, would give me the stamp of respectability.

England is a great country, and I pay my homage to the greatness of her people, but I must be excused if I did not appreciate it at the moment. For an Indian boy such as I was, left there alone in the depth of winter when the birds were silent and the sun so miserly with its gifts, the country seemed on every side like a visible spirit of rude refusal. I was homesick and extremely shy. I was frightened at the sombrely dressed people who stared at me. From my lodging-house, facing Regent's Park, I would gaze with a feeling of bewilderment at its monotony of leaflessness through the mists, the fogs, and the drizzle. In a word, I was young—too young to enter into the spirit of England at that time. I merely glanced at the surface of things with my distracted heart always yearning for its own nest across the sea.

After a few months' stay, I went back home to India. But I dare not here give a recital of my idle days which followed to those of you who are young, and for whom the example of a studiously strenuous life of usefulness would perhaps be more beneficial. I avoided all kinds of educational training that could give me any sort of standardized culture stamped with a university degree. I dreamt, wrote verses, stories and plays, lived in solitude on the banks of the Ganges, and hardly knew anything of the movements and counter-movements of forces in the great world.

Whilst I was in the midst of my creative work, there came to me an inner message asking me to come out of my seclusion and seek life in the heart of the crowd. I knew not what I could do. I had a love for children, so that I called them round me, in order to rescue them from the dismal dungeons of the educational department, and find for them that atmosphere of sympathy and freedom which they needed most. I chose a beautiful and secluded spot where, in collaboration with Mother Nature, it was possible to bring up these boys in a spirit of wisdom and love.

While I was still busy doing service to children I do not know what possessed me all of a sudden. From some far-away sky came to me a call of pilgrimage reminding me that we are all born pilgrims—pilgrims of this green earth. A voice questioned me: 'Have you been to the sacred shrine where Divinity reveals itself in the thoughts and dreams and deeds of Man?' I thought possibly it was in Europe where I must seek it and know the full meaning of my birth as a human being in this world. And so for the second time I came to this continent.

But, meanwhile, I had grown up and learnt much of the history of man. I had sighed with the great poet Wordsworth, who became sad when he saw what man had done to man. We too have suffered at the hands of man—not tigers and snakes, not elemental forces of nature, but human beings. Men are ever the greatest enemy of Man. I had felt and known it; all the same, there was a hope, deep in my heart, that I should find some place, some temple, where the immortal spirit of man dwelt hidden like the sun behind clouds.

Yet, when I arrived in the land of my quest, I could not stop the insistent question which kept troubling me with a sense of despair: 'Why is it that Europe with all her power of mind is racked with unrest? How is it that she is overcome with such a whirlwind of suspicion and jealousy and greed? Why is it that her greatness itself offers a vast field for fiercely contending passions to have their devil-dance in the lurid light of conflagration?'

When I travelled from Italy to Calais I saw the beautiful scenery on both sides of the railway. These men, I thought, have the ability to love their soil; and what a great power is this love! How they have beautified and made fruitful the whole continent with heroic sacrifice! With the force of their love they have fully won their country for themselves, and this ever-active service of their devotion, for generations, has given rise in them to an irresistible power. For love is the highest human truth, and truth gives fulness of life. The earth is overwhelmed by it, not because of man's covetousness, but because of this life-giving shower of heart and mind that he has poured around him. How he has struggled to eradicate the obstinate barrenness from the inert! How he has fought and defeated at every step the evil in everything that was hostile in his surroundings! Why then this dark misery lowering over Europe, why this widespread menace of doom in her sky?

Because the love for her own soil and children will no longer suffice for her. So long as destiny offered to her only a limited problem, Europe did more or less satisfactorily solve it. Her answer was patriotism, nationalism—that is to say, love only for that and those to whom she happened to be related. According to the degree of truth in this love she has reaped her harvest of welfare. But to-day, through the help of science, the whole world has been given to her for a problem. How to answer it in the fulness of truth she has yet to learn. Because the problem has become vast, the wrong answer is fraught with immense danger.

A great truth has been laid bare to you, and according to your dealing with it you will attain the fulfilment of your destiny. If you do not have the strength to accept it in the right spirit, your humanity will rapidly degenerate; your love of freedom, love of justice, love of truth, love of beauty, will wither at the root; and you will be rejected of God.

Do you not realize how a rigid ugliness is everywhere apparent—in your cities, in your commerce, the same monotonous mask—so that nowhere is there room for a living expression of the spirit? This is the creeping in of death, limb by limb, in the body of your civilization.

Love can be patient. Beauty is moulded and matured by patience. Your great artists knew it in the days when they could gladly modulate all the riches of their leisure into some tiny detail of beauty. The greedy man can never do this. Factories are the triumph of ugliness, for no one has the patience to try to give them the touch of grace; and so, everywhere in God's world to-day, we are faced with what is called progress, a progress towards inhospitable ugliness, towards the eddy of a bottomless passion which is voracity. Can you call to mind any great voice speaking out of the human heart in these modern days?

We have no doubt reason to be proud of Science. We offer to Europe our homage in return for her gift of science, now bequeathed to posterity. Our sages have said: 'The Infinite has to be known and realized. For man, the Infinite is the only true source of happiness.' Europe has come face to face with the Infinite in the world of extension, the domain of external Nature.

I do not cry down the material world. I fully realize that this is the nurse and the cradle of the Spirit. By achieving the Infinite in the heart of the material world you have made this world more generous than it ever was. But merely coming to a rich fact does not give us the right to own it. The great Science which you have discovered still awaits your meriting. Through what you have gained outwardly you may become successful, but you may miss greatness in spite of the success.

Because you have strenuously cultivated your mind in Europe, because of your accuracy of observation and the development of your reasoning faculties, these discoveries you have undoubtedly deserved. But discoveries have to be realized by a complete humanity—Knowing has to be brought under the control of Being—before Truth can be fully honoured. But our Being, the fundamental reality in the human world, with which all other truths have to be brought into harmony at any cost, is not within the domain of Science. Truth when not properly treated turns back on us to destroy us. Your very science is thus becoming your destroyer.

If you have acquired a thunderbolt for yourself, you must earn the right arm of a god to be safe. You have failed to cultivate those qualities which would give you full sovereign right over science and therefore you have missed peace. You cry for peace, and only build another frightful machine, some new powerful combination. Quiet may be imposed by outside compulsion for a time, but Peace comes from the inner spirit, from the power of sympathy, the power of self-sacrifice—not of organization.

I have great faith in humanity. Like the sun it can be clouded, but never extinguished. I admit that at this time when the human races have met together as never before, the baser elements appear predominant. The powerful are exulting at the number of their victims. They take the name of science to cultivate the schoolboy superstition that they have certain physical signs indicating their eternal right to rule, as the explosive force of the earthquake once might have claimed, with enough of evidence, its never-ending sway over the destiny of this earth. But they in their turn will be disappointed.

Theirs is the cry of a past that is already exhausted, a past that has thrived upon the exclusive spirit of national individualism which will no longer be able to keep the balance in its perpetual disharmony with its surroundings. Only those races will prosper who, for the sake of their own perfection and permanent safety, are ready to cultivate the spiritual magnanimity of mind that enables the soul of man to be realized in the heart of all races.

For men to come near to one another and yet to continue to ignore the claims of humanity is a sure process of suicide. We are waiting for the time when the spirit of the age will be incarnated in a complete human truth and the meeting of men will be translated into the Unity of Man.

I have come to your door seeking the voice of humanity, which must sound its solemn challenge and overcome the clamour of the greedy crowd of slave-drivers. Perhaps it is already being uttered in whispers behind closed doors, and will grow in volume till it bursts forth in a thundering cry of judgment, and the vulgar shout of brute force is silenced in awe.

1925

The Indian Ideal of Marriage

A request has come to me from Europe to say something about the Indian idea of marriage. This puts me in mind of the difference between the European and the Indian idea,—a difference which is not merely of outer method, but of inner purpose.

Like all distinctive features of civilized societies, the marriage system is an attempt at compromise between the biological purposes of Nature and the sociological purposes of Man; and both its outer form and inner aim depends upon the divergence between these two. For, in his individual as well as in his social life, man is governed by this Diarchy.

Thus, where society is complex with a network of widely-ramified relationships, the natural propensities have to be kept in check by social pressure from every side. While, where wants are numerous and their supply difficult, and man is compelled to venture forth to distant places to make a living, there the social obligations need must be light, and the nature and extent of the mutual claims of individuals over one another cannot be rigidly prescribed by society, but must be left to be adjusted by the individuals themselves.

It is a matter of comment by Europeans that we use no word like 'thanks' in our own language, for expressing gratitude; and they jump to the conclusion that our character must be free from that troublesome feeling. But the fact is, that in our society the obligation of the giver of help is held to be stronger than that of the recipient. On him who has acquired learning is cast the duty of giving to others,—that is not taken as a favour done by teacher to student. The offering of hospitality even to the casual visitor, is incumbent on the householder for his own sake. Each of the domestic ceremonies, from the birth-celebration to the funeral, is but an expression of the debt which each member owes to his community. From this it becomes evident that our society is not like a stream on which its members float in comparative freedom, but like the earth in whose depths their root-system is held secure.

The Aryans of India were at first forest dwellers. Then as the dense screen of forest was lifted off the stage of their history, India's broad, river-served plains were converted from sylvan shelters of patriarchal communities into monarchical territories; and agriculture became the mainstay of her growing settlements. On the one hand, the close neighbourhood of peoples, racially different, giving rise to perpetual cultural conflict; and, on the other, the agricultural civilization claiming co-operation and the complex regulations of stable life,—these are the two forces that moulded Hindu society and still guide its course. Such a society can never exist and perform its functions unless peace is maintained amongst its members by a perfect system of mutual adjustment of rights.

In the beginning of India's history, of which we gain glimpses in the Rāmāyaṇa, three different parties are to be distinguished,—the Aryans, the barbarians (variously called monkeys, bears, etc.) and the powerful, cultured Rākshasas. While all these were at daggers drawn, their constant dissensions precluded the establishment of any common social polity. Then as the conquering Kshatriyas extended their sway, and populous settlements grew up in their wake, the need for peace was felt and its merits were exalted. So, broadly speaking, the establishment of relationships between the Aryans, the barbarians and the Rākshasas, form the main theme of the Rāmāyaṇa.

Courage, in the ethics of Peace, means the courage of self-sacrifice; there, bravery has for its object the triumph Renunciation. And, in societies where such sacrifice and renunciation are cultivated, not the individual but the household is the primary unit, and such household is broad, not narrow conception and content. That is why, as the Rāmāyaṇa evolves from a collection of ballads into an epic, its main function is transformed from a narration of struggles against the outrages offered to the cult of tillage *(sītā)* into the exaltation of the Ethics of the Household. The unfaltering strength of self-renunciation which is needful for keeping true the varied relations between king and subject, father and son, brother and brother, husband and wife, master and servant, and among neighbours different in colour and character,—that is what it really glorifies.

Wherever many men have congregated, not for the purpose of attacking others, but for mutual benefit, there is evolved a mentality which eventually transcends all considerations of expediency and envisages Supreme Good as an absolute fulfilment. And so, in our country, there was a day when the household was glorified, not as a comfortable home, not as the enjoyment of proprietary right, but as the means of living the fullest communal life, and through it of attaining supreme liberation at the end.

The intimacy of relationship with wife and child is but natural, and so may hardly help to loosen the bonds of self,—rather it serves to strengthen them. But the household wherein even the most distant of kinsmen have a recognized right, where one's own earnings have to be shared by those who are almost strangers, where it is a matter of shame and censure if differences be made between near and distant relations,—there the claims of moral welfare override those of natural affection, and give rise to certain special qualities of heart. These gradually grow so powerful that both the individual as well as the social conscience refuse to tolerate any personal claims when these conflict with those of the household *dharma*.

Therefore the home of the Indian has never been looked upon as his castle, the place where he is lord and master. No doubt the duty, there cast on him, of considering the rights of others on any and every occasion, has involved him in expenditure of time and money but his accounts have ever been cast up, not in terms of self-interest, but of social and spiritual welfare.

In societies where the household is founded on the comfort and convenience of the individual, his acceptance or non-acceptance of the householders' estate remains optional. If any such should say that he does not care for domestic joys, but prefers the freedom of irresponsibility, no room for objection is left. But in Hindu India, because the household is an essential element in its social structure, marriage is almost compulsory,—like conscription in Europe on the threat of war.

According to our Lawgivers, anyone making gifts to, or taking gifts from, a Brahmin who remains a householder, but does not marry, goes to hell. Says Atri: 'No hospitality should be accepted from an unmarried householder.' The household has been compared, in our *shāstras,* to a great tree; for, just as the roots of the latter support its branches, twigs and foliage, so does the life of the household maintain the different institutions of society; and the Lawgiver lays it down that the King should do honour to the upholder of the householders' estate. But the mere fact of setting up a household, anyhow, does not constitute that estate according to our *shāstras:*

Grihasthopi kriyāyukto na grihena grihāsrami,
Na chaiva putradārena svakarma parivarjita.

Not by the house is made the household but by the performance of the householders' duties,—nor even by wife and children, if the householder be wanting in his own *karma.*

Karma here does not mean the looking after his family interests, but the performance of his specific duty,—the fulfilment of his obligation to society.

Tathā tathaiva kāryāni na kālastu vidhīyate,
Asminneva prayuñjáno hyasminneva tu liyate.

With society are we connected, in it do we terminate this life, therefore should we do our duty as it arises, and not await our own convenience.

To perform the duties of a householder is in fact looked upon as a spiritual discipline. Says Vasistha:

Grihastha eva yajate grihasthastapyate tapah,
Chaturnāmāsramānāntu grihasthastu vishishyate.

That is to say, because the life of a householder is a life of self-abnegation having its manifold obligations to gods and men therefore of all the four *āsramas,* the *āsrama* or estate of the householder is specially distinguished.

In societies where the household is but the means of ensuring the comfort and security of the individual, the notion of property also becomes intensely individualistic; for the right of property is at the base of the householders' estate. And when property is viewed as dedicated to individual enjoyment, it ceases as such to be a joy to the others who own it not, but becomes rather an object of their envy. Not only that, but in the process of its acquisition the question of social or moral welfare is lost sight of, and the spirit of rivalry and competition acknowledges no limit. And so, in ancient India, the class of merchants whose object in life was to acquire wealth in excess of the requirements of their livelihood, were held in contempt. Even to-day, water touched by such is deemed to be impure.

A school of thought has arisen in Europe which looks upon property as inherently vicious, and would advise its forcible extirpation. For, there, the irresponsible ownership of property is a potent factor in maintaining the antagonism between the claims of universal humanity and of individual man. And, so far, Western Politics has devoted its forces to the protection of the rights of the proprietor. Hence the need for this counter-movement.

But many substances which are now good food, were once unpalatable or even poisonous. Man, however, did not reject those at the outset, but made them wholesome and toothsome by a long process of culture. India, likewise, cultivated the viciousness out of property by converting the household into a field for spiritual discipline. And thus society in India stably maintained itself for centuries on the basis of the individual ownership of property; in fact India's wealth of food and clothing, education, morals and religion were all so acquired,—by virtue of that original precautionary measure.

When the welfare of society is left to depend on the voluntary generosity of its wealthy members, then is the vicious aspect of property brought out; for the indiscriminate acceptance of charity spoils the recipient. But, in India, expenditure by the householder for social welfare was not a matter of generosity, but of primary duty in the interests of his own fulfilment. Such duty was cast not only on the rich, but also on the poor, according to their means. Manu says: 'The *rishis,* the forefathers, the gods, the guests, and all living creatures, expect to be maintained by the householder. Knowing this, he should act accordingly.' By many such injunctions and in diverse other ways, are the Indian people kept reminded that the *dharma* of the householder consists in fulfilling the various claims of humanity. And further, in Manu's opinion, those who are of weak character and have no control over their passions,—they are not worthy of the householders' high estate.

In order to understand the principle underlying Hindu marriage, it is necessary first to come to a true appreciation of this principle underlying the Hindu social system. It will then become clear that, in this type of society, having for its object the perfection of communal life, there is danger in allowing marriage to pursue the path of self-will. Such a society can only withstand the encroachments of Nature, if its marriage system is walled round with a protective embankment. So the Hindu ideal of marriage has no regard for individual taste on inclination,—it is, rather, afraid of them.

If any European would really understand the psychology behind this, let him bethink himself of the state of things that obtained during the last war. Ordinarily, in Europe, there is no bar to international marriages. But, when the one objective of the war overshadowed all other considerations, marriage with the subject of an enemy country became an impossibility; so much so, that European society felt no compunction in cruelly severing even long-standing marriage ties of this description. Not only was the marriage question so affected, but during war conditions, food and all other amenities of life had to be cut down to a uniform standard. The personal liberty and elasticity of occupation, so characteristic of Western civilization, tended wholly to disappear.

These war conditions afford a good parallel to the permanent conditions which govern Hindu society, where the encroachment of alien cultures has always been a constant danger to be guarded against. This vital objective of the twice-born leaders, who practically represented the whole people, therefore runs as a steady undercurrent through our society. The problem of keeping its civilization pure having been acknowledged as all-important, and its solution thus sought by India, her society has had to claim of its members the severe and permanent curbing of their individual liberty of choice and action.

Indian society, however, did not reach this stage all at once. It was gradually evolved through successive adaptations to changing circumstances. Meanwhile many relics of earlier stages survived into the later. Therefore Manu had to recognize, in his treatise, different other forms of marriage, such as the *Gāndharva* (by mutual choice), *Rākshasa* (by conquest), *Asur* (by purchase), *Paishācha* (by taking advantage of helplessness). In none of these is the social will manifest, but only the desire of the individual; for force whether of arms, or money, or circumstances, is arrogant and passion refuses to submit to extraneous considerations. But, while recording these forms, Manu censured them.

Though the Gāndharva marriage, founded on mutual attraction, was also one of those which did not find favour with the Lawgiver, it nevertheless long persisted in Indian society, as our epics and other literature make clear. This only shows that, however conservatively stable a society may be, the principle of stability cannot be equally strong amongst all the classes which it comprises. In the Kshatriya character, especially, the cultivation of self-suppression was least likely to attain its fullest development. It is not possible to keep confined in a complex net of social obligations the warrior spirit which ever seeks fresh fields for expansion. It is for this reason that our *shāstras* prohibited the crossing of the sea. Any adventurous activity whatsoever, that may loosen our mind from its mooring and disturb the fixed habit of our thought and belief and behaviour, is bound to undermine the very foundation of our society.

Not only sea voyage, but also residence in foreign countries with antagonistic social ideals, was prohibited and penalised. In the West we find now-a-days all kinds of forcible attempts being made to prevent the intrusion of Bolshevic ideas. This is comparable with our prohibition of foreign travel. No penalty is deemed too severe if it but keep in check the propaganda which, it is apprehended, may destroy the elements essential for the stability of the orthodox Western social system. The liberty of the people form their own opinions, to regulate their own conduct, is here no longer respected. The terrorist organization called Fascism, which seems to be daily gaining ground in Europe, is the exact counterpart of our rigorous social injunctions. There was a day in India when for the Sudra to aspire to the path of the Brahmin entailed the death penalty. The same psychological phenomenon is seen in the West in the cruel forms of Lynching, Fascism, Ku-Klux-Klanism, and the like.

It is no doubt conducive to a certain strength if all the members of a society are, in the main, moulded in accordance with some uniform standard. That may be a bar to the fullest development of its individuals, but it certainly does help to keep the society, as a whole, in a state of stable equilibrium. And, if any society, on the cessation of its growth, should come to pride itself on being, not like a growing tree, but like a temple of which its securely established immoveableness is its gory, it will inevitably feel the moving of a single one of its bricks to be a loss. Nevertheless it is not possible to keep all the members of any society uniformly bound in such unalterable fixity—that is against the nature of man and destructive of the principle of life itself. So that, so long as any people is vigorously alive, they or some of them cannot but keep breaking through the rules and prohibitions imposed by their society. Both in its biological and sociological phases, these opposing forces of conservation and experimentation, are characteristic of Life.

Anyhow, so long as the Kshatriyas were real Kshatriyas it was not found possible to keep them rigorously bound down to the habitual performance of the prescribed rules for daily observance. That is why, in the history of ancient India, at the bottom of all the social and religious revolutions, were the Kshatriyas. We must remember that Buddha was a Kshatriya that Māhavīra was a Kshatriya; and that the clan, to which Srīkrishna himself belonged, was not famous for observing the precepts and prohibitions most esteemed by the Lawgivers. As we read through the Mahābhārata, we are reminded at every turn that, however determined may have been the endeavour to protect society behind a permanent embankment, there was not a single kingly clan of note which did not break through the walls. It was only in comparatively recent times, when the

Kshatriyas had lost their virility and the Brahmins had gained almost unquestioned ascendancy, that it became possible to make the social bonds so rigorously inert.

Manu gives the name of *Gāndharva* to marriage by mutual choice, and signifies his disapprobation by stigmatising it as 'born of desire'. The way to marriage, which is shown by the torchlight of passion, has not for its goal the welfare of society, but the satisfaction of desire. Even in Europe, where the obligation of the individual to society is much lighter, it is well known how the mingling of the sexes under the impulse of passion often gives rise to antisocial difficulties; but there, society being mobile, the effects are not so deep as with us. In our *shāstras,* therefore, the *Brāhma* marriage is considered to be the best. According to this, the bride should be given to a man who had not solicited her. If the institution of marriage has to be regulated strictly from the social standpoint, room cannot be found for the personal wishes of the people concerned. So, the system which obtains in the case of the Royal Houses of Europe, is the system which prevails throughout Hindu society.

Another way for the better understanding by the European of the mentality underlying our marriage system, would be by reference to the discussions on eugenics, which are a feature of modern Europe. The science of Eugenics, like all other sciences, attaches but little weight to personal sentiment. According to it, selection by personal inclination must be rigorously regulated for the sake of the progeny. If the principle involved be once admitted, marriage needs must be rescued from the control of the heart, and brought under the province of the intellect, otherwise insoluble problems will keep on arising; for passion recks not consequences, nor brooks interference by outside judges.

To return to our Kshatriyas, they were, as I have indicated, not in the habit of observing with any strictness the social rules relating to marriage. But it becomes clear from the poems of Kalidasa, that there was a struggle of protest in his mind against this laxity of their observance. The Poet keenly felt the value of the eugenic restrictions which were directed towards maintaining the racial ideals pure, and yet his heart could not fail to be moved by the beauty of the play of the natural loves of man and woman against the background of the exuberance of the Universal Life. In most of the great works of Kalidasa are treated the conflict of these opposites. The coming of the line of the Bhāratas was a great event in the History of India. But though the prelude of unbridled desire, which ushered in the founder of the line, has been viewed by the Poet in its aspect of Beauty in the first part of the play, he has corrected it from the standpoint of the Good towards the conclusion.

Amidst the natural beauty of the forest hermitage, Sakuntalā's youth blossoms out in prodigal curves of body and mind, along with the ecstasy of form and movement in the flowering trees and creepers around her. Everywhere in this retreat does Nature beckon, but Society, as yet, has found no loophole through which to obtrude the warning of her uplifted finger. Sakuntalā's secret union with King Dushyanta, which takes place amidst these surroundings, is not in harmony with the rest of society. So, according to the Poet, the curse comes upon her. She overlooks, in her self-absorption, the duty of hospitality; for when Nature is busy securing any special purpose, she throws all other purposes into the background. Society thereupon exacts its penalty and, in the Kings' audience hall, the inevitable thunderbolt of insult and rejection falls upon Sakuntalā.

In the seventh Act, the picture which the Poet draws of the hermitage, in which is consummated King Dushyanta's final union with Sakuntalā, now purified by discipline, is everywhere full of the rigour of renunciation, eclipsing the life-play of Nature. In the opening scene, the King is informed that the *Rishi* is busy expounding the *dharma* of the wifely estate Sakuntalā, here, is seen as the emblem of devotion, the Mother. It is clear that the Poet's object was vividly to contrast these two pictures of the relations of woman to man, the one carrying the bondage of desire, the other the detachment of *dharma*.

Motherhood, in so far as it is concerned with the physical nurture of offspring, is not essentially different in man and the lower animals, being a function of biological, not of sociological life, governed by instincts which are of nature, not by man's own creative power. But where the mother undergoes voluntary penance for the elevation of the human race, keeping her natural instincts in rigorous subordination to the dictates of mind and soul, there indeed is her own creative power at work. Now-a-days in the West, we often find women feeling a certain degradation in becoming subject to Maternity; that is to say, they feel the insult of having to submit to this tyranny of Nature over their sex. But the way for woman to avoid such insult is not by abjuring Motherhood, but by making it subserve her ideal, by bringing it under the control of her own intellect and conscience. How far India's conscious activity in the past—this striving of hers for the best possible progeny—was fully consonant with the conclusions of modern science, is not the question here. The point is, that just by such intellectual and spiritual vigilance can the human Mother achieve her true dignity.

In his Kumāra-sambhava it is the same thing that the Poet tells us. There he has shown the divine aspect of the eternal love of man and woman. When the Titans have won paradise, and banished the gods therefrom, the love of man and woman, transformed into ascetic striving, wins back heaven from the insult of defeat. The gods are eternally awaiting the birth of Kumāra, the conqueror of evil. And, in order to achieve this birth, the passion of desire must be transmuted into pure, disciplined endeavour. The rigorous aspect of such achievement is the truth which is beauty. The beauty of Illusion is gorgeous in its adornment, the beauty of Freedom is naked.

In all the three of his works, the Raghu-vamsa, the Kumāra-sambhava and Sakuntalā, India's Poet has looked upon marriage as a state of discipline, not intended for gaining individual happiness but of which the method is the control of desire and the object to bring about the birth of the Slayer of Evil, the superman who will make possible the achievement of heaven on earth. The agony of the Poet which we glimpse in each of these, springs from his consciousness of the degeneracy which was overtaking society through the flagrant disregard by the Kshatriya kings of the Aryan ideal of marriage. And the Poet sends out his call to bring away the union of man and woman from the realm of Kandarpa *(Eros)* into the hermitage of Shiva, the Good. This Indian ideal of marriage can be much more vividly understood from the works of the Poet than from any Dharma-shāstra.

Here the question arises that, if desire be banished from the very threshold of marriage, how can love find any place in the wedded life? Those who have no true acquaintance with our country, and whose marriage system is entirely different, take it for granted that the Hindu marriage is loveless. But do we not know of our own knowledge how false is such conclusion?

If we accept the institution of marriage, we must also admit that no system can be devised to ensure that its original object shall remain true throughout the long period covered by the life of the wedded couple. That is why, both law and public opinion have to keep such vigilant watch from the outside. But when external compulsion tries to bind together those whom only mutual love can truly unite, it makes their relations inherently impure,—in fact, no greater insult can be offered to man. Yet, all over the civilized world, man submits even to this for the sake of the welfare of his children. So far, no society has been able to claim that it has arrived at a faultless solution of the difficulty. In entering the married state we have all to make our plunge into the doubtful and leave it to providence whether we shall sink, or swim through.

The 'desire', however, against which India's solution of the marriage problem declared war, is one of Nature's most powerful fighters; consequently, the question of how to overcome it was not an easy one. There is a particular age, said India, at which this attraction between the sexes reaches its height, so if marriage is to be regulated according to the social will, it must be finished with before such age. Hence the Indian custom of early marriage.

This brings to my mind the conversation I once had with an Agriculturist. I was complaining to him of the lack of common grazing grounds in our villages, whereupon he told me that it was a mistake to suppose that a cow would thrive best if allowed to graze at will. Scientific feeding with specially cultivated fodder-crops could only yield the best results. These must have been the lines of argument, in regard to married love, pursued in our country. For the purpose of marriage, spontaneous love is unreliable, its proper cultivation should yield the best results,—such was the conclusion,—and this cultivation should begin before marriage. Therefore from their earliest years, the husband as an idea, is held up before our girls, in verse and story, through ceremonial and worship. When at length they get this 'husband', he is to them not a person but a principle, like Loyalty, Patriotism, or such other abstractions which owe their immense strength to the fact that the best part of them is our own creation and therefore part of our inner being.

There is also in our society the glorification of the *Satī,* the ideal wife; and, accordingly, a real reverence for woman, as the embodiment of housewifely virtues, is not rare in our country. The idea was, in both cases, to replace the natural passion of sexual love by the cultivated emotion of wedded love. But, it must be admitted that woman being emotional by nature, it has not been as easy for man thus to idealise the married state as it has been for her. It must also be admitted that the restraints and restrictions prescribed in the case of the man have not been so rigorous as those for the woman.

Therefore, in coming to our judgment on the marriage system of India, we must not fail to recognize the fact that therein the man and the woman are not on a footing of equality. Such inequality would have utterly humiliated her, but that, for the wife, the husband is an idea. She has not surrendered herself to the brute force of another, but voluntarily consecrated herself to the service of her own ideal. And if the husband is a man of sensitive soul the flame of this ideal love is transmitted to his own life also. Such mutual illumination it has often been our lot to witness.

There is yet another vital element in India's culture which we must keep in mind. In spite of her exaltation of the household estate, India did not look upon this as man's ultimate stage. According to India's ideal, even the home must be given up in due course, in quest of the Infinite,—the household, in fact, is only to be set up as an important stage in this quest. Even to-day, we see our householders, when their children are grown up, leaving their home to spend the rest of their life in some place of pilgrimage. Here is another pair of opposites which India attempted to reconcile. On the one hand, her civilization is essentially bound up in the home, albeit a home in which a wide circle of relationships find their place. On the other, its endeavour is, one by one, to snap all earthly ties in its pursuit of the liberation of the soul. In fact, it recognizes the social bonds because it is only through their acceptance that they can be transcended. In order to get rid of the natural desires of man, they must be used up; that is to say, guided by the spirit of renunciation to their own extinction. Here we find the difference between Hinduism and Buddhism. In its relations with Nature, Buddhism is uncompromisingly anarchist from the very outset.

The weakness of the Hindu system lies in the fact that its complex web is too closely knit, and that the least loosening of its fibre, in any of its parts, tends to its disruption. It is afraid of the contact of the outside because the bond which holds it together is that of external regulation, whose strength depends upon habitual conformity. But self-segregation for any society is no longer practicable in this age. For, while it may be possible to prevent the man on this side of the sea from crossing to the other, what about preventing those on the other side from coming over here?

So have alien ideas, alien systems, alien customs, breaking in through her embankments, dashed upon India in a multitudinous flood, making visible breaches in all the habits and beliefs which were the pillars of her social system. Further, apart from this disturbance of her inward life, there has been the more effective attack of an alien economic system; for without a sufficiency of food, it is impossible for the various relationships of her complex society to be kept together. And, just as foreign ideas come pouring in on our mental world, so do our foodstuffs, caught up in various currents of commerce, keep flowing away towards foreign lands. So that the people of our country, in their social dealings, are now compelled to keep careful count of their meagre resources. Lastly, there is the nemesis of the unrealized ideal, which overtakes any civilization when, by reason of flagging vitality, it fails in the earnestness of its pursuit, and lapses into the stagnation of mechanical habits. Every living organism is constantly confronted with the waste products of its own fatigue, for which its vital forces, while active, find natural means of elimination. The adoption of complex external devices is of no avail when vitality is on the wane, for they only tend to weaken the natural functions still further, if not to create new forms of weakness and disease. The civilizations which flourished for a time, and have disappeared, are those which committed suicide, clinging on to their own toxic products, by suppressing, under the urgence of their special purposes, the cleansing impulses provided by Nature.

Anyhow, the special qualities of head and heart, which once found varied support in our broad social system, are now dying out for lack of opportunity for their exercise; meanwhile it has not been possible to effect a corresponding change in the structure of our society; with the result, that while all its restrictions keep on hampering us, their original object and justification have become impossible of acknowledgement. And so, on every side, are the members of this vast society overwhelmed with futility. In particular, the very basis of our marriage system having been undermined, there is no longer any harmony of adjustment between the underlying ideals and the actual facts of our modern marriages. One section of our people keeps crying out for a return of the *Satya-yuga*, but that golden age refuses to respond to their call. The time has, therefore, come for us to think out our problems afresh, to correlate our thoughts and conclusions with those of all humanity.

The gulf of separation, which Nature has contrived between the sexes, has preserved in its atmosphere the varied play of a powerful mutual attraction. This force which is creative,—but destructive as well,—continually sends its awakening message to our souls from behind the veil. If we screen off society from its forceful activity, that may conduce to its own safety, but will surely reduce it to passivity. In our language we call the power of woman over man by the name of *shakti*. Deprived of *shakti* the creative process in society languishes, and man, losing his vitality, becomes mechanical in his habits. In such case, though he may still retain many a passive quality, all energy of activity forsakes him. The manner in which the relations between the sexes have been regulated in our country, has left no room for the action of this *shakti;* for, as we have seen, our society, with immovable stability as its objective, has been busy cultivating the passive qualities, ever in dread of individual forcefulness. Now that our country has awakened to outside influences, she finds herself powerless to resist alien aggression. She has even lost the faculty of recognizing that her weakness proceeds from within her own social system, and is not the outcome of any outward accident.

In every society, its civilization is the territory conquered in its contest with Nature. And since in our country this contest was long and bitter, everywhere we find its fences more in evidence than its roads. But because there was once a good reason for this state of things, it does not help to save her when the reason has ceased to exist. Her barriers which kept the outsider off, now keep herself confined.

It seems that in the age which has now come upon us, man is thinking of giving up the desperate hope of victoriously keeping up this constant struggle. He would now make his peace with Nature,—and that duty has been entrusted to Science. But the marriage system of every society belongs to an age when, in the Parliament of Life, man was sitting on the opposition benches against Nature's government. And Nature has ever retaliated against his obstructive tactics. Up to now they have nowhere come to any satisfactory agreement. That is why these ubiquitous attempts at the external regulation of man's most intimate relations, have been insulting his best feelings and degrading the greatest of his institutions, all over the world.

Let me, as an individual Indian, offer in conclusion my own personal contribution to the discussion of the marriage question generally.

There are two parallel activities in the human world, the one which carries forward the stream of population: the other, the civilization of man. The first chiefly belongs to the realm of Life, and the second to that of Mind. In the creation of progeny, man's part though essential, is secondary. After he has once roused the passive seed, in woman's keeping, to vital activity, all the travail of child-bearing and parturition are hers alone. It is because of this comparative lightness of the male function in the propagation of the species, that we find instances of the killing off of superfluous males in the insect world, and of the keeping down of the number of male beasts by internecine struggles due to the savage jealousy which is their characteristic; shewing the minor importance of this sex for the purpose of biological creation.

But, when Mind evolved itself into greatness, man found the opportunity to gain glory for his sex in the scheme of human development. For, while woman remained entangled in the specific duties which Life had assigned to her, man, with his greater freedom therefrom, was able to respond to the call of his intellect and engage in various work of creation in the world of Mind,—in fact he created the sphere of his own usefulness. In this, the first chapter of civilization, when Mind was in the ascendant, woman in her turn dropped into the second place, not only as less useful, but even as an actual impediment; for the world which was her special creation, constantly sought to throw its toils round the adventurous spirit of man as well. This comparative unimportance of woman in the birth stage of civilization, clings to her still. That is why the rebellious section of womankind would curtail her responsibilities in the region of Life, in order to enable her to claim equality with man in the work of his creation of society.

Opportunities, however, cannot be artificially created. The propensities of heart, strongly ingrained in woman's nature, cannot be dislodged by attacks from the outside. The tendency of these propensities of hers are towards holding fast, and not progressing onwards. So it is only by adherence to the cult of preservation that woman can attain her true welfare. If she desperately engages in adventurous pursuits, she will at every step come into conflict with her own inner nature, and thus constantly distracted, she can never succeed in competing with man in his own special sphere. But just as man, after a long period of subordination during the ascendancy of Life, was enabled to get rid of his disabilities in a subsequent stage, so woman too may look forward to a yet higher regime whereunder she will have the right to emerge from her present subjection. It is difficult to decide what to call this next stage; for the word '*spiritual*' is so beset with controversy regarding its true meaning. However, let me for my present purpose give it that name.

The inner qualities of the woman's heart, result in an important byproduct, which may be called *charm.* This charm like light, is a force. Intangible, imponderable though it be, the strivings of our intellect may not attain fruition if deprived of its life-giving touch. The nourishment which the tree draws though its roots may be classified and measured,—not so the vitality which is the gift of the sunlight, and without which its functioning becomes altogether impossible.

This ineffable emanation of woman's nature has, from the first, played its part in the creations of man, unobtrusively but inevitably. Had man's mind not been energised by the inner working of woman's vital charm, he would never have attained his successes. Of all the higher achievements of civilization,—the devotion of the toiler, the valour of the brave, the creations of the artist,—the secret spring is to be found in woman's influence. In the clash and battle of primitive civilization, the action of woman's *shakti* is not clearly manifest; but, as civilization becomes spiritual in the course of its development, and the union of man with man is acknowledged to be more important than the differences between them, the charm of woman gets the opportunity to become the predominant factor. Such spiritual civilization can only be upheld if the emotion of woman and the intellect of man are contributed in usual shares for its purposes. Then their respective contributions may combine gloriously in ever-fresh creations, and their difference will no longer make for inequality.

Woman, let me repeat, has two aspects,—in one she is the Mother; in the other, the Beloved. I have already spoken of the spiritual endeavour that characterises the first, viz., the striving, not merely for giving birth to her child, but for creating the best possible child,—not as an addition to the number of men, but as one of the heroic souls who may win victory in man's eternal fight against evil in his social life and natural surroundings. As the Beloved, it is woman's part to infuse life into all the aspirations of man; and the spiritual power that enables her to do so I have called *charm,* and was known in India by the name of *shakti.*

There is a poem called *Ānanda-laharū* (The stream of Delight), attributed to Shankarāchārya. She who is glorified therein is the *Shakti* in the heart of the Universe, the Giver of Joy, the Inspirer of Activity. On the one hand, we know and use the world; on the other we are related to it by ties of disinterested joy. We can know the world because it is a manifestation of Truth: we rejoice in it because it is an expression of Joy. 'Who would have striven for life,' says the *Rishi,* 'if this *ānanda* (joy) had not filled the sky.' It seems to me that the 'Intellectual Beauty', whose praises Shelley has sung, is identical with this *Ānanda.* And it is this same *ānanda* which the poet of *ānanda-laharū* has visualised as the woman; that is to say, in his view, this Universal *Shakti* is manifest in human Society in the nature of Woman. In this manifestation is her charm. Let no one confuse this *shakti* with mere 'sweetness', for in this charm there is a combination of several qualities,—patience, self-abnegation, sensitive intelligence, grace in thought, word and behaviour,—the reticent expression of rhythmic life, the tenderness and terribleness of love; at its core, moreover, is that self-radiant Spirit of Delight which ever gives itself up.

This *shakti,* this joy-giving power of woman as the Beloved, has up to now largely been dissipated by the greed of man, who has sought to use it for the purposes of his individual enjoyment, corrupting it, confining it, like his property, within jealously-guarded limits. That has also obstructed for woman herself her inward realization of the full glory of her own *shakti.* Her personality has been insulted at every turn by being made to display its power of delectation within a circumscribed arena. It is because she has not found her true place in the great world, that she sometimes tries to capture man's special estate as a desperate means of coming into her own. But it is not by coming out of her home that woman can gain her liberty. Her liberation can only be effected in a society where her true *shakti,* her *ānanda,* is given the widest and highest scope for its activity. Man has already achieved the means of self-expansion in public activity without giving up his individual concerns. When, likewise, any society shall be able to offer a larger field for the creative work of woman's special faculty, without detracting from her creative work in the home, then in such society will the true union of man and woman become possible.

The marriage system all over the world, from the earliest ages till now, is a barrier in the way of such true union. That is why woman's *shakti,* in all existing societies, is so shamefully wasted and corrupted. That is why, in every country marriage is still more or less of a prison house for the confinement of woman,—with all its guards wearing the badge of the dominant male. That is why man, by dint of his efforts to bind woman, has made her the strongest of fetters for his own bondage. That is why woman is debarred from adding to the spiritual wealth of society by the perfection of her own nature, and all human societies are weighed down with the burden of the resulting poverty.

The civilization of man has not, up to now, loyally recognized the reign of the Spirit. Therefore the married state is still one of the most fruitful sources of the unhappiness and downfall of man, of his disgrace and humiliation. But those who believe that society is a manifestation of the spirit, will assuredly not rest in their endeavours till they have rescued human marriage relations from outrage by the brute forces of society,—till they have thereby given free play to the force of Love in all the concerns of humanity.

1925

The Cult of the Charka

Acharya Prafulla Chandra Ray has marked me with his censure in printer's ink, for that I have been unable to display enthusiasm in the turning of the Charka. But because it is impossible for him to be pitiless to me, even when awarding punishment, he has provided me with a companion in my ignominy in the illustrious person of Acharya Brajendra Nath Seal. That has taken away the pain of it, and also given me fresh proof of the eternal human truth, that we are in agreement with some people and with some others we are not. It only proves that while creating man's mind, God did not have for his model the spider mentality doomed to a perpetual conformity in its production of web and that it is an outrage upon human nature to force it through a mill and reduce it to some standardised commodity of uniform size and shape and purpose.

When in my younger days I used to go boating on the river, the boatmen of Jagannath Ghat would swarm around, each pressing on me the service of his own particular vessel. My selection once made, however, there would be no further trouble; for, if the boats were many, so were the passengers; and the places to go to were likewise various. But suppose one of the boats had been specially hallmarked, as the one and only sacred ferry by some dream emanating from the shrine of Tarakeswar, then indeed it would have been difficult to withstand the extortion of its touts, despite the inner conviction of the travellers that though the shore opposite may be one, its landing places are many and diversely situate.

Our *shastras* tell us that the divine *shakti* is many-sided, so that a host of different factors operate in the work of creation. In death these merge into sameness; for chaos alone is uniform. God has given to man the same many-sided *shakti,* for which reason the civilizations of his creation have their divine wealth of diversity. It is God's purpose that in the societies of man the various should be strung together into a garland of unity; while often the mortal providence of our public life, greedy for particular results, seeks to knead them all into a lump of uniformity. That is why we see in the concerns of this world so many identically-liveried, machine-made workers, so many marionettes pulled by the same string: and on the other hand, wherever the human spirit has not been reduced to the coldness of collapse, we also see perpetual rebelliousness against this mechanical, mortar-pounded homogeneity.

If in any country we find no symptom of such rebellion, if we find its people submissively or contentedly prone on the dust, in dumb terror of some master's bludgeon, or blind acceptance of some *guru's* injunction, then indeed should we know that for such a country, *in extremis,* it is high time to mourn.

In our country this ominous process of being levelled down into sameness has long been at work. Every individual of every caste has his function assigned to him, together with the obsession into which he has been hypnotised, that, since he is bound by some divine mandate, accepted by his first ancestor, it would be sinful for him to seek relief therefrom. This imitation of the social scheme of ant-life makes very easy the performance of petty routine duties, but specially difficult the attainment of manhood's estate. It imparts skill to the limbs of the man who is a bondsman, whose labour is drudgery; but it kills the mind of a man who is a doer, whose work is creation. So in India, during long ages past, we have the spectacle of only a repetition of that which has gone before.

In the process of this continuous grind India has acquired a distaste for very existence. In dread of the perpetuation of this same grind, through the eternal repetition of births, she is ready to intern all mental facilities in absolute inaction in order to cut at the root of *Karma* itself. For only too well has she realized, in the dreary round of her daily habit, the terribleness of this everlasting re-canitulation. Moreover, this dreariness is not the only loss sustained by those who have suffered themselves to be reduced to a machine-like existence; for they have also lost all power to combat aggression or exploitation. From age to age they have been assaulted by the strong, defrauded by the cunning, and deluded by the *gurus* to whom their conscience was surrendered. Such a state of abject passivity has become easy because of the teaching that through an immutable decree of providence they have been set adrift on the sea of Time, upon the raft of a monotonous living death, burdened with a vocation that makes no allowance for variation in human nature.

But whatever our *shastras* may or may not have said, this popular conception of the Creator's doing is the very opposite of what he really did do to man at the moment of his creation. Instead of furnishing him with an automatically revolving grindstone, God slipped into his constitution that most lively sprightly thing called Mind. And unless man can be made to get rid of this mind, it will remain impossible to convert him into a machine. In so far as the men at the top succeeded in paralysing the people's minds by fear, or greed or hypnotic texts, they succeeded in extorting, from one class of them, only textiles from their looms; from another class, only pots from their wheels; from a third, only oil from their mills. Now when from such persons as these it becomes necessary to demand the application of their mind to any big work on hand, they stand aghast. 'Mind!' cry they, 'What on earth is that? Why don't you order us what to do and give some text for us to repeat from mouth to mouth and age to age?'

Our mind, in doing duty only as a hedge to prevent the encroachment of living ideas, had been kept evenly clipped short for the purpose. If, in spite of that, in this age of self-assertion, we find mischievous branches trying to make room for the disturbance of the spruceness of the trimming,—if all our minds refuse incessantly to reverberate some one set *mantram*, in the droning chirp of the cicadas of the night,—let no one be annoyed or alarmed; for only because of this does the attainment of Swaraj become thinkable!

That is why I am not ashamed,—though there is every reason to be afraid,—to admit that the depths of my mind have not been moved by the *charka* agitation. This may be counted by many as sheer presumption on my part. They may even wax abusive; for swearing is a much needed relief for the feelings when even one stray fish happens to elude the all-embracing net. Still I cannot help hoping that there are others who are in the same plight as myself,—though it is difficult to find them all out. For even where hands are reluctant to work the spindle, mouths are all the more busy spinning its praises.

I am strongly of opinion that all intense pressure of persuasion brought upon the crowd psychology is unhealthy for it. Some strong and widespread intoxication of belief among a vast number of men can suddenly produce a convenient uniformity of purpose immense and powerful. It seems for the moment a miracle of a wholesale conversion; and a catastrophic phenomenon of this nature stuns our rational mind, raising high some hope of easy realization which is very much like a boom in the business market. The amazingly immediate success is no criterion of its reality,—the very dimension of its triumph having a dangerous effect of producing a sudden and universal eclipse of our judgment. Human nature has its elasticity; and in the name of urgency, it can be forced towards a particular direction far beyond its normal and wholesome limits. But the rebound is sure to follow, and the consequent disillusionment will leave behind it a desert track of demoralisation. We have had our experience of this in the tremendous exultation lately produced by the imaginary easy prospect of Hindu-Muslim unity. And therefore I am afraid of a blind faith on a very large scale in the *charka,* in a country which is so liable to succumb to the lure of short cuts when pointed out by a personality about whose moral earnestness they can have no doubt.

Anyhow, what I say is this. If, today, poverty has come upon our country, we should know that the root cause is complexly ramified and it dwells within ourselves. For the whole country to fall upon only one of its external symptoms with the application of one and the same remedy, will not serve to fight the demon away. If man had been a mindless image of stone, a defect in his features might have been cured with hammer and chisel; but when his shrunken features bespeak vital poverty, the cure must be constitutional, not formal; and repeated hammer strokes upon some one particular external point will only damage that same life still more.

In the days when our country had to bear the brunt of Moghul and Pathan, the little jerry-built edifices of Hindu sovereignty fell to pieces on every side. There was then no dearth of home-spun thread, but that did not serve to bind these into stability. And, yet, in those days, there was no economic antagonism between the people and their rulers. The throne of the latter was established on the soil of the country, so that the ripe fruits fell to the ground where the tree stood. Can it then be today—when we have not one or two kings, but a veritable flood of them, sweeping away our life-stuffs across the seas away from our motherland, causing it to lose both its fruits and its fertility,—can it be, I say, that the lack of sufficient thread prevents our stemming this current? Is it not rather our lack of vitality, our lack of union?

Some will urge that though in the days of Moghul and Pathan we had not sovereign power, we had at least a sufficiency of food and clothing. When the river is not flowing, it may be possible to bank up little pools in its bed to hold water enough for our needs, conveniently at hand for each. But can such banks guarding our scanty economic resources for local use withstand the shocks which come upon it today from far and near? No longer will it be possible to hide ourselves away from commerce with the outside world; moreover such isolation itself would be the greatest of deprivations for us. If, therefore, we cannot rouse the forces of our mind, in adequate strength, to take our due part in this traffic of exchanging commodities, our grain will continue to be consumed by others, leaving only the chaff as our own portion. In Bengal we have a nursery rhyme which soothes the infant with the assurance that it will get the lollipop if only it twirls its hands. But is it a likely policy to reassure grown-up people by telling them that they will get their Swaraj,—that is to say, get rid of all poverty, in spite of their social habits that are a perpetual impediment and mental habits producing inertia of intellect and will,—by simply twirling away with their hands? No! If we have to get rid of this poverty, which is visible outside, it can only be done by rousing our inward forces of wisdom, of fellowship and mutual trust which make for co-operation.

But it may be argued, does not external work react on the mind? It does, only if it has its constant suggestions to our intellect, which is the master, and not merely its commands for our muscles, which are slaves. In this clerk-ridden country, for instance, we all know that the routine of clerkship is not mentally stimulating. By doing the same thing day after day mechanical skill may be acquired; but the mind, like a mill-turning bullock, will be kept going round and round a narrow range of habit. That is why, in every country, man has looked down on work which involves this kind of mechanical repetition. Carlyle may have proclaimed the dignity of labour in his stentorian accents, but a still louder cry has gone up from humanity, age after age, testifying to its indignity, 'The wise man sacrifices the half to avert a total loss',—so says our Sanskrit proverb. Rather than die of starvation, one can understand a man preferring to allow his mind to be killed. But it would be a cruel joke to try to console him by talking of the dignity of such sacrifice.

In fact, humanity has ever been beset with the grave problem, how to rescue the large majority of the people from being reduced to the stage of machines. It is my belief that all the civilizations which have ceased to be, have come by their death when the mind of the majority got killed under some pressure by the minority; for the truest wealth of man is his mind. No amount of respect outwardly accorded, can save man from the inherent ingloriousness of labour divorced from mind. Only those who feel that they have become inwardly small can be belittled by others, and the numbers of the higher castes have ever dominated over those of the lower, not because they have any accidental advantage of power, but because the latter are themselves humbly conscious of their dwarfed humanity. If the cultivation of science by Europe has any moral significance, it is in its rescue of man from outrage by nature,—not its use of man as a machine, but its use of the machine to harness the forces of nature in man's service. One thing is certain, that the all-embracing poverty which has overwhelmed our country cannot be removed by working with our hands to the neglect of science. Nothing can be more undignified drudgery than that man's *knowing* should stop dead and his *doing* go on for ever.

It was a great day for man when he discovered the wheel. The facility of motion thus given to inert matter enabled it to bear much of man's burden. This was but right, for Matter is the true Sudra; while with his dual existence in body and mind, Man is a *Dwija*. Man has to maintain both his inner and outer life. Whatever functions he cannot perform by material means, are left as an additional burden on himself, bringing him to this extent down to the level of matter, and making him a Sudra. Such Sudras cannot obtain glory by being merely glorified in words.

Thus, whether in the shape of the spinning wheel, or the potters' wheel, or the wheel of a vehicle, the wheel has rescued innumerable men from the Sudra's estate and lightened their burdens. No wealth is greater than this lightening of man's material burdens. This fact man has realized ever more and more, since the time when he turned his first wheel; for his wealth has thereupon gone on compounding itself in ever-increasing rotation, refusing to be confined to the limited advantage of the original *charka*.

Is there no permanent truth underlying these facts? One aspect of Vishnu's *shakti* is the *padma,* the beautiful lotus; another is the *chakra,* the moveable discus. The one is the complete ideal of perfection, the other is the process of movement, the ever-active power seeking fulfilment. When man attained touch with this moving *shakti* of Vishnu, he was liberated from that inertia which is the origin of all poverty. All divine power is infinite. Man has not yet come to the end of the power of the revolving wheel. So, if we are taught that in the pristine *charka* we have exhausted all the means of spinning thread, we shall not gain the full favour of Vishnu. Neither will his spouse Lakshmi smile on us. When we forget that science is spreading the domain of Vishnu's *chakra,* those who have honoured the Discus-Bearer to better purpose will spread their dominion over us. If we are wilfully blind to the grand vision of whirling forces, which science has revealed, the *charka* will cease to have any message for us. The hum of the spinning-wheel, which once carried us so long a distance on the path of wealth, will no longer talk to us of progress.

Some have protested that they never preached that only the turning of the *charka* should be engaged in. But they have not spoken of any other necessary work. Only one means of attaining *Swaraj* has been definitely ordered and the rest is a vast silence. Does not such silence amount to a speech stronger than any uttered word? Is not the *charka* thrust out against the background of this silence into undue prominence? Is it really so big as all that? Has it really the divinity which may enable it to appropriate the single-minded devotion of all the millions of India, despite their diversity of temperament and talent? Repeated efforts, even unto violence and bloodshed, have been made, all the world over, to bring mankind together on the basis of the common worship of a common Deity, but even these have not been successful. Neither has a common God been found, nor a common form of worship. Can it then be expected, that, in the shrine *of Swaraj*, the *charka* goddess will attract to herself alone the offerings of every devotee? Surely such expectation amounts to a distrust of human nature, a disrespect for India's people.

In my childhood, I had an up-country servant, called Gopee, who used to tell us how once he went to Puri on a pilgrimage, and was at a loss what fruit to offer to Jagannath, since any fruit so offered could not be eaten by him any more. After repeatedly going over the list of edible fruits known to him, he suddenly bethought himself of the tomato (which had very little fascination for him) and the tomato it was which he offered, never having reason to repent of such clever abnegation. But to call upon man to make the easiest of offerings to the smallest of gods is the greatest of insults to his manhood. To ask all the millions of our people to spin the *charka* is as bad as offering the tomato to Jagannath. I do hope and trust that there are not thirty-three crores of Gopees in India. When man receives the call of the great to make some sacrifice, he is indeed exalted; for then he comes to himself with a start of revelation,—to find that he too has been bearing his hidden resource of greatness.

Our country is the land of rites and ceremonials, so that we have more faith in worshipping the feet of the priest than the Divinity whom he serves. We cannot get rid of the conviction that we can safely cheat our inner self of its claims, if we can but bribe some outside agency. This reliance on outward help is a symptom of slavishness, for no habit can more easily destroy all reliance on self. Only to such a country can come the *charka* as the emblem of her deliverance; and the people dazed into obedience by some specious temptation go on turning their *charka* in the seclusion of their corners, dreaming all the while that the car of *Swaraj* of itself rolls onward in triumphal progress at every turn of their wheel.

And so it becomes necessary to restate afresh the old truth that the foundation of *Swaraj* cannot be based on any external conformity, but only on the internal union of hearts. If a great union is to be achieved, its field must be great likewise. But it, out of the whole field of economic endeavour, only one fractional portion be selected for special concentration thereon, then we may get home-spun thread, and even genuine *khaddar,* but we shall not have united, in the pursuit of one great complete purpose, the lives of our countrymen.

In India, it is not possible for every one to unite in the realm of religion. The attempt to unite on the political platform is of recent growth, and will yet take long to permeate the masses. So that the religion of economics is where we should above all try to bring about this union of ours. It is certainly the largest field available to us; for here high and low, learned and ignorant, all have their scope. If this field cease to be one of warfare, if there we can prove, that not competition, but co-operation is the real truth, then indeed we can reclaim from the hands of the Evil One an immense territory for the reign of peace and goodwill. It is important to remember, moreover, that this is the ground whereon our village communities had actually practised unity in the past. What if the thread of the old union has snapped? It may again be joined together; for such former practice has left in our character the potentiality of its renewal.

As is livelihood for the individual, so is politics for a particular people,—a field for the exercise of their business instincts of patriotism. All this time, just as business has implied antagonism, so has politics been concerned with the self-interest of a pugnacious nationalism. The forging of arms and of false documents has been its main activity. The burden of competitive armaments has been increasing apace, with no end to it in sight, no peace for the world in prospect.

When it becomes clear to man that in the co-operation of nations lies the true interest of each,—for man is established in mutuality—then only can politics become a field for true endeavour. Then will the same means which the individual recognizes as moral and therefore true, be also recognized as such by the nations. They will know that cheating, robbery and the exclusive pursuit of self-aggrandisement are as harmful for the purposes of this world as they are deemed to be for those of the next. It may be that the League of Nations will prove to be the first step in the process of this realization.

Again, just as the present-day politics is a manifestation of extreme individualism in nations, so is the process of gaining a livelihood an expression of the extreme selfishness of individuals. That is why man has descended to such depths of deceit and cruelty in his indiscriminate competition. And yet since man is man, even in his business he ought to have cultivated his humanity rather than the powers of exploitation. In working for his livelihood he ought to have earned not only his daily bread, but also his eternal truth.

When, years ago, I first became acquainted with the principles of co-operation in the field of business, one of the knots of a tangled problem which had long perplexed my mind seemed to have been unravelled. I felt that the separateness of self-interest, which had so long contemptuously ignored the claims of the truth of man, was at length to be replaced by a combination of common interests which would help to uphold that truth, proclaiming that poverty lay in the separation, and wealth in the union of man and man. For myself I had never believed that this original truth of man could find its limit in any region of his activity.

The co-operative principle tells us, in the field of man's livelihood, that only when he arrives at his truth can he get rid of his poverty,—not by any external means. And the manhood of man is at length honoured by the enunciation of this principle. Co-operation is an ideal, not a mere system, and therefore it can give rise to innumerable methods of its application. It leads us into no blind alley; for at every step it communes with our spirit. And so, it seemed to me, in its wake would come, not merely food, but the goddess of plenty herself, in whom all kinds of material food are established in an essential moral oneness.

It was while some of us were thinking of the ways and means of adopting this principle in our institution that I came across the book called 'The National Being' written by that Irish idealist. A.E., who has a rare combination in himself of poetry and practical wisdom. There I could see a great concrete realization of the co-operative living of my dreams. It became vividly clear to me what varied results could flow therefrom, how full the life of man could be made thereby. I could understand how great the concrete truth was in any plane of life, the truth that in separation is bondage, in union is liberation. It has been said in the Upanishad that *Brahma* is reason, *Brahma* is spirit, but *Anna* also is *Brahma,* which means that Food also represents an eternal truth, and therefore through it we may arrive at a great realization, if we travel along the true path.

I know there will be many to tax me with indicating a solution of great difficulty. To give concrete shape to the ideal of co-operation on so vast a scale will involve endless toil in experiment and failure, before at length it may become an accomplished fact. No doubt it is difficult. Nothing great can be got cheap. We only cheat ourselves when we try to acquire things that are precious with a price that is inadequate. The problem of our poverty being complex, with its origin in our ignorance and unwisdom, in the inaptitude of our habits, the weakness of our character, it can only be effectively attacked by taking in hand our life as a whole and finding both internal and external remedies for the malady which afflicts it. How can there be an easy solution?

There are many who assert and some who believe that *Swaraj* can be attained by the *charka;* but I have yet to meet a person who has a clear idea of the process. That is why there is no discussion, but only quarrelling over the question. If I state that it is not possible to repel foreign invaders armed with guns and cannons by the indigenous bow and arrow, there will I suppose be still some to contradict me asking, 'Why not?' It has already been said by some, 'Would not the foreigners be drowned, even if everyone of our three hundred and thirty millions were only to spit at them?' While not denying the fearsomeness of such a flood, or the efficacy of such a suggestion, for throwing odium on foreign military science, the difficulty which my mind feels to be insuperable is that you can never get all these millions even to spit in unison. It is too simple for human beings. The same difficulty applies to the *charka* solution.

The disappointments, the failures, the recommencements that Sir Horace Plunkett had to face when he set to work to apply the co-operative principle in the economic reconstruction of Ireland, are a matter of history. But though it takes time to start a fire, once alight it spreads rapidly. That is the way with truth as well. In whatever corner of the earth it may take root, the range of its seeds is world-wide, and everywhere they may find soil for growth and give of their fruit to each locality. Sir Horace Plunkett's success was not confined to Ireland alone; he achieved also the possibility of success for India. If any true devotee of our motherland should be able to eradicate the poverty of only one of her villages, he will have given permanent wealth to the thirty-three crores of his countrymen. Those who are wont to measure truth by its size get only an outside view, and fail to realize that each seed, in its tiny vital spark, brings divine authority to conquer the whole world.

As I am writing this, a friend objects that even though I may be right in thinking that the *charka* is not competent to bring us *Swaraj*, or remove the whole of our poverty, why ignore such virtues as it admittedly possesses? Every farmer, every householder, has a great deal of leisure left over after his ordinary work is done; so that if everyone would utilise such spare time in productive work, much could be done towards the alleviation of our poverty. Why not glorify the *charka* as one of the instruments of such a desirable consummation? This reminds me of a similar proposition I have heard before. Most of our people throw away the water in which their rice is boiled. If everyone conserved this nutritious fluid that would go a long way to solve the food problem. I admit there is truth in this contention. The slight change of taste required for eating boiled rice with its water retained should not be very difficult to acquire, in view of the object sought to be gained. Many other similar savings could be effected which are doubtless worth the effort and should be looked upon as a duty. But has any one ever suggested that the conservation of rice-water should be made a plank in the platform of *Swaraj-work?* And is there no good reason for the omission?

In order to make my point clear, let me take an instance from the case of religion. If a preacher should repeatedly and insistently urge that the drinking of water from any and every well is the cause of the degeneracy of our religion, then the chief objection to his teaching would be its tendency to debase the value of moral action as a factor in religion. No doubt there is the chance of some well or other containing impure water; impure water destroys health; a diseased body begets a diseased mind; and therefore spiritual welfare is in danger. I am not concerned to dispute the truth in all this, yet I must repeat that to give undue value to the comparatively unimportant, lowers the value of the important. And so we find that there are numbers of Hindus who would not hesitate even to kill a Mohamedan if he came to draw water from their own well. If the small be put on an equal footing with the big, it is not content to rest there, but needs must push its way higher up. That is how the injunction: 'Thou shalt not drink dubious water' gets the better of the commandment: 'Thou shalt not kill.' There is no end to the perversions of value which have thus weakened our minds, and it is only because we have become habituated to their facile intrusion that no one is surprised to see the *charka* stalk the land, with uplifted club, in the garb of *Swaraj* itself. The *charka* is doing harm because of the undue prominence which it has thus usurped, whereby it only adds fuel to the smouldering weakness that is eating into our vitals. Suppose some mighty voice should next proclaim that the rice-water waster must not be suffered to enter our councils. Given requisite forcefulness, that may lead to the flow of rice-water being followed by the flow of human blood, in the sacred name of political purity. If the idea of the impurity of foreign textiles should effect a lodgement in our mind along with the numerous fixed ideas already there, in regard to the impurity of certain foods and waters, the Id riots, to which we are accustomed, might pale before the sanguinary strife that may eventually be set ablaze between the so-called unclean lot who may use foreign cloth and those politically pure souls who do not. The danger to my mind is that the contagion of 'untouchability', which was hitherto confined to our society, may extend to the economic and political spheres as well.

Someone whispers to me that to combine in *charka*-spinning is co-operation itself. I beg to disagree. If all the higher caste people of the Hindu community combine in keeping their well-water undefiled from use of the lower ones, this practice in itself does not give it the dignity of Bacteriology. It is a particular action isolated from the comprehensive vision of this science. And therefore while we keep our wells reserved for the cleaner sect, we allow our ponds to get polluted, the ditches round our houses to harbour messengers of death. Those who intimately know Bengal also know that at the time of preparing a special kind of pickle our women take extra precaution in keeping themselves clean. In fact they go through a kind of ceremonial of ablution and other forms of purification. For such extra care their pickle survives the ravage of time, while their villages are devastated by epidemics. For while there may remain some Pasteur's law invisible at the depth of this pickle-making precaution, the diseased spleens in the neighbourhood make themselves only too evident by their magnitude. The universal application of Pasteur's law in the production of pickle has some similarity to the application of the principle of a co-operation method of livelihood in turning the spinning-wheel. It may produce enormous quantity of yarn, but the blind suppression of intellect which guards our poverty in its dark dungeon will remain inviolate. This narrow activity will shed light only upon one detached piece of fact keeping its great background of truth densely dark.

It is extremely distasteful to me to have to differ from Mahatma Gandhi in regard to any matter of principle or method. Not that, from a higher standpoint, there is anything wrong in so doing: but my heart shrinks from it. For what could be a greater joy than to join hands in the field of work with one for whom one has such love and reverence? Nothing is more wonderful to me than Mahatmaji's great moral personality. In him divine providence has given us a burning thunderbolt of *shakti*. May this *shakti* give power to India,—not overwhelm her,—that is my prayer! The difference in our standpoints and temperaments has made the Mahatma look upon Rammohun Roy as a pygmy, while I revere him as a giant. The same difference makes the Mahatma's field of work one which my conscience cannot accept as its own. That is a regret which will abide with me always. It is, however, God's will that man's paths of endeavour shall be various, else why these differences of mentality?

How often have my personal feelings of regard strongly urged me to accept at Mahatma Gandhi's hands my enlistment as a follower of the *charka* cult, but as often have my reason and conscience restrained me, lest I should be a party to the raising of the *charka* to a higher place than is its due, thereby distracting attention from other more important factors in our task of all-round reconstruction. I feel sure that Mahatmaji himself will not fail to understand me, and keep for me the same forbearance, which he has always had. Acharya Roy, I also believe, has respect for independence of opinion, even when unpopular; so that, although when carried away by the fervour of his own propaganda he may now and then give me a scolding, I doubt not he retains for me a soft corner in his heart. As for my countrymen, the public,—accustomed as they are to drown, under the facile flow of their minds, both past services and past disservices done to them,—if today they cannot find it in their hearts to forgive, they will forget to-morrow. Even if they do not,—if for me their displeasure is fated to be permanent, then just as to-day I have Acharya Seal as my fellow-culprit, so to-morrow I may find at my side persons rejected by their own country whose radiance reveals the black unreality of any stigma of popular disapprobation.

1925

Judgment

The young generation of men in the East are everywhere attracted by what they imagine is modern. And they have convinced themselves that Western life is modern. They are seeking from its manners and mentality the magic formula of how to grow modern. They believe that what is called modern represents the principle of indefinite growth and freedom,—it is youth, it is life.

If that is the definition of modern, then we must know that its essential element does not consist in a particular time, but in a particular truth, lacking which a thing of the latest pattern and polish may in reality be out of date and condemned to perish. A number of nations have so perished who were too late in realizing that the raft of time, to which they clung believing it to be modern, had already become of the past. Are we sure that the same thing has not happened to the West, and that the atmosphere of turmoil which we find there is not due to the conflict between, their present history, which is no longer modern, and the messenger of the future, which was come with its sovereign claim?

Even the paling darkness of the dawn is immensely distant from the morning light, though they are in immediate contact; and who knows if the present history of the West is not already as old as the day of the deluge?

All that is deeply human is never old. It has the perpetual freshness of imperishable life. Only the acquisitiveness which is not of growth but of hoarding, the cleverness which wins in the game of life with false cards up its sleeve, is crabbed and wrinkled. The business of slave hunting, however up to date in form and profitable in practice, is old; cannibalism, crude or subtle, direct or indirect, with Christian surname or heathen, is never modern, not even in its beginning.

How can we ever believe that the spirit of the hungry Nation from the west, which for over a century has robbed and humiliated us in the eastern hemisphere, has found the secret of everlasting life in its reckless power? Have we lost all faith in the teaching of the wise: that the passions which mock the eternal and things that defiantly grow out of proportion with their surroundings, can never be lasting?

However that may be, the fact cannot be denied that the outstanding feature of the present age is the way of which the West has spread its physical dominance over the whole world, and is still imposing its mind upon other continents. All the great countries of the East, in some period or other of their history, had to submit to foreign invasion and foreign rule, but such alien contact was either milder in its driving force, or was more in harmony with local tradition and environment, and therefore did not attack the inner bonds of unity which maintained the personality of the people.

A complete change of condition has been brought about by the easy means of communication effected by modern science. It is no longer some resourceful individual, who comes like a comet with a host of mercenary soldiers forming his tail, suddenly crossing the path of a strange people and eventually getting entangled and assimilated; but an entire predatory nation which is able to clutch in its titanic grip the vitals of other races for whom it has no feeling of kinship.

Men who do not come as representatives of some organization, political, commercial or religious, have their simple human sentiments; they are not like ghosts who haunt human habitations and yet do not dwell in them, who obsess living beings and yet do not live their life. Such real individuals naturally tend to establish personal relationships with their neighbours and gradually attain their common unity. But Europe's connection with Asiatic countries has not yet developed that personal character in its organizations,—it is like the pressure of some callous outgrowth of her nature, which has not the creative touch of life, but only mechanical skilfulness.

The West has come to us like an engineer who lays stone-paved roads across our meadows and orchards, over our trampled verdure, with the primary object of making easy his work of exploitation. However marvellous and convenient this may be, the overwhelming dominance of mere method and skill in our surroundings is demoralising. It so often makes us forget that, compared to life, the machine is too simple, its action too obvious its results measurable in an indubitably definite manner, its concentrated influence directed only towards the surface of our nature.

For the same reason we often witness in western countries the demonstration of immense esteem, approaching hero-worship, for some winner in a game of skill or strength. This has increased to such an inordinate degree, that a professional organizer of such games can claim better remuneration than a cultured teacher, even in an educational institution. The very superficiality inherent in mere proficiency, produces its immediate impression upon the multitude, hiding from them the higher manifestation of truth that has no definite standard of measurement.

The barbarous in us occupies a large place in human nature; it is idolatrous in its instincts, ready to prostrate itself before all representations of power that are external, that compel us to acknowledge them through our greed, or our fear, or our primitive crudity of thought and feeling. In fact the constant sight and contemplation of any success that has colossal magnitude produces the same mentality in us, as in the savage does the fetish, made emphatically apparent by its barbarity of decoration.

However, the West, which has thrust itself upon us, is the utilitarian adventurer, imbued with the idolatry of the Nation; it carries an elaborate paraphernalia of self worship, and claims other continents for its victims of sacrifice. The loudest of all the messages that it has brought to ourselves is: *You are none of us.* For this reason, even its best gifts carry for us an insult, and it is for this very reason that, when we cannot help accepting them, we feel so small. The West has hurt us deeply with the shock of its greatness. Its very magnificence faces us with its stony gesture of refusal, allowing us to approach it as the earth does the meteorites, merely to feed with them its own dust.

The moral distance which we impose upon men to whose physical proximity we come for exploitation, is immense. This makes them appear so ridiculously diminutive as to be but dimly recognizable by our conscience. It smooths our path of self-seeking to be able to think that others are absolutely other than ourselves, that their human value is represented in coins that have an utterly different mintage from those which we claim for our own. The West, in its relationship with non-western peoples, has for its constant meditation-text: *They are radically and eternally different from ourselves.* Its cult of separateness, which is the cult of the Nation, bristles with doctrines of disdain. It displays its system of canine teeth in the barbed wire fencing round its inhospitable world, in the name of the inborn right to be supercilious, characteristic of a superior civilization.

Asia, in its dignity of age-long tradition, at first refused to acknowledge Europe's claim of superiority. But gradually it had to own defeat at the hand of the organized power and indomitable self-assertion of the Nation, the latest-born progeny of the West. The spectacle of gigantic success with its unsheathed claws and teeth sank deeper and deeper into Eastern consciousness. The contemptuous sneer which accompanied it rankled in Asia's heart, never allowing it for a moment to remain in forgetfulness of this apparition; till a day has arrived when Asia, overcome by the stupendous coil of muscle, has gradually yielded itself to the licking tongue of this monster: Organization of Power.

There has been related in one of our Bengali epics the legend of a merchant who was a devout worshipper of Shiva the Good, the Pure,—Shiva who represents the principle of renunciation and the power of self-control. This man was perpetually persecuted by a deity, the fierce Snake-goddess, who in order to divert his allegiance to herself inflicted the endless power of her malignance upon her victim. Through a series of failures, deaths and disasters he was at last compelled to acknowledge the superior merit of the divinity of frightfulness. The tragedy does not lie in the external fact of the transfer of homage from one shrine to the other, but in the moral defeat implied in the ascribing of a higher value of truth to the goddess of success,—

the personification of unscrupulous egotism,—rather than to the god of moral perfection.

So long as the West herself believed in this latest evolution of her indomitable self-assertion, and was certain that it was going to give her an indefinite extension of the monopoly of all earthly privileges, we in Asia also humbly believed in her. The western people convinced us at the point of their bayonets that they were the chosen people of God, and that the right to inherit the earth was inherent in their race because of a quality which was contrary to that of meekness. We bowed our head to the belief that external success was the ultimate criterion of truth, and I still remember the shock of surprise I felt when a rumour first came to India about Japan's readiness to accept Christianity because it was the religion of a triumphant success, the religion that had unlimited cash in the banks of its devotees and frightful machines of destruction in their arsenal. The moral humiliation of Asia could go on further, and for a moment I was frightened at the prospect of a whole world some day bringing its homage to the shrine of the Snake-goddess, deserting that of Shiva, the Good.

At that time it was difficult for western people to realize that there was anything lacking in their civilization,—for they were so fatuously prosperous and comfortable, so smugly respectable in their behaviour among their own kinsmen. They were never tired of smiling at themselves and saying that they were good, because their drawing rooms were crowded with irrelevancy, their roads geometrically straight, their minds clever, methods efficient, arrangements convenient; because their women had pet dogs, pet schemes of benevolence and head-dresses for which creatures of rare beauty from the most inaccessible regions of the earth had paid toll with their lives.

We, who belong to other continent than theirs, dwell in the obscurity of their shadow, which swallows up our hemisphere, giving us very little chance to bask in the sunshine of their success. For the attitude of success is exclusive, it is by nature suspicious and arrogant. They do not care to come into the heart of our humanity, for it is not needful for their purpose;

and they can be excruciatingly funny when they talk about the peculiarity of the smell of our dwelling places, the inscrutability of our countenances, some mannerisms in our code of behaviour, or any exaggerations in our language or gesture which are different from the exaggerations customary with them and therefore unconscious. Even after this they become sincerely amazed when their energetic acquaintance with us fails to evoke in our mind a grateful feeling of adoration, on when their victims show signs of unhappiness. These they ascribe either to the machination of some interested third party, or to the incomprehensible idiosyncrasies of the people with whom they deal.

It is because we are so imperfectly real to them that they try to boast of their beneficence by making a long list of the railway lines, telegraph posts, coal mines, tea plantations, and the law and order inflicted upon our lands. Their minds are so densely callous to the needs of our humanity that they are ready to punish us when we do not bless them for what they have done to ourselves, in the way of helping us with the commodities which we hardly need and which they vomit forth because they are a great deal more than they can consume themselves.

Let me quote some lines from an article on 'Christian Missions' which came to my notice:

> The last century has contained instance after instance, in the Far East, in Africa, and in the islands of the sea, in which the preaching of the Gospel has seemed to the natives only preliminary to political or economic outrage. Sometimes the two have gone hand in hand. Not soon will educated Chinese forget that the charter under which the Christian missionary operates in his land was a part of that same Treaty of Nanking that legalised the importation of opium. So it is that these peoples wonder in bewilderment why the bodies that proclaim their devotion to the setting up of the rule of God can be content with the individual type of missions, while sins that give the very Christian concept of God the lie grow luxuriant.

About the political relations of West and East the writer quotes Tyler Dennet who says:

> No nation has escaped the valid charge of bad faith. The guilt of all parties being clearly proven, it has seemed profitless to continue the discussion of guilt with a view to determining the relative degree of wickedness. Each Nation, the United States not excepted, has made its contribution to the welter of evil which now comprises the Far Eastern Question.

Speaking of economic exploitation the same writer observes:

> The ruthless manner in which the ancient handicrafts of India were destroyed to favour the mill-owners of England is a matter of parliamentary record. And the tale of the developing industrial life of India, China and Africa is being written in blood. Western business demands, and secures, all sorts of governmental exemptions and favours to ensure its profits when it goes abroad. And again and again, when there, it follows a policy of inhuman hours and starvation wages that is sowing the wind against the future. It is probable that the West thinks of Sir John Bowring—when it thinks of him at all—as the man who wrote:
>
> In the Cross of Christ I glory
> Towering o'er the wrecks of time.
>
> But the East remembers him as the indefatigable diplomat whose labours contributed so much to the legalisation of the opium traffic in China.

I agree with the author when he says that 'This is the sort of international sin that most grievously besets the future—political injustice, economic exploitation, racial discrimination, material standards of success.' But what to my mind is the source of a greater mischief is the fact that bribery on a prodigious scale is being used to persuade whole peoples in the East to sell their future. As the opium has shackled the mind of the coming generation of China in fetters of stupor, the silver narcotic injected into the people's constitution is creating a chronic national helplessness, inducing a habit which will make the motherland sell her own children. The bribery which has the sanctimonious appearance of benevolence is the most dangerous form of banditry; for through its unctuous exuberance a huge load of ransom noiselessly drags the country to a bottomless insolvency.

We have seen in the late war the moral camouflage creates useful delusion not only in the minds of the opponents but in those of one's own party, and for the same reason a vast ethical department is necessary as an adjunct to the organization of exploitation. For the hand that draws blood is greatly helped if it is guided by the idea that it is translating some Sunday School lesson into a beautiful practice. In olden times there were tribes of men who throve upon other people's possessions. Not having that sense of decency which wears a protective decoration they used very little material or moral clothing. They are described in history as savage tribes with criminal tendencies. They remained isolated; no respectable peoples copied their manners. Such narrowness of seclusion itself made their mischievous power short-lived and restricted it to a small area.

In modern times they have changed their names and methods, and even while a great portion of the world is being, ripped open by the iron claws of their organization they have no hesitation in believing in the sure foundation of their civilization and the perfection of its superstructure. It produces such a moral confusion that even we, who are their victims, are willing to copy them.

In fact we are beginning to be ashamed of our trust in what we call *dharma*, the sovereignty of the inner world of ideals. We think that it is a sign of the possession of some brand-new type of cleverness, shiningly up-to-date; to be able to join in the chorus of cynical laughter at a faith in the reality of moral truth.

So we watched for long the outer horizon and there saw no portent of storm-clouds overtaking the fair weather in the West; in fact, all our meteorological misgivings pointed their arrow-heads to the thunder-bearing forces from the West carrying menace in other directions. We had been witnessing for too long the triumph in human history of the law of natural selection prevalent in the biological world, the elbowing out of the less offensive by the aggressive pressure of a superior pushfulness. All our calculations come to be based upon the working of that law till, at last, the man in us made his final obeisance to the brute in us and uttered in awe: *Hail, unholy Might!*

While such a hymn of praise was being raised in all the countries of the world, both by the victors and the vanquished, while the races favoured by fortune dreamt of nothing else but the sharpening of their military fangs and the lengthening of their commercial suckers; while the defeated peoples were cherishing the hope, and secretly preparing, to be able one day to contribute their own share of devilry to the political nightmare of the modern cult of nationalism; the most devastating war that ever happened tore into tatters the enormous self-satisfaction of Europe. She has lately been startled into realizing that its origin was not from outside.

Up to this moment she had been at the zenith of her power and brilliancy; to outward seeming she had conquered endless time for her boundless prosperity, while she had been moulding with a pitiless success the destiny of millions of alien people fashion her own footstool and keep it permanently secure. The barometer which recorded the external condition of the atmosphere foreboded a perpetual monotony of fair weather. There had been, no doubt, angry flashes of lightning from the friction created by colliding greeds, but it was firmly believed that the urging of an intelligent self-interest was itself sufficient to check any of these violent gestures from ending in a catastrophe.

Then came the day when everything that had given her supremacy in the world seemed to turn against her and the Science which she had tamed for a hunting expedition tore ugly rents in her own limbs, which still show no sign of healing. So her proud mind has had to come to the conclusion that her present suffering is not due to any lack of intellectual attainment or material advantage, but to some cancerous growth within her own moral nature.

This has, at length, given us in Asia the opportunity of judging Europe with our mind freed from the hypnotism of success,—an opportunity necessary for our own salvation. This judgment must not be in a spirit of retaliation, which chuckles at the chance of hurling back at the West some part of the evil-smelling mud which she was never tired of flinging at the unprotected Orient. Nevertheless we must have the courage to judge. For the standard of moral judgment is the true helm of our life. Lately it has been laughed at by the modern young person for being stationary, and our hold upon it has been slackened. We must regain our confidence in it, knowing that this helm is more necessary for us to-day than ever before, because we are overtaken by a current that is sudden and swift, by winds that are changing, and because we must move among breakers.

Fight there must be in this world. We cannot make truce with impunity. Our evolution towards the perfect has been and has to be through a series of fights. Our moral judgment is the best weapon we have in the warfare for the preservation of humanity. With it we have to resist, and even to hurt, for the cause of justice.

Have we not noticed in the modern East how the people, who have a highly developed instinct for turning out things of perfect beauty for their daily life show utter crudity in their selection of western articles for show or for use? They completely forget the dignity of the true born aristocracy which they possess in the world of craftsmanship when they try to acquire or imitate the furniture and other western appliances that bear the brand of the outcast. They carelessly allow the aggression of weeds into their garden where flowers have been nourished by the love and the sensitive understanding of generations of their forefathers. It has been made possible because they have blindly surrendered their judgment of excellence overwhelmed by the spectacle of a robust success. In their infatuation they rob Apollo of his homage in order to offer it to the image of Hercules.

My heart was filled with shame and pain when I passed by the ruined mounds of the Summer Palace of Peking, brought to the dust by those who were furiously loud in their condemnation of the destruction of some ancient cathedrals of Europe by their enemies. Yet they can be forgiven, for they knew not what they had been doing. They merely personated an unintelligent storm of fury which had a scientific thoroughness of brutality, and they wantonly destroyed buildings, pictures and objects of art the like of which was never seen before nor will be in the future.

But it fills my heart with despair when I realize that the modern Chinese are themselves helping in the devastation of the genius of China, daily growing used to things that are merely convenient and forgetting the miracle of creative touch which their fingers have acquired. It shows a laziness of apathy which is uncivilized. True civilization knows the value of things that belong to the higher nature of man and is ever ready to take trouble to produce them, use them, and maintain them in their excellence. To succumb to the temptation of cheap production and hasty utility is the sign of the shallow mind that seeks its release from the strenuous claim of high aspiration in the vulgar comfort of standardised respectability. The educated China of to-day seems to have surrendered its judgment of taste and through this defeat is threatened with a desert of white monotony swallowing up the colours and features of its civilization.

The surrender of moral judgment is also a defeat through which the invasion of the West is laying its stony road across the soul of the East, leading most of its traffic of ideas to the gambling den of commerce and politics, to the furious competition of suicide in the arena of military lunacy. Shady paths that ran into various avenues of life carrying the invitation of hearts and the call of co-operation, are one by one being closed. This also is helping the monotonous extension of that aspect of the West which is not fruit-bearing.

But we must not allow this to go on. We must find our voice to be able to say to the West: 'You may force your things into our homes, you may obstruct our prospects of life,—but *we judge you*. You may ignore our judgment. Materially it will not injure you, nor check you in your climbing up the dizzy precipice of profit and power, but it will save us from moral degradation. We refuse to humiliate ourselves by saying that you are worthy of obedience because you are strong, worthy of respect because you are rich.'

What I have discussed above only shows that in its relation to the eastern peoples the aspect of western character which has come uppermost is not only insulting to us but to the West itself. Nothing could have been more unfortunate in the history of man than this. For all meetings of men should reveal some great truth which is worthy of a permanent memorial, such, as for instance, had been the case of India's meeting with China in the ancient time.

At the moment when the West came to our door, the whole of Asia was asleep, the darkness of night had fallen over her life. Her lights were dim, her voice mute. She had stored up in her vaults her treasure, no longer growing. She had her wisdom shut in her books. She was not producing living thoughts of fresh forms of beauty. She was not moving forward but endlessly revolving round her past. She was not ready to receive the West in all her majesty of soul.

The best in us attracts the best in others: our weakness attracts violence to our neighbourhood, as thinness in the air attracts a storm. To remain in the fulness of our manifestation is our duty, not only for ourselves but for others. We have not seen the great in the West because we have failed to bring out the great that we have in us and we delude ourselves into thinking that we can hide this deficiency behind borrowed feathers.

Yet, through all our shame and our suffering, we have to acknowledge that the West is great. With her science she has offered a grand illumination to the path of reason. Some people in the East are in the habit of reviling science, calling it materialistic. They may as well say that incendiarism is in the fire. Science is truth. It is immaterial. It gives us freedom in the realm of matter. It brings our mind into touch with the eternal at the uttermost brink of the finite. What if science can help some temperaments solely to cultivate materialism,—cannot religion do the same? We have witnessed in the East the grossest form of materialism and the cruellest form of inhumanity stalking abroad in our society wearing the uniform of spiritual culture. We constantly see the epicureanism of religious emotion, indulged in by self-centred individuals, admired by simple-minded people as piety in full blossom.

On the other hand, the usual form of spiritual expression we find in the lives of the best individuals in western countries is their love of humanity, their spirit working through their character; their keen intellect and their indomitable will leaguing together for human welfare. In their individuals it reveals itself in loyalty to the cause of truth for which so many of them are ready to suffer martyrdom, often standing heroically alone against some fury of their national insanity. When their wide human interest, which is intellectual, takes a moral direction, it grows into a fulness of intelligent service of man that can ignore all geographical limits and racial habits of tradition. The goodness which is undaunted in its chivalrous adventure, and love of truth, variedly active and widespread in its ministration, we do not see in the East.

But, because in their individual lives the western peoples have raised the tower of their moral standard so high, the ravage of their national unrighteousness at the base is fraught with dangerous consequence. Bespattering the whole world with their diplomatic lies, continually adding to the number of victims for their man-eating prosperity, scientifically crushing the human rights of large continents of races, spreading a contagion of ugly carbuncles all over the earth with the impurity of their utilitarian touch, keeping their snarling nastiness bared at the entrance of their miserly national mansion,—they have, in all these, an ever increasing gravitational pull against the top of their greatness. The fall will be terrific.

But what is most unfortunate for us in Asia is the fact that the advent of the West into our continent has been accompanied not only by science, which is truth and therefore welcome, but by an impious use of truth for the violent purpose of self-seeking which converts it into a disruptive force. It is producing in the countries with which it is in contact a diseased mentality that refuses moral ideals, considering them to be unworthy of those who aspire to be rulers of men, and who must furiously cultivate their fitness to survive. That such a philosophy of survival, fit for the world of tigers, cannot but bring a fatal catastrophe in the human world, they do not see. They become violently angry at those who protest against it, fearing that such a protest might weaken in them the animal that should be allowed to survive for eternity.

Doctors know that infusion of animal blood into human veins does not give vigour to man but produces death, and the intrusion of the animal into humanity will never be for its survival. But faith in man is weakening even in the East, for we have seen that science has enabled the inhuman to prosper, the lie to thrive, the machine to rule in the place of *Dharma.* Therefore in order to save us from the anarchy of weak faith we must stand up to-day and judge the West.

But we must guard against antipathy that produces blindness. We must not disable ourselves from receiving truth. For the West has appeared before the present-day world not only with her dynamite of passion and cargo of things but with her gift of truth. Until we fully accept it in a right spirit we shall never even discover what is true in our own civilization and make it generously fruitful by offering it to the world. The culture, the humanity of the West do not belong to the Nation but to the People.

While nations fight for their exclusive possessions, the peoples share with one another their true wealth. And the highest spirit of the peoples of the West, their loyal love of truth and active love of man, we must try to make our own in order to impart to our life a movement and to our ideals a vitality that shall give them the impulse to produce new flower and fruit.

1925

The Philosophy of Our People

My timidity makes it difficult for me properly to enjoy the honour you have done me to-day by offering a chair which I cannot legitimately claim as my own. It has often made me wonder, since I had my invitation, whether it would suit my dignity to occupy such a precarious position on an ephemeral eminence, deservedly incurring anger from some and ridicule from others. While debating in my mind as to whether I should avoid this risk with the help of the doctor's certificate, it occurred to me that possibly my ignorance of philosophy was the best recommendation for this place in a philosophers' meeting,—that you wanted for your president a man who was blankly neutral and who consciously owed no allegiance to any particular system of metaphysics, being impartially innocent of them all. The most convenient thing about me is that the degree of my qualification is beyond the range of a comparative discussion,—it is so utterly negative. In my present situation, I may be compared to a candlestick that has none of the luminous qualities of a candle and, therefore, suitable for its allotted function, which is to remain darkly inactive.

But, unfortunately, you do not allow me to remain silent even in the circumstance when silence was declared to be prudent by one of our ancient sages. The only thing which encourages me to overcome my diffidence, and give expression in a speech to my unsophisticated mind, is the fact that in India all the *vidyās,*—poesy as well as philosophy,—live in a joint family. They never have the jealous sense of individualism maintaining the punitive regulations against trespass that seem to be so rife in the West.

Plato as a philosopher decreed the banishment of poets from his ideal Republic. But, in India, philosophy ever sought alliance with poetry, because its mission was to occupy the people's life and not merely the learned seclusion of scholarship. Therefore, our tradition, though unsupported by historical evidence, has no hesitation in ascribing numerous verses to the great Shankarāchārya, a metaphysician whom Plato would find it extremely difficult to exclude from his Utopia with the help of any inhospitable Immigration Law. Many of these poems may not have high poetical value, but no lover of literature ever blames the sage for infringement of propriety in condescending to manufacture verse.

According to our people, poetry naturally falls within the scope of a philosopher, when his reason is illumined into a vision. We have our great epic Mahābhārata, which is unique in world literature, not only because of the marvellous variety of human characters, great and small, discussed in its pages in all variety of psychological circumstances, but because of the ease with which it carries in its comprehensive capaciousness all kinds of speculation about ethics, politics and philosophy of life. Such an improvident generosity on the part of poesy, the risk of exceeding its own proper limits of accommodation, has only been possible in India where a spirit of communism prevails the different individual groups of literature. In fact the Mahābhārata is a universe in itself in which various sphere of mind's creation find ample space for their complex dance rhythm. It does not represent the idiosyncrasy of a particular poet but the normal mentality of the people who are willingly be led along the many branched path of a whole world thoughts, held together in a gigantic orb of narrative surrounded by innumerable satellites of episodes.

The numerous saints that India successively produced during the Mohammedan rule have all been singers whose are aflame with the fire of imagination. Their religious emotion had its spring in the depth of a philosophy that deals with fundamental questions,—with the ultimate meaning of existence. That may not be remarkable in itself; but when we find that these songs are not specially meant for some exclusive pundits' gathering, but that they are sung in villages and listened to by men and women who are illiterate, we realize how philosophy has permeated the life of the people in India, how it has sunk deep into the sub-conscious mind of the country.

In my childhood I once heard from a singer, who was a devout Hindu, the following song of Kabir:

When I hear of a fish in the water dying of thirst, it makes
me laugh.
If it be true that the infinite Brahma pervades all space,
What is the meaning of the places of pilgrimage like
Mathura or Kashi?

This laughter of Kabir did not hurt in the least the pious susceptibilities of the Hindu singer; on the contrary, he was ready to join the poet with his own. For he, by the philosophical freedom of his mind, was fully aware that Mathura or Kashi, as sites of God, did not have an absolute value of truth, though they had their symbolical importance. Therefore, while he himself was eager to make a pilgrimage to those places, he had no doubt in his mind that, if it were in his power directly to realize *Brahma* as an all-pervading reality, there would have been no necessity for him to visit any particular place for the quickening of his spiritual consciousness. He acknowledged the psychological necessity for such shrines, where generations of devotees have chosen to gather for the purpose of worship, in the same way as he felt the special efficacy for our mind of the time-honoured sacred texts made living by the voice of ages.

It is a village poet of East Bengal who in his songs preaches the philosophical doctrine that the universe has its reality in its relation to the Person. He sings:

The sky and the earth are born of mine own eyes.
The hardness and softness, the cold and the heat
are the products of my own body;
The sweet smell and the bad are of my own nose.

This poet sings of the Eternal Person within him, coming out and appearing before his eyes just as the Vedic Rishi speaks of the Person, who is in him, dwelling also in the heart of the Sun.

I have seen the vision,
The vision of mine own revealing itself,
Coming out from within me.

The significant fact about these philosophical poems is that they are of crude construction, written in a popular dialect and disclaimed by the academic literature; they are sung to the people, as composed by one of them who is dead, but whose songs have not followed him. Yet these singers almost arrogantly disown their direct obligation to philosophy, and there is a story of one of our rural poets who, after some learned text of the Vaishnava philosophy of emotion was explained to him, composed a song containing the following lines:

Alas, a jeweller has come into the flower garden!—
He wants to appraise the truth of a lotus by rubbing it against his touchstone.

The members of the *Baül* sect belong to that mass of the people in Bengal who are not educated in the prevalent senses of the word. I remember how troubled they were, when I asked some of them to write down for me a collection of their songs. When they *did* venture to attempt it, I found it almost impossible to decipher their writing—the spelling and lettering were so outrageously unconventional. Yet their spiritual practices are founded upon a mystic philosophy of the human body, abstrusely technical. These people roam about singing their songs, one of which I heard years ago from my roadside window, the first two lines remaining inscribed in my memory:

Nobody can tell whence the bird unknown
Comes into the cage and goes out.
I would feign put round its feet the fetter of my mind,
Could I but capture it.

This village poet evidently agrees with our sage of the Upanishad who says that our mind comes back baffled in its attempt to reach the Unknown Being; and yet this poet like the ancient sage does not give up his adventure of the infinite, thus implying that there is a way to its realization. It reminds me of Shelley's poem in which he sings of the mystical spirit of Beauty:

The awful shadow of some unseen Bower
Floats, though unseen, among us visiting
This various world with as inconstant wing

As summer winds that creep from flower to flower.
Like moonbeams that behind some piny mountain shower,
It visits with inconstant glance
Each human heart and countenance.

That this Unknown is the profoundest reality, though difficult of comprehension, is equally admitted by the English poet as by the nameless village singer of Bengal in whose music vibrate the wing beats of the unknown bird,—only Shelley's utterance is for the cultured few while the Baül song is for the tillers of the soil, for the simple folk of our village households, who are never bored by its mystic transcendentalism.

All this is owing to the wonderful system of mass education which has prevailed for ages in India, and which to-day is in danger of becoming extinct. We have our academic seats of learning where students flock round their famous teachers from distant parts of the country. These places are like lakes, full of deep but still water, which have to be approached through difficult paths. But the constant evaporation from them, forming clouds, is carried by the wind from field to field, across hills and dales and through all the different divisions of the land. Operas based upon legendary poems, recitations and story-telling by trained men, the lyrical wealth of the popular literature distributed far and wide by the agency of mendicant singers,—these are the clouds that help to irrigate the minds of the people with the ideas which in their original form belonged to difficult doctrines of metaphysics. Profound speculations contained in the systems of Sānkhya, Vedānta and Yôga are transformed into the living harvest of the people's literature, brought to the door of those who can never have the leisure and training to pursue these thoughts to their fountain-head.

In order to enable a civilized community to carry on its complex functions, there must be a large number of men who have to take charge of its material needs, however onerous such task may be. Their vocation gives them no opportunity to cultivate their mind. Yet they form the vast multitude, compelled to turn themselves into unthinking machines of production so that a few may have the time to think great thoughts, create immortal forms of art and to lead humanity to spiritual altitudes.

India has never neglected these social martyrs, but has tried to bring light into the grimy obscurity of their life-long toil, and has always acknowledged its duty to supply them with mental and spiritual food in assimilable form through the medium of a variety of ceremonies. This process is not carried on by any specially organized association of public service, but by a spontaneous social adjustment which acts like circulation of blood in our bodily system. Because of this, the work continues even when the original purpose ceases to exist.

Once when I was on a visit to a small Bengal village mostly inhabited by Mohammedan cultivators, the villagers entertained me with an opera performance the literature of which belonged to an obsolete religious sect that had wide influence centuries ago. Though the religion itself is dead, its voice still continues preaching its philosophy to a people who in spite of their different culture are not tired of listening. It discussed according to its own doctrine the different elements, material and transcendental, that constitute human personality, comprehending the body, the self and the soul. Then came a dialogue during the course of which was related the incident of a person who wanted to make a journey to *Brindāban*, the Garden of Bliss, but was prevented by a watchman who startled him with an accusation of theft. The thieving was proved when it was shown that inside his clothes he was secretly trying to smuggle into the garden the *self,* passing it on as his own and not admitting that it is for his master. The culprit was caught with the incriminating bundle in his possession which barred-for him his passage to the supreme goal. Under a tattered canopy held on bamboo poles and lighted by a few smoking kerosene lamps, the village crowd, occasionally interrupted by howls of jackals in the neighbouring paddy fields, attended with untired interest, till the small hours of the morning, the performance of a drama, that discussed the ultimate meaning of all things in a seemingly incongruous setting of dance, music and humorous dialogue.

These illustrations will show how naturally, in India, poetry and philosophy have walked hand in hand, only because the latter has claimed its right to guide men to the practical path of their life's fulfilment. What is that fulfilment? It is our freedom in truth, which has for its prayer:

Lead us from the unreal to Reality.

For *satyam is ānandam,* the real is joy.

From my vocation as an artist in verse, I have come to my own idea about the joy of the real. For to give us the taste of reality through freedom of mind is the nature of all arts. When in relation to them we talk of aesthetics we must know that it is not about beauty in its ordinary meaning, but in that deeper meaning which a poet has expressed in his utterance: 'Truth is beauty, beauty truth.' An artist may paint a picture of a decrepit person not pleasant to look at, and yet we call it perfect when we become intensely conscious of its reality. The mind of the jealous woman in Browning's poem, watching the preparation of poison and in imagination gloating over its possible effect upon her rival, is not beautiful; but when it stands vividly real before our consciousness, through the unity of consistency in its idea and form, we have our enjoyment. The character of Karna, the great warrior of the Mahābhārata, gives us a deeper delight through its occasional outbursts of meanness, than it would if it were a model picture of unadulterated magnanimity. The very contradictions which hurt the completeness of a moral ideal have helped us to feel the reality of the character, and this gives us joy, not because it is pleasant in itself, but because it is definite in its creation.

It is not wholly true that art has its value for us because in it we realize all that we fail to attain in our life; but the fact is that the function of art is to bring us, with its creations, into immediate touch with reality. These need not resemble actual facts of our experience, and yet they do delight our heart because they are made true to us. In the world of art, our consciousness being freed from the tangle of self-interest, we gain an unobstructed vision of unity, the incarnation of the real, which is a joy for ever.

As in the world of art, so in God's world, our soul waits for its freedom from the ego to reach that disinterested joy which is the source and goal of creation. It cries for its *mukti* into the unity of truth from the mirage of appearances endlessly pursued by the thirsty self. This idea of *mukti,* based upon metaphysics, has affected our life in India, touched the springs of our emotions, and supplications for it soar heavenward on the wings of poesy. We constantly hear men of scanty learning, and simple faith singing in their prayer to *Tara,* the Goddess Redeemer:

> *For what sin should I be compelled to remain in this dungeon of the world of appearance?*

They are afraid of being alienated from the world of truth afraid of their perpetual drifting amidst the froth and foam of things, of being tossed about by the tidal waves of pleasure and pain and never reaching the ultimate meaning of life. Of these men, one may be a carter driving his cart to market, another a fisherman plying his net. They may not be prompt with an intelligent answer, if questioned about the deeper import of the song they sing, but they have no doubt in their mind, that the abiding cause of all misery is not so much in the lack of life furniture as in the obscurity of life's significance. It is common topic with such to decry an undue emphasis upon *me* and *mine,* which falsifies the perspective of truth. For have they not often seen men, who are not above their own level in social position or intellectual acquirement, going on to seek Truth, leaving everything that they have behind them.

They know that the object of these adventurers is not betterment in worldly wealth and power,—it is *mukti,* freedom. They possibly know some poor fellow villager of their own craft, who remains in the world carrying on his daily vocation, and yet has the reputation of being emancipated in the heart of the Eternal. I myself have come across a fisherman singing with an inward absorption of mind, while fishing all day in the Ganges, who was pointed out to me by my boatmen, with awe, as a man of liberated spirit. He is out of reach of the conventional prices which are set upon men by society, and which classify them like toys arranged in the shop-windows according to the market standard of value.

When the figure of this fisherman comes to my mind, I cannot but think that their number is not small who with their lives sing the epic of the unfettered soul, but will never be known in history. These unsophisticated Indian peasants know that in Emperor is a decorated slave remaining chained to his Empire, that a millionaire is kept pilloried by his fate in the golden cage of his wealth, while this fisherman is free in the realm of light. When, groping in the dark, we stumble against objects, we cling to them believing them to be our only hope. When light comes we slacken our hold, finding them to be mere parts of the all to which we are related. The simple man of the village knows what freedom is—freedom from the isolation of self, from the isolation of things which imparts a fierce intensity to our sense of possession. He knows that this freedom is not in the mere negation of bondage, in the bareness of belongings, but in some positive realization which gives pure joy to our being, and he sings:

To him who sinks into the deep, nothing remains unattained.
Let my two minds meet and combine
And lead me to the City Wonderful.

When the one mind of ours which wanders in search of things in the outer region of the varied, and the other which seeks the inward vision of unity, are no longer in conflict, they help us to realize the *ajab,* the *anirvachanīya,* the ineffable. The poet saint Kabir has also the same message when he sings:

By saying that Supreme Reality only, dwells in the inner realm of spirit we shame the outer world of matter, and also when we say that he is only in the outside we do not speak the truth.

According to these singers, truth is in unity and therefore freedom is in its realization. The texts of our daily worship and meditation are for training our mind to overcome the barrier of separateness from the rest of existence and to realize *advaitam,* the Supreme Unity which is *anantam,* infinitude. It is philosophical wisdom having its universal radiation in the popular mind in India but inspires our prayer, our daily spiritual practices. It has its constant urging for us to go beyond the world of appearances in which facts as facts are alien to us, like the mere sounds of a foreign music; it speaks to us of an emancipation in the inner truth of all things in which the endless *many* reveals the *One,* as the multitude of notes, when we understand them, reveal to us the inner unity which is music.

But because this freedom is in truth itself and not in an appearance of it, no hurried path of success, forcibly cut out by the greed of result, can be a true path. And an obscure village poet, unknown to the world of recognized respectability, untramelled by the standardised learning of the Education Department, sings:

> *O cruel man of urgent need, must you scorch with fire the mind which, still is a bud? You will burst it into bits, destroy its perfume in your impatience. Do you not see that my lord, the Supreme Teacher, takes ages to perfect the flower and never is in a fury of haste? But because of your terrible greed you only rely on force, and what hope is there for you, O man of urgent need? 'Prithee!' says Madan the poet. 'Hurt not the mind of my Teacher. Know that only he who follows the simple current and loses himself can hear the voice, O man of urgent need.'*

This poet knows that there is no external means of taking freedom by the throat. It is the inward process of losing ourselves that leads us to it. Bondage in all its forms has its stronghold in the inner self and not in the outside world; it is in the dimming of our consciousness, in the narrowing of our perspective, in the wrong valuation of things.

The proof of this we find in the modern civilization whose motive force has become a ceaseless urgency of need. Its freedom is only the apparent freedom of inertia which does not know how and where to stop. There are some primitive people who have put an artificial value on human scalps and they develop an arithmetical fury which does not allow them to stop in the gathering of their trophies. They are driven by some cruel fate into an endless exaggeration which makes them ceaselessly run on an interminable path of addition. Such a freedom in their wild course of collection is the worst form of bondage. The cruel urgency of need is all the more aggravated in their case because of the lack of truth in its object. Similarly it should be realized that a mere addition to the rate of speed, to the paraphernalia of fat living and display of furniture, to the frightfulness of destructive armaments, only leads to an insensate orgy of a caricature of bigness. The links of bondage go on multiplying themselves, threatening to shackle the whole world with the chain forged by such unmeaning and unending urgency of need.

The idea of *mukti* in Christian theology is liberation from a punishment which we carry with our birth. In India it is from the dark enclosure of ignorance which causes the illusion of a self that seems final. But the enlightenment which frees us from this ignorance must not merely be negative. Freedom is not in an emptiness of its contents, it is in the harmony of communication through which we find no obstruction in realizing our own being in the surrounding world. It is of this harmony, and not of a bare and barren isolation, that the Upanishad speaks, when it says that the truth no longer remains hidden in him who finds himself in the All.

Freedom in the material world has also the same meaning expressed in its own language. When nature's phenomena appeared to us as manifestations of an obscure and irrational caprice, we lived in an alien world never dreaming of our *swaraj* within its territory. With the discovery of the harmony of its working with that of our reason, we realize our unity with it and, therefore, freedom. It is *avidyā,* ignorance, which causes our disunion with our surroundings. It is *vidyā,* the knowledge of the *Brahma* manifested in the material universe that makes us realize *advaitam,* the spirit of unity in the world of matter.

Those who have been brought up in a misunderstanding of this world's process, not knowing that it is his by his right of intelligence, are trained as cowards by a hopeless faith in the ordinance of a destiny darkly dealing its blows, offering no room for appeal. They submit without struggle when human rights are denied them, being accustomed to imagine themselves born as outlaws in a world constantly thrusting upon them incomprehensible surprises of accidents.

Also in the social or political field, the lack of freedom is based upon the spirit of alienation, on the imperfect realization of *advaitam*. There our bondage is in the tortured link of union. One may imagine that an individual who succeeds in dissociating himself from his fellows attains real freedom, inasmuch as all ties of relationship imply obligation to others. But we know that, though it may sound paradoxical, it is true that in the human world only a perfect arrangement of interdependence gives rise to freedom. The most individualistic of human beings, who own no responsibility, are the savages who fail to attain their fulness of manifestation. They live immersed in obscurity, like an ill-lighted fire that cannot liberate itself, from its envelope of smoke. Only those may attain their freedom from the segregation of an eclipsed life, who have the power to cultivate mutual understanding the cooperation. The history of the growth of freedom is the history of the perfection of human relationship.

The strongest barrier against freedom in all departments of life is the selfishness of individuals or groups. Civilization, whose object is to afford humanity its greatest possible opportunity of complete manifestation, perishes when some selfish passion, in place of a moral ideal, is allowed to exploit its resources unopposed, for its own purposes. For the greed of acquisition and the living principle of creation are antagonist to each other. Life has brought with it the first triumph of freedom in the world of the inert, because it is an inner expression and not merely an external fact, because it must always exceed the limits of its substance, never allowing its materials to clog its spirit, and yet ever keeping to the limits of its truth. Its accumulation must not suppress its harmony of growth, the harmony that unites the *in* and the *out,* the end and the means, the *what is* and the *what is to come.*

Life does not store up but assimilates; its spirit and its substance, its work and itself, are intimately united. When the non-living elements of our surroundings are stupendously disproportionate, when they are mechanical systems and hoarded possessions, then the mutual discord between our life and our world ends in the defeat of the former. The gulf thus created by the receding stream of soul we try to replenish with a continuous shower of wealth which may have the power to fill but not the power to unite. Therefore the gap is dangerously concealed under the glittering quick-sands of things which by their own accumulating weight cause a sudden subsidence, while we are in the depth of our sleep.

But the real tragedy does not lie in the destruction of our material security, it is in the obscuration of man himself in the human world. In his creative activities man makes his surroundings instinct with his own life and love. But in his utilitarian ambition he deforms and defiles it with the callous handling of his voracity. This world of man's manufacture with its discordant shrieks and mechanical movements, reacts upon his own nature, incessantly suggesting to him a scheme of universe which is an abstract system. In such a world there can be no question of *mukti,* because it is solidly solitary fact, because the cage is all that we have, and no sky beyond it. In all appearance the world to us *is* a closed world, like a seed within its hard cover. But in the core of the seed there is the cry of *Life* for *mukti* even when the proof of its possibility is darkly silent. When some huge temptation tramples into stillness this living aspiration after *mukti,* then does civilization die like a seed that has lost its urging for germination.

It is not altogether true that the ideal of *mukti* in India is based upon a philosophy of passivity. The Ishopanishad has strongly asserted that man must wish to live a hundred years and go on doing his work; for, according to it, the complete truth is in the harmony of the infinite and the finite, the passive ideal of perfection and the active process of its revealment; according to it, he who pursues the knowledge of the infinite as an absolute truth sinks even into a deeper darkness than he who pursues the cult of the finite as complete in itself. He who thinks that a mere aggregation of changing notes has the ultimate value of unchanging music, is no doubt foolish; but his foolishness is exceeded by that of one who thinks that true music is devoid of all notes. But where is the reconciliation? Through what means does the music which is transcendental turn the facts of the detached notes into a vehicle of its expression? It is through the rhythm, the very limit of its composition. We reach the infinite through crossing the path that is definite. It is this that is meant in the following verse of the Isha:

> *He who knows the truth of the infinite and that of the finite both united together, crosses death by the help of* avidyā, *and by the help* of vidyā *reaches immortality.*

The regulated life is the rhythm of the finite through whose very restrictions we pass to the immortal life. This *amritam,* the immortal life, is not a mere prolongation of physical existence, it is in the realization of the perfect, it is in the well-proportioned beautiful definition of life which every moment surpasses its own limits and expresses the Eternal. In the very first verse of the Isha, the injunction is given to us *mā gridhah. Thou shalt not covet.* But why should we not? Because greed, having no limit, smothers the rhythm of life—the rhythm which is expressive of the limitless.

The modern civilization is largely composed of *atmahanojanāh* who are spiritual suicides. It has lost its will for limiting its desires, for restraining its perpetual self-exaggeration. Because it has lost its philosophy of life, it loses its art of living. Like poetasters it mistakes skill for power and realism for reality. In the Middle Ages when Europe believed in the kingdom of heaven, she struggled to modulate her life's forces to effect their harmonious relation to this ideal, which always sent its call to her activities in the midst of the boisterous conflict of her passions. There was in this endeavour an ever present scheme of creation, something which was positive, which had the authority to say: *Thou shalt not covet, thou must find thy true limits.* To-day there is only a furious rage for raising numberless brick-kilns in place of buildings. The great scheme of the master-builder has been smothered under the heaps of brick-dust. It proves the severance of *avidyā* from her union with *vidyā* giving rise to an unrhythmic power, ignoring all creative plan, igniting a flame that has heat but no light.

Creation is in rhythm,—the rhythm which is the border on which *vidyāncha avidyāncha,* the infinite and the finite, meet. We do not know how, from the indeterminate, the lotus flower finds its being. So long as it is merged in the vague it is nothing to us, and yet it must have been everywhere. Somehow from the vast it has been captured in a perfect rhythmical limit forming an eddy in our consciousness, arousing within us a recognition of delight at the touch of the infinite which finitude gives. It is the limiting process which is the work of a creator, who finds his freedom through his restraints, the truth of the boundless through the reality of the bounds. The insatiable idolatory of material, that runs along an ever-lengthening line of extravagance, is inexpressive; it belongs to those regions which are *andhênatamasāvritah*, enveloped in darkness, which ever carry the load of their inarticulate bulk. The true prayer of man is for the Real not for the big, for the Light which is not in incendiarism but in illumination, for Immortality which is not in duration of time, but in the eternity of the perfect.

Only because we have closed our path to the inner world of *mukti,* has the outer world become terrible in its exactions. It is a slavery to continue to live in a sphere where things are, yet where their meaning is obstructed. It has become possible for men to say that existence is evil, only because in our blindness we have missed something in which our existence has its truth. If a bird tries to soar in the sky with only one of its wings, it is offended with the wind for buffeting it down to the dust. All broken truths are evil. They hurt because they suggest something, which they do not offer. Death does not hurt us, but disease does, because disease constantly reminds us of health and yet withholds it from us. And life in a half world is evil, because it feigns finality when it is obviously incomplete, giving us the cup, but not the draught of life. All tragedies consist in truth remaining fragmentary, its cycle not being completed.

Let me close with a *Baül* song, over a century old, in which the poet sings of the eternal bond of union between the infinite and the finite soul, from which there can be no *mukti,* because it is an interrelation which makes truth complete, because love is ultimate, because absolute independence is the blankness of utter sterility. The idea in it is the same as we have in the

Upanishad that truth is neither in pure *vidyā* nor in *avidyā,* but in their union:

> *It goes on blossoming for ages; the soul-lotus in which I am bound, as well as thou, without escape. There is no end to the opening of its petals, and the honey in it has such sweetness that thou like an enchanted bee canst never desert it, and therefore thou art bound, and I am, and mukti is nowhere.*

1926

The Rule of the Giant

Wrongs can be seen and felt separately, but most often their one common source remains hidden, and so ignored. I have tried to describe in this paper what I consider to be the parent ill of the present age.

The fact comprising the non-human comes under neither good nor bad. All that can be said about it is that it persists in space and time. The reality of its existence is judged by a criterion that can count, measure and weigh. The fact of human personality is not judged by any value that lies in quantity of force or substance, or duration of time. It has its significance in an ideal of perfection according to which it is either good or bad. Since the secret of nature's forces has been revealed to man, wealth and power have grown so stupendously big that the barbarous in him has been stricken with awe at their enormity. Peoples are set dreaming of the big wealth of millions and the big power of imperialism. The standard of quantity is every day getting the better of the standard of perfection and truth. The idolatry of bigness has occupied the altar of greatness. As the human world is the world of personality, such desecration, if tolerated, will reduce men into mere things, and things into dust.

It is the hugely disproportionate growth, in modern civilization, of the not-life, of which the bulk of overshadowing life and whose weight is crushing it. We are every day growing more and more tolerant of the disharmony produced between Man and his organization, between his means and end, thereby offering to unbalanced bigness more and more temptation to insult the ideal of fulness that gives us equilibrium in things and equanimity in mind.

Life has its own special cadence with which the environment that it creates for itself should be in accord. Otherwise the whole thing becomes like a melody whose accompaniment, in a sudden frenzy, has developed a different pitch and time of its own. Whereupon the man who seeks his fulfilment finds noise in place of music and self-assertion bullying self-expression into silence.

In the present age when human society has the tendency to swell up into overgrown organizations, the weight of their bulk cannot but obstruct the spirit's modulations. Possibly they are scientifically adapted to one or more special purposes. But the ultimate purpose which is the perfect expression of personality is forgotten, making it possible for man to pay all his attention to the golden eggs, and to do away with the inconvenient bird that claims attention to its life. The knife that kills it is exquisitely efficient, the hand that wields the knife is accurately dexterous, and the crowd is exultant at this marvel of achievement, at this triumph of the efficiency in its apparatus and dexterity in its agents. It requires courage to disturb this jubilant self-gratulation with the question: 'What about the bird? Where is the complete man, the Person?' Such a question seems so out of date; the concern about the bird is so old fashioned and sentimental; what is so gloriously modern is the big knife and the complex technicality.

There is a radical difference between man's ambition and his aspiration. Aspiration seeks growth as a whole; it is the process of life itself, the life which has its balance of proportion, its poetry of limits. Ambition goes on adding to the parts; it is an arithmetical process. In its greed for fuel it has no compunction in smothering the Fire. Our body needs clothing; yet because it is not a wardrobe, but a living organism, the clothes must have sufficient lightness and flexibility to be able to move easily with life's movements. But if the clothing be a heavy suit of mail, then it may serve a particular purpose for a special contingency, but not the full purpose of life. It looks formidable; it denotes power in a man who wears it; it evokes admiration in the juvenile heart; but all the while it weighs upon life like death itself. In the same manner a society, that produces a hugeness of organization in its politics, commerce, religion, education and amusement, which fetters its living limbs and smothers the movements of its spiritual expression, continually builds round itself its own tomb, albeit for the time being this appears like its tower of victory.

The boastful hugeness, which always tries to exceed life's simplicity of limits, is an exaggeration: it is puffed up by the crowding of the non-essential, which like a noxious weed grows only to choke the essential into insignificance. Thus overladen, the education that is bursting with a miscellany of subjects, is fostered at the cost of true culture, a prodigious quantity of printed stuff is continually poured upon the mind of the people, allowing the fertile soil of creation to be buried under the debris of the heterogeneous. The commerce, which is abnormally big, is busily engaged in over-production and in trying to dig channels for its torrents of surplus across the unwilling breast of the earth. It diverts an enormous part of time and energy from life's field of creation to the imbecility of an endless repetition of things. A constant process of suicide has thus to be kept going on under conditions in which the utmost output is being extorted from machinery regulated to a speed and power far beyond life's natural rhythm.

In this perpetual race with the machine that is keeping a different measure of time, Life is hurt and humiliated. Our senses need a certain allowance of time in order to fulfil their functions properly. If we see too hastily, we do not really see; if we do not give enough time to our mind to brood over its observations or problems, it cannot produce true thoughts. But the wheels of our modern organizations drag us whirling through space and time for the sake of results that can only satisfy the miser in us, who loves to glut himself on number and quantity. The journalistic mentality, the outcome of a breathless haste, is like some shallow river bed, through which sensational floods rush off to a complete exhaustion leaving the startled banks thirsty and barren, shrouded in sand. These floods always seem to be counting the pebbles of number over which they pour themselves, heedless of the harvest that they might have helped in producing.

I remember sometime ago there appeared in the papers an account of a bird shoot in which a party of merry-makers, belonging to a high position, took part. The number of their innocent victims ran into thousands. Blood flowed abundantly; but, I am sure, not the tinge of a blush was evident in the distinguished cheeks of these people who were proud of their appalling success. It is what they call a breaking of records, the most amazingly superficial of all satisfactions for a rational being, paying to unmeaning quantity a homage worthy of a head hunter. You all know with what an excitement of reverence these number-pickers keep count of some latest addition to their list of records, measuring even to a fraction of an inch, of a minute, of a particle. This shallowness of mind is productive of cruelty and deception.

When we artificially develop a longing for number for its own sake, a purely abstract sense of possession, then a standard of wrong valuation is established and the sacredness of human sentiments is minimised. When a newspaper of already unnecessary length advertises the great event of the publication of its two further daily editions, then it merely exploits this childish crudity in the modern mind, its fascination for the more and more in number. It helps to add one more huge organization to a host of others and, in order to startle its readers' minds into a spirit of veneration, declares how a few more inches have been added to the length of its columns and how some extra hundred copies, over and above the output of its rivals, can be printed in a minute by its own up-to-date press, thereby rousing to a pitch of ecstasy the feeling of worship for the record-breaker.

I am told that a bronze statue has been erected near the Westminster abbey, as a memorial to the British machine-gunners killed in the late war, with the following inscription on the pedestal, chosen very likely by some devout reader of the Bible: *Soul has slain thousands, but David tens of thousands.* Such an impious homage to blood-stained numbers has been made possible in the present day, when civilization takes the enormous variety of inflated disproportion from which it suffers, to be the measure of its excellence,—when its critics are claiming the first prize in the race of bloatedness before onlookers with gaping mouths. Whatever we may think of the cannibal feeding upon his fellow beings, it is some satisfaction to know that it allays his hunger and nourishes him. But when we realize that numberless individuals are made to offer their very life blood, not to fulfil human need, but to help in the increase of some record-breaking enormity of the non-essential, then we cannot help hoping that God's vengeance will strike down to the dust, from its blood-soaked altar, the demon of production, so preposterously prolific.

Once in my life, I had a very clear sight of this demon feeding upon the carcass of its victim. I have described it in another paper and must do so once more. It was when I took a trip down the Ganges between banks which were dearly familiar to me in my boyhood. The rare beauty of those spots held in the deepest reverence by centuries of lovers and worshippers lay dead and desecrated, tortured by cloven-footed commerce. The thought that the whole future generation of men would never know how divinely great it had been, was heart-breaking. But the impiety of this sacrilege does not touch in the least the profit-maker's heart, lying safe in his bulging pockets. The bare fact of this particular happening, however painful to the lovers of this majestic river, is not however the important thing; but the deadening tendency of mind which is the cause of it, is terribly significant. In the temple of a living principle has been enshrined an iron monster, productive of things and destructive of life.

There was a time when the profession of fighting and the business of profit-gathering were restricted to specially trained groups of men, while the rest of the people had full freedom to cultivate their human personality. But because the scientific facility of communication has to-day spread its conquest in every realm of the elements, the field for fighting and profit making has also become boundless in dimension. And therefore the organization of offensive and defensive measures is taxing a large part of the resources of the whole population of the country. It means that what is merely technical is crowding into a narrow corner what is purely human. From the outside it offers an imposing spectacle; for organizations can be made symmetrical and accurate. You can make them supernormally big if only you have enough material; for they are voracious in their hunger for materials. To satisfy the growing claims of the military machine of monstrous proportions we need a devastating amount of money. And for that we need to multiply our money-making machines, which in their turn, in order too keep pace, need a parallel organization of whips and shouts in the donkey race of military expansion. The new reverence for the Deity of the Multiplication Table does not allow us to see the working of this huge joke played by the Devil himself against human destiny, with his special compound of blindness of passion joined to cleverness of science. He is trying experiments with it in the present day world, making the people knock their heads against each other automatically, and damaging things of living value in a dangerously comic manner.

We cannot maintain that detachment of mind necessary for being amused at this spectacle. For weal or for woe, the races of man *have* come close to each other; and if human history at the end is going to prove itself to be a farce, then we in India, shall also have to take part in it, if not as the funny man who deals enormous slaps, then as the other funny one whose flaming cheek produces a diverting sound at the concussion. Henceforward all our problems are world problems. It is no consolation for us to be able to say, when our own roof is burning, that the fire originated in the house of our neighbour who dwells on the opposite side of the road.

We are dangerously becoming accustomed to the fact of how easily the adorers of the big ignore the value of the human, how their infatuation produces the tragic mentality that has its worshipful tenderness for the automaton. The money that is recklessly lavished in order to manufacture and maintain the unproductive military doll has to be forcibly snatched away from the hungry, from the sick, from the tillers of the soil, who must sell their plough-bullocks to make their contribution.

I have had my experience of what water scarcity means for people who live under the tropical sun, when drinking water has to be extorted from the grip of the miserly mud, when a chance spark burns down a whole village to ashes with not a drop of water in the neighbourhood, save tear-drops, for quenching the fire. The daily suffering, during the sultry months of summer, of numberless men and women is intense and widespread. But care is taken that this suffering must not, in the least, touch the imperfectly human, the mutilated souls, who dwell in the barracks and the offices of the organization agency.

Those whose function it is to carry on the unbroken stream of life from age to age are made to sacrifice their very life stuff in order to maintain an ample supply of saw-dust for the gigantic Doll. This equipment, a great part of which is meaningless, serves merely to fill up time and space for the purpose of giving the idol an imposing appearance of amplitude. Life is being constantly bled white merely for swelling the girth of that which is not life, which is even against life.

The complexity which leans too far away from the natural centre of gravity of the social system is compelled to build external props which themselves are unwieldy. The conflicting forces in a living society maintain their equilibrium by the help of the unwritten convention that becomes organic in the memory of the race. Things of vital importance to society should never become too difficult of comprehension for the average intelligence of the people. For that creates a profound chasm between life's need and the means of its satisfaction, and in that gaping hole all kinds of mischief find their lodging because it is beyond the reach of the entire mind of the people. The vast dimensions and the technical character of our present day written legal codes only prove what an elaborately painful arrangements of chains and screws, requiring expert help at every turn, is necessary to keep the lumbering modern deadness together.

It is useless to grumble against this; but what strikes me as a sign of extreme fanatical loyalty to the Lifeless, is the fact that while the services of learned advocates are secured for the mechanical organization called Government, living individuals, who are sensitive to pains and losses, are left to their own poor devices to come out whole from the meshes of law after safely accomplishing their journey through the heart-breaking maze of legal pathways. When it is said that before the law everybody is equal, we must know that such praise can only be reserved for God's sunlight, not merely because it is universal, but because it is simple; because it does not require the help of a professional interpreter to explain it, the next moment to be contradicted by his professional opponent helping another professional man who is a judge to a conclusion which may be very learnedly inconclusive. In fact, the uncertainty of justice which is the inevitable consequence of these difficult and complex technicalities has made the Law Court an unlicensed gambling hall in which the chances of success most often learn toward the rich.

Those who cannot imagine that civilization can ever become simple are sure to question me as to what should be done. This question expects from its answer the means as to how a path can be made, though the wilderness should remain untouched. That, of course, I do not know. But I do know that the age has come which, through its moral earthquakes, has given warning to the pilers of dead things that the obstruction has to be removed and the way kept open for the chariot of new life to pass through its triumphal gate.

'Simplicity is primitive', exclaims the schoolboy. No, on the contrary, it is the barbarous which is not simple, which is absurdly heterogeneous. True simplicity dwells in the white light, not because its wealth of colour is meagre, but because it has all the colour rays perfectly harmonized. Difficult technicalities only reveal some deficiency in our natural function of coordination. This function is the function of wisdom and not that of knowledge. When it is lacking then the huge and the heavy make themselves conspicuous and challenge our admiration. The acrobat in all his manoeuvres shows a skill on which the signature of technical training is displayed in prominent letters. There are people who enjoy such exhibitions more than the grace which does not spur our attention by the constant obtrusion of its points, but woos our heart by its reticent completeness, running the risk of being overlooked.

As a boy, I was familiar with a picture of simplicity which was the manifestation of a complex that had found its perfection. It was the picture of the mistress of a family, the mother of an Indian household. According to the custom of the old-world Indian family life, which is vast and intricate, there lived in the same house a large number of men and women belonging to a common circle of kinship. It had, like the solar world, its concentric planetary orbits, some very close to the centre, some extending to a vague and far-away distance. Some of the members were bigly important with their bulk and weight, and some like meteors, insignificant, yet claiming their places along with the others. There were also a great many dependents as well as numerous relatives living in separate houses, who nevertheless had their right of citizenship in the family universe. In its heart reigned its mistress, with a dignity that was graceful, with a mellowed sweetness of nature that seemed to have been maturing for ages before she had been born. The duties and responsibilities were endless and difficult; the code of behaviour was varied and subtle, but she bore it all with a simple majesty like the sun surrounded by planets which also have their own family of satellites. What was the meaning of that perfect simplicity of hers which was so beautiful? It was the ideal of unity which she had within her; she had the natural power and training to enable her to comprehend the multitudinous diversity of the whole family life in her own life. She was made one with this world, not through mechanical adjustments, but through sentiments which belong to creative life, spontaneously permeating the branching limbs of an organic body. And therefore, through her, this large household found the pliant delicacy and tenderness of a living creation. It was not an aggregate of parts, but an assimilation in which all the parts lost their dividing limits.

The doubt may be felt whether the mistress of this household did not owe the beauty of her simple personality to her ignorance of many things that are being constantly added to our knowledge in the present time. My answer is, that perfection is something which is positive, it can never be based upon an emptiness of negation. It is not right to say that the ancient civilization of Greece had its perfect form only because in those days the Greeks did not know a good many things that our modern schoolboys know. It is never true that only the savages can evolve a harmony of life in their society. The Greeks, through their intellect and imagination brought all their thoughts, acquirements and surroundings to conform to the rhythm of a central life. If the Indian mother of the old type had been taught that the earth goes round the sun, or had been trained in an intelligent appreciation of the hygienic laws of living, it would have been all the better for her. But what was even more valuable in her was that gift which by life's magic could bring the miscellaneous into a perfection of balance.

Our personality is our own field of creation. And in order to make it perfect we must know that in all art every display of power is vulgar, that an artist is truly humble in his own creation. He despises making a show of material in his work and a parade of the difficulty in its process. For the power which accumulates things and manipulates them is fundamentally different from the genius which transmutes them into a perfect unity.

God is humble in his creation. He does not keep his muscles bared; nor does he go out of his way to attract our attention to the store of his things or to the account book of their cost. He gives out *himself* in the abundance of his nature. His last message of harmony in this material world in brought by Life which has her mission to simplify the materials that are numerous and forces that are desultory. She wins the hard heart of a rocky soil and covers its naked barbarity with her merciful green. Thus in the patient course of ages she has been spreading her ministration of beauty and fruitfulness over an earth which once had been destitute, though huge and multifarious in its constitution. When this life is menaced then the whole future of a self-sustaining plenitude is in danger.

We know the slow progress of the history of the desert. The trees are cut down with an extravagant ruthlessness, countless herds of goats and other animals are allowed to destroy in a wholesale manner the struggling shoots of life over vast tract of land. The forest of noble trees is reduced to paper pulp for the production of journalism, a great part of which circulates lies in its news and advertisements, and carries disease germs for the moral man. The loss of trees affects the rainfall, it lets loose floods that tear down the fertile soil from the breast of the earth, it interferes with the work of storing water by provident Nature in her sub-soil reservoirs. During some period of such exploitation of life the outer magnificence of civilization shows an amazing result in its buildings and ships and furniture. At last the dragon of the desert suddenly shows its parched white tongue on the horizon, creeping nearer and nearer to our habitations, sweeping away with its gigantic tail the hoarded capital of life to its last penny.

To-day there are vast stretches of desert on this earth where we see from the traces of dry river beds that once water flowed, trees flourished, rain fell, and that food was grown for cities now lying buried. It is evident that, with the complexity of living, through the disproportionate growth of non-life, the non-essential constantly extorted taxes from life, till life itself was made bankrupt by the extravagant egoism of man. There are invisible writings on the blank pages of these desolate places which tell the story of how some civilization had for ages elaborately busied itself in preparing its own burial ground.

The same thing has been going on in the moral and spiritual region of society for a long time, and all life-giving sentiments, all creative faith is being laid low by the clever, by the greedy. The huge and hungry organizations are rudely elbowing out the personal man. Before long humanity will surely realize that its life-stuff has been exhausted, that the office has swallowed up the home and that the progress of the fast spreading dominion of death can no longer be checked.

We have observed in the primitive art of prehistoric times how nearly all its pictures represent animal life. They are full of the touch that shows an intense interest in the subject. We see among the savages how they have some special animal for their tribal deity to whom they trace their ancestry. The reason is that man at that time had not completely outgrown the animal; he was not too proudly conscious of the fact that he was human. The animals have their greater perfection than man, as animals. During our brute stage we could proudly imagine ourselves to be like lions or bulls and therefore better than the others who were mere men. In the initial stage of man's growth this animal mentality gave him strength in the struggle for existence. The primitive man's admiration of animals for their superior physical efficiency is transferred to-day to the machine, and the modern man is busy reducing himself into a mechanical perfection. In the remote time, when he imagined that he was a noble animal, he still had in his future a vast field of life full of colour and music. Now when he imagines, with an unbounded sense of admiration that he is a sub-wheel of an efficient machine, he has before him only that colossal office hall where King Death holds his puppet dance with dead hearts.

Organizations we must have. These help to simplify the application of energy for attaining our purpose. They are our tools and men are tool-making creatures. And yet, we must never forget that we are living beings and that our tools are non-living. They should not be allowed to overwhelm our life with the space and time they occupy, the burden they impose, the special mentality they produce, and the obstruction they offer to the expression of personality. When our tools are in harmony with our life, they become an extension of our body, they acquire the rhythm of our hand; our mind thinks, our heart throbs through them. Life, when it has unity with its agents, its materials, finds efficiency without losing freedom. Our body has its skeleton, its organization of bones, which is non-living, ugly, inexpressive. But because it yields to the dominance of life, it helps not only in life's purposes but in its expression. Occasionally the skeletal system tries to overstep its limits; ossification sets in and shackles and strangles life till it is dead. There was a time when men used heavy armour in their battles. This was an artificial extension of bones, where bones were not. Men suffered this imposition for the sake of a purpose. The use of armour was limited to a comparatively few persons and to short periods of time. But even then it was found that those who dispensed with it won in the end.

We can see from this, that life's alliance with the non-living may become so necessary for certain purposes, that the latter is allowed to proclaim its own martial law where its place was once that of a servant. For the sake of life the rule of such law should occupy the least possible space and time. But when some universal passion, some ambitious purpose, becomes the dominant force in a society, man's tools grow in power and weight more than his life.

There was a time when man's innate love for pomp and power found its vicarious satisfaction in the magnificence of the military glory of kings and ruling classes. Then he could see the manifestation of his wealth in his temples, and in his religious and communal ceremonies. His prosperity found its shrine in a common enjoyment, and enriched his social life. Freed from the giddy round of competition and the burden of personal luxury, the people as a whole had an ample field for cultivating their social life, which is the completeness of life. They occasionally suffered from the tyranny of the king and his representatives, but they accepted or resisted it as they do the visitations of famine or flood; it did not come from their own midst. They suffered from it, but were not a party to it. This enabled their social life to survive the rise and fall of kingly dynasties and saved it from the self-multiplying hydra-headed tyranny of the non-human. When society is living, moral value becomes for it the highest value. Therefore, under ideal conditions, the best men gifted with spiritual qualities find their homage from the people. Such homage is never degrading for those who offer it. On the contrary, through acknowledgement of the best in man they participate in it. But to-day there are whole multitudes of voluntary slaves, who wear their lives out for the unworthy ones, for the profit-makers, for those who know how to clothe their falsehood in immaculate tailoring. The multitude has come to imagine that all this is civilization and that it is good.

There are those in the East who have slavishly come to believe that superstitions which are modern denote progress. They are proudly ready to be yoked to the car of the exploiter, of the ambitious, and think that the burden they bear is being transmuted into merit in some fools' paradise of their own imagining. They suspect, when I say this, that I am a reactionary, —one of those fanatical conservatives who blame the sun for keeping time that does not agree with their own family watch, the watch which they have forgotten to wind for centuries. But those who know me know that I have ever fought against obedience to the unmeaning, to traditions that are dead; against all imitations that only succeed in increasing intellectual and moral snobbishness. I believe in life, only when it is progressive; and in progress, only when it is in harmony with life. I preach the freedom of man from the servitude of the fetish of hugeness, the non-human. I refuse to be styled an enemy of enlightenment because I do not stand on the side of the giant who swallows life, but on the side of Jack, the human, who defies the big, the gross, and wins victory at the end.

I conclude with a quotation from one of Po-Chu-I's poems in which the great Chinese poet has shown into what vulgar mouths the offerings of false worship find their destination:

Deep the waters of the Black Pool, coloured like ink;
They say a Holy Dragon lives there, whom men have never seen,
Beside the pool they have built a shrine; the authorities have established a ritual;
A dragon by itself remains a dragon, but men make it a God.
Meats lie stacked on the rocks of the Pool's shore;
Wine flows on the grass in front of the shrine,
I do not know, of all those offerings, how much the Dragon eats;
But the mice of the woods and the foxes of the hills are continually drunk and sated.
Why are the foxes so lucky?
What have the sucking pigs done,
That year by year they should be killed, merely to glut the foxes?
That the foxes are robbing the Sacred Dragon and eating his sucking-pig,
Beneath the nine-fold depths of this Pool, does he know or not?

(*Waley's Translation*)

The modern meaning of this poem is, that meat and drink are offered at the shrine of Democracy, innumerable lives are sacrificed, but only plutocrats and autocrats in various disguise thrive on them; the idol does not know it, and the pious worshippers smile in foolish satisfaction.

1926

The Meaning of Art

There is a remarkable verse in the Atharva Veda which attributes all that is great in the human world to superfluity. It says:

Ritam satyam tapo rashtram sramo dharmascha karmacha,
Bhūtam bhavishyat ucchiste viryam lakshmīrbalam bale

Righteousness, truth, great endeavours, empire, religion, enterprise, heroism and prosperity, the past and the future dwell in the surpassing strength of the surplus.

The meaning of it is that man expresses himself through his superabundance which largely overlaps his absolute need.

The renowned Vedic commentator, Sāyaṇāchārya, says:

Yajñe hutasishtasya odanasya sarvajagatkāranabhūta
Brahmābhedena stutih kriyate.

The food offering which is left over after the completion of sacrificial rites is praised because it is symbolical of Brahma, the original source of the universe.

According to this explanation, Brahma is boundless in his superfluity which inevitably finds its expression in the eternal world process. Here we have the doctrine of the genesis of creation, and therefore of the origin of art. Of all living creatures in the world man has his vital and mental energy vastly in excess of his need, which urges him to work in various lines of creation for its own sake. Like Brahma himself, he takes joy in productions that are unnecessary to him, and therefore representing his extravagance and not his hand-to-mouth penury. The voice that is just enough can speak and cry to the extent needed for every day use, but that which is abundant sings, and in it we find our joy. Art reveals man's wealth of life, which seeks its freedom in forms of perfection which are an end in themselves.

All that is inert and inanimate is limited to the bare fact of existence. Life is perpetually creative because it contains in itself that surplus which ever overflows the boundaries of the immediate time and space, restlessly pursuing its adventure of expression in the varied forms of self-realization. Our living body has its vital organs that are important in maintaining its efficiency, but this body is not a mere convenient sac for the purpose of holding stomach, heart, lungs and brains; it is an image,—its highest value is in the fact that it communicates its personality. It has colour, shape and movement, most of which belong to the superfluous, that are needed only for self-expression and not for self-preservation.

At the root of all creation there is a paradox, a logical contradiction. Its process is in the perpetual reconciliation of two contrary forces. We have already said that the natural urging of the surplus, the *ucchista,* is the motive force of all that makes for perfection. But the boundless overflow must yield to the bounds of finitude for its manifestation. Truth must become real by the definition of the infinite. We have two contradictory utterances in the Upanishad about the origin of all things. On the one hand, it has been said:

Anandādhyeva khalvimāni bhūtāni jāyante.

The universe has come out of joy.

On the other hand, there is the verse which says:

Sa tapo'tapyatah sa tapastaptvā sarvamasrijat yadidam kincha.

God made penance, and with the heat generated therefrom he created all that there is.

The freedom of joy and the restraint of *tapasyā,* both are equally true in the creative expression of Brahma.

This limitation of the unlimited is personality: God is personal where he creates.

Kavirmanīshī paribhūh svayambhūryatatathyāto'rthan
Vyadadhāt shāswatibhyah samābhyah.

Where he dispenses the inner necessities of existence in an accurate measure and for all time he is the poet, the lord of mind, the sovereign power, the self-creator.

He accepts the limits of his own law and the play goes on which is this world whose reality is in its relation to the Person. Things are distinct not in their essence but in their appearance, in other words, in their relation to one to whom they appear. This is art, the truth of which is not in substance or logic, but in expression. Abstract truth may belong to science and metaphysics, but the world of reality belongs to art.

The world as an art is the play of the Supreme Person revelling in image making. Try to find out the ingredients of the image—they elude you, they never reveal to you the eternal secret of appearance. In your effort to capture life as expressed in living tissue, you will find carbon, nitrogen and many other things utterly unlike life, but never life itself. The appearance does not offer any commentary of itself through its material. You may call it *māyā* and pretend to disbelieve it, but the great artist, the *Māyāvin,* is not hurt. For art is *maya,* it has no other explanation but that it seems to be what it is. It never tries to conceal its evasiveness, it mocks, even its own definition and plays the game of hide and seek through its constant flight in changes.

And thus life, which is an incessant explosion of freedom, finds its metre in a continual falling back in death. Every day is a death, every moment even. If not, there would be an amorphous desert of deathlessness eternally dumb and still. So life is *máyá,* —as moralists love to say, it *is* and *is not.* All that we find in it is the rhythm through which it shows itself. Are rocks and minerals any better? Has not science shown us the fact that the ultimate difference between one element and another is only that of rhythm? The fundamental distinction of gold from mercury lies merely in the difference of rhythm in their respective atomic constitution, like the distinction of the king from his subject which is not in their different constituents, but in the different metres of their situation and circumstance. There you find behind the scene the Artist, the Magician of rhythm, who imparts an appearance of substance to the unsubstantial.

What is this rhythm? It is the movement generated and regulated by harmonious restriction. This is the creative force in the hand of the artist. So long as words remain in uncadenced prose form, they do not give any lasting feeling of reality. The moment they are taken and put into rhythm they vibrate into a radiance. It is the same with the rose. In the pulp of its petals you may find everything that went to make the rose, but the rose which is *māyā,* an image, is lost; its finality which has the touch of the infinite is gone. The rose appears to me to be still, but because of its metre of composition it has a lyric of movement within that stillness, which is the same as the dynamic quality of a picture that has a perfect harmony. It produces a music in our consciousness by giving it a swing of motion synchronous with its own. Had the picture consisted of a disharmonious aggregate of colours and lines, it would be deadly still.

In perfect rhythm, the art-form becomes like the stars which in their seeming stillness are never still, like a motionless flame that is nothing but movement. A great picture is always speaking, but news from a newspaper, even of some tragic happening, is still-born. Some news may be a mere commonplace in the obscurity of a journal; but give it a proper rhythm and it will never cease to shine. That is art. It has the magic wand which gives undying reality to all things it touches, and relates them to the personal being in us. We stand before its productions and say: I know you as I know myself, you are real.

Let me repeat here my remark about the function of art from a previous paper of mine: 'When we talk of aesthetics in relation to arts we must know that it is not about beauty in its ordinary meaning but in that deeper meaning which a poet has expressed in his utterance: truth is beauty, beauty truth. An artist may paint a picture of a decrepit person not pleasing to the eye, and yet we call it perfect when we become deeply conscious of its reality.'

Hopeless tragedies of life can never technically be called beautiful, but when appearing on the background of art they delight us because of the convincingness of their reality. It only proves that every object which fully asserts its existence to us because of its inherent finality, is beautiful; it is what is called in Sanskrit *manohara,* the stealer of the mind,—the mind which stands between the knower and the known. We have our primal sympathy for all things that exist, for when realized they stimulate the consciousness of our own existence. The fact that we exist has its truth in the fact that everything else does exist.

The *I am* in me realizes its own extension, its own infinity whenever it truly realizes something else. Unfortunately, owing to our limitations and a thousand and one pre-occupations, a great part of our world, though closely surrounding us, is far away from the lamp-post of our attention; it is dim, it passes by us, a caravan of shadows, like the landscape seen in the night from the window of an illuminated railway compartment: the passenger knows that the outside world exists, that it is important, but for the time being the railway carriage for him is far more significant. If among the innumerable objects in this world there be a few that come under the full illumination of our soul and thus assume reality for us, they constantly cry to our creative mind for a permanent representation. They belong to the same domain as the desire of ours which represents the longing for the permanence of our own self.

I do not mean to say that things to which we are bound by the tie of self-interest have the inspiration of reality: on the contrary, these are eclipsed by the shadow of our own self. The servant is not more real to us than the beloved. The narrow emphasis of utility diverts our attention from the complete man to the merely useful man. The thick label of market price obliterates the ultimate value of reality. It has been said in the *Brihad-Aranyaka:*

> *The desire for the son does not make him dear, the son is dear for the sake of the self.*

That is to say, in the son the father becomes conscious of a reality which is immediately and profoundly within him. He is delighted not because his son is perfect and beautiful, but because his son is indubitably real to him,—our joy, as I have said before, being the disinterested perception of the real. This is the source of our delight in all arts and literature, where reality is presented to us on the pedestal of its own absolute value.

All the deep impressions in our mind are accompanied by some emotions which set up their own variety of tremors in our consciousness. This agitation modulates our voice and movements and impels us to all creative display of colours, forms and sounds. This reminds me of the occasion when I saw inscribed on the wall of a school building, in exaggerated characters: 'Bipin is an egregious ass!' It amused me, and at the same time offered me an answer to the question, *what is art*.

No one takes the least trouble to proclaim the information that Bipin is tall, or that he suffers from a cold. Ordinarily our mind is soberly grey in its impression of Bipin. But when we love him or hate him, the fact of Bipin's existence becomes glowingly evident on the agitated background of passion. Then our mind can no longer remain neutral; it detaches the idea of Bipin from the immense multitude of what is non-significant to us, and according to its own power our mind tries to make him as unavoidably real to others as he is to ourselves.

The boy who angrily longed to give permanence to his indignant estimate of Bipin and make it universally accepted had nothing but his inadequate charcoal and ineffectual training, whereas his forefathers of the primitive age, when excited to anger, not only could give vent to it effectively in action, but also in an expression of gorgeous ferocity by the help of pigments, feathers, tinsel and war dance. That writing on the school wall, craving immortality, sadly begged for colours and rhythmic lines to be like its glorious congeners, the fresco paintings of the world-renowned caves, where the artists attempted to emphasise their estimate of certain personalities, and of sundry incidents, into permanence.

As art creations are emotional representations of facts and ideas they can never be like the product of a photographic camera which is passively receptive of lights and shadows in all their indiscriminate details. Our scientific mind is unbiased; it accepts facts with a cold-blooded curiosity that has no preference. The artistic mind is strongly biased, and that bias not only guides it in its fastidious selection of the subject, but also in that of its details. It throws coloured lights of emphasis on its theme in such a manner that it attains a character which clearly distinguishes it from its fellows. The skylarks of science offer corroboration of their truth through their similarity, the skylarks of artists and poets through their dissimilarity. If Shelley's poem on this bird were just like that of Wordsworth, it should have been rejected for its lack of truth.

As art embodies our personal, estimate of a thing, or character, or circumstance, the artist in his work does not follow nature in its capacious heterogeneity, but his own human nature which is selective. By leaving out whatever is non-essential for his own purpose of expression and intensifying what is significant, he brings out the truth of his creation much more vividly than he would if he copied actuality which is strictly impartial to whatever exists. The wholeness of God's creation is immensely vast and it is not possible for any detail to be too defiantly discrepant in its relation to it. But the background of human expression is small and therefore it is never possible to accommodate nature's details in our art compositions. It is childish to expect the primeval forest in the perspective of our garden plot, or an illustration of natural history in our works which modulate fact to the tune of our personality.

Once the question had been asked to me as to the place I assigned to music in my theory of art. I am bound to answer it, and I take this opportunity to offer my explanation.

Music is the most abstract of all arts, as mathematics is in the region of science. In fact, these two have a deep relationship with each other. Mathematics as the logic of number and dimension is the basis of our scientific knowledge. When taken out of its concrete associations with cosmic phenomena and reduced to symbols it reveals its grand structural majesty, the inevitableness of its own perfect concord. But there is also such a thing as the magic of mathematics which works at the root of all appearances, producing harmony of unity,—the cadence of inter-relation of the parts bringing them under the dominion of the whole. This rhythm of harmony has been extracted from its usual context and exhibited through the medium of sound. And thus the pure essence of expressiveness in existence is offered in music. In sound it finds the least resistance and has a freedom unencumbered by the burden of facts and thoughts. It gives it a power to arouse in us an intense feeling of reality; it seems to lead us into the soul of all things and make us feel the very breath of inspiration flowing from the supreme creative joy.

In the pictorial, plastic and verbal arts the object and our feelings with regard to it are closely associated, like the rose and its perfume. In music the feeling, extracted in sound, becomes itself an independent object. It assumes a tune-form which is definite, but a meaning which is indefinable and yet grips our mind with a sense of absolute truth.

There came a time, centuries ago, in Bengal, when the divine love drama that had its eternal play in human souls was vividly revealed by a personality radiating its intimate realization of God. The mind of a whole people was stirred by the vision of the world as an instrument through which sounded our invitation to the meeting of bliss. The ineffable mystery of God's love-call taking shape in an endless panorama of colours and forms, finding its chorus in the symphony of human affections, inspired activity in a music that overflowed the restrictions of classical conventionalism. Our *kirtan* music in Bengal came to its being like a star flung up by a burning whirlpool of emotion in the heart of a whole people.

There come in our history occasions when the consciousness of a large multitude becomes suddenly illumined with the recognition of something which rises far above the triviality of daily happenings. Such an occasion there was when the voice of Buddha reached distant shores across all physical and moral impediments. Then our life and our world found their profound meaning of reality in their relation to the central person who offered us emancipation of love. And men, in order to make this great human experience ever memorable, determined to do the impossible; they made rocks to speak, stones to sing, caves to remember; the cry of joy and hope took immortal forms along hills and deserts, across barren solitudes and populous cities. A gigantic creative endeavour built up its triumph in stupendous carvings, defying obstacles that were overwhelming. Such heroic activity over the greater part of the Eastern continent clearly answers the question: *What is art?*—It is the response of man's creative soul to the call of the real.

But the individual mind according to its temperament and training has its own recognition or reality in some of its special aspects. We can see from the Gandhara figures of Buddha that the artistic influence of Greece put its emphasis on the scientific aspect, on anatomical accuracy, while the purely Indian mind dwelt on the symbolic aspect and tried to give expression to the soul of Buddha, never acknowledging the limitations of realism. For the adventurous spirit of the great European sculptor, Rodin, the most significant aspect of reality is the unceasing struggle of the incomplete for its freedom from the fetters of imperfection, whereas before the naturally introspective mind of the Eastern artist the real appears in its ideal form of fulfilment.

Therefore, when we talk of such a fact as Indian Art, it indicates some truth based upon the Indian tradition and temperament. At the same time we must know that there is no such thing as absolute caste restriction in human cultures; they ever have the power to combine and produce new variations, and such combinations have been going on for ages proving the truth of the deep unity of human psychology. It is admitted that in Indian art the Persian element found no obstacles, and there are signs of various other alien influences. China and Japan have no hesitation in acknowledging their debt to India in their artistic and spiritual growth of life. Fortunately for our civilizations all such intermingling happened when professional art critics were not rampant and artists were not constantly nudged by the warning elbow of classifiers in their choice of inspiration. Our artists were never tiresomely reminded of the obvious fact that they were Indian; and in consequence they had the freedom to be naturally Indian in spite of all the borrowings that they indulged in.

The sign of greatness in great geniuses is their enormous capacity for borrowing, very often without their knowing it; they have unlimited credit in the world market of culture. Only mediocrities are ashamed and afraid of borrowing, for they do not know how to pay back the debt in their own coin. Even the most foolish of critics does not dare blame Shakespeare for what he openly appropriated from outside his own national inheritance. The human soul is proud of its comprehensive sensitiveness; it claims its freedom of entry everywhere when it is fully alive and awake. We congratulate ourselves on the fact, and consider it a sign of our being alive in soul, that European thoughts and literary forms found immediate hospitality in Bengali literature from the very beginning of its contact with our mind. It ushered in a great revolution in the realm of our literary expression.

Enormous changes have taken place, but our Indian soul has survived the shock and has vigorously thriven upon this cataclysm. It only shows that though human mentality, like the earth's atmosphere, has undoubtedly different temperatures in different geographical zones, yet it is not walled up into impassable compartments and the circulation of the common air over the entire globe continues to have its wholesome effect. So let us take heart and make daring experiments, venture out into the open road in the face of all risks, go through experiences in the great world of human mind defying unholy prohibitions preached by prudent little critics, laughing at them when in their tender solicitude for our safety they ask our artists to behave the good children and never to cross the threshold of their school-room.

Fearfully trying always to conform to a conventional type is a sign of immaturity. Only in babies is individuality of physiognomy blurred, and therefore personal distinction not strongly marked. Childishness is a mentality that can easily be generalised: children's babbling has the same sound-tottering everywhere, their toys are very nearly similar. But adult age is difficult of classification, it is composed of individuals who claim recognition of their personal individuality which is shown not only in its own uniqueness of manner but also in its own special response to all stimulations from outside.

I strongly urge our artists, vehemently to deny their obligation carefully to produce something that can be labelled as Indian art according to some old world mannerism. Let them proudly refuse to be herded into a pen like branded beasts that are treated as cattle and not as cows. Science is impersonal, it has its one aspect which is merely universal and therefore abstract; but art is personal and, therefore, through it the universal manifests itself in the guise of the individual, physiology expresses itself in physiognomy, philology in literature. Science is a passenger in a railway train of generalization; there reasoning minds from all directions come to make their journey together in a similar conveyance. Art is a solitary pedestrian, who walks alone among the multitude, continually assimilating various experiences, unclassifiable and uncatalogued.

There was a time when human races lived in comparative segregation and therefore the art adventurers had their experience within a narrow range of limits deeply-cut grooves of certain common characteristics. But to-day that range has vastly widened, claiming from us a much greater power of receptivity than what we were compelled to cultivate in former ages. If to-day we have a living soul that is sensitive to ideas and to beauty of form, let it prove its capacity by accepting all that is worthy of acceptance, not according to some blind injunction of custom or fashion, but in following one's instinct for eternal value—the instinct which is a God-given gift to all real artists. Even then our art is sure to have a quality which is Indian, but it must be an inner quality and not an artificially fostered formalism, and therefore not be too obtrusively obvious and abnormally self-conscious.

When in the name of Indian art we cultivate with deliberate aggressiveness a certain bigotry born of the habit of a past generation, we smother our soul under idiosyncrasies unearthed from buried centuries. These are like masks with exaggerated grimaces, that fail to respond to the ever changing play of life.

Art is not a gorgeous sepulchre immovably brooding over a lonely eternity of vanished years. It belongs to the procession of life, making constant adjustment with surprises, exploring unknown shrines of reality along its path of pilgrimage to a future which is as different from the past as the tree from the seed. Art represents the inexhaustible magnificence of creative spirit; it is generous in its acceptance and generous in its bestowal; it is unique in its manner and universal in its appeal; it is hospitable to the All because it has the wealth which is its own; its vision is new though its view may be old; it carries its special criterion of excellence within itself and therefore contemptuously refuses to be brow-beaten into conformity with a rhetoric manufactured by those who are not in the secret of the subtle mysteries of creation, who want to simplify through their academic code of law that which is absolutely simple through its spontaneity.

The art ideal of a people may take fixed root in a narrow soil of tradition developing a vegetable character, producing a monotonous type of leaves and flowers in a continuous round of repetitions. Because it is not disturbed by a mind which ever seeks the unattained, and because it is held firm by a habit which piously discourages allurements of all adventures, it is neither helped by the growing life of the people nor does it help to enrich that life. It remains confined to coteries of specialists who nourish it with delicate attention and feel proud of the ancient flavour of its aristocratic exclusiveness. It is not a stream that flows through and fertilises the soil, but a rare wine stored in a dark cellar underground, acquiring a special stimulation through its artificially nurtured, barren antiquity. In exchange for a freedom of movement which is the prerogative of vigorous youth, we may gain a static perfection of senility that has minted its wisdom into hard and rounded maxims. Unfortunately, there are those who believe it an advantage for a child to be able to borrow its grandparents' age and be spared the trouble and risk of growing, and think that it is a sign of wealthy respectability for an artist lazily to cultivate a monotonously easy success by means of some hoarded patrimony of tradition.

And yet we may go too far if we altogether reject tradition in the cultivation of art, and it is an incomplete statement of truth to say that habits have the sole effect of deadening our mind. The tradition which is helpful is like a channel that helps the current to flow. It is open where the water runs onward, guarding it only where there is danger in deviation. The bee's life in its channel of habit has no opening,—it revolves within a narrow circle of perfection. Man's life has time-honoured institutions which are its organized habits. When these act as enclosures, then the result may be perfect, like a beehive of wonderful precision of form, but unsuitable for the mind which has unlimited possibilities of progress.

Before I close my address let me take this opportunity to ask our artists to realize the greatness of their vocation: it is to take a creative part in the festival of life, the festival which is to give expression to the infinite in man. In our everyday world we live in poverty; our resources have to be husbanded with care; our strength becomes exhausted and we come to our God as beggars. On festival days, we display our wealth and say to Him that we are even as He is; and we are not afraid to spend. This is the day when we bring to Him our gift of joy. For we truly meet God, when we come to Him, with our offerings and not our wants, and such offerings need Art for its vehicle.

I need have no anxiety about the great world to which I have been born. The sun does not wait to be trimmed by me. But from the early morning all my thoughts are occupied by the little world of my *self*. Its importance is owing to the fact that I have a world given to me which is *mine,* which depends for its perfection on my own creative soul. It is great because I have the power to make it worthy of its relationship with me; it is great, because by its help I can offer my own hospitality to the God of all the world.

1926

Notes and Comments

This age is like a precocious child delighting in its up-to-date toy of a megaphone that mercilessly exaggerates fugitive whispers, making them overheard by the whole world. It helps to keep up the ceaseless hubbub of a dust storm that has the same sweeping welcome for flowers as for rotten leaves. In the days when the means of publicity were limited, literature could easily maintain its dignity, shunning the contact of hourly gossip and still-born rumours by allowing a scanty and distant hospitality on its fringe for all literary immigrants not worthy of permanent citizenship. But the contrary is the case to-day, when vast accommodation is offered to the vagabond and the non-descript, bringing them into daily intimacy with public life unheedful of possible contamination. World-wide organizations of news-pickers and paragraph-makers have been established with the object of catering for an abnormally busy people with an unwholesome craving four promiscuous facts and desultory topics,—a veritable intellectual drug habit.

The constant demand for a mental narcotic that ends in smoke and ashes, that destroys delicacy of taste and healthy appetite for nutrition, encourages illicit traffic and adulteration. I have had my personal experience of it once, when on a lecturing tour in the United States. Some persons belonging to a detective agency, evidently in the pay of interested individuals, came to me with the news that the Hindu revolutionist party in San Francisco had decided to kill me owing to their disagreement with my political views. This canard went round the papers and when I sent a protest, expressing my disbelief, it was not published, possibly in deference to a political need for strengthening the prejudice against Hindu settlers in America on the eve of an anti-Asiatic legislation, or because the news was too rich in sensation to allow any doubt to rob it of its sparkle for the sake of mere justice.

Shortly after my return to India the news reached me, through Japanese papers, that a law suit had been instituted against the above-mentioned party, accusing it of secret attempts at overthrowing British rule in India. My name was dragged into this case alleging that I had taken money from the Germans deceitfully to serve their purpose while in America, and at the same time to dig for my own country underground tunnels of dark politics. I began to receive letters from your people full of reproaches for having betrayed the trust of a confiding nation whose guest I had been in the disguise of an idealist. I sent an explanatory cablegram to President Wilson, asking for his protection, which remained unacknowledged.

This was the time when the American people all of a sudden seemed furiously to remember that blood was thicker than water and to forget that it was they who had forcibly severed their political connection with a nation to which they were related by blood. The idea that struck me, through various such instances, made me think that while Aristocracy strenuously cultivates self-respect, often at the cost of material profit, and guards a high standard of culture against deterioration, undiluted Democracy has a tendency to glide down to the lazy level of the average, for all its struggle is to add to its rights, not to build up a high tower of excellence. It makes a deliberate study of the laws of the dark patches in the human intellect, wherewith to help itself to create an atmosphere of delusion through hints, gestures, yells and startling lies, for the purpose of stupefying the popular mind. Once when I was in Chicago I saw everywhere on the town walls once single name blazened in big letters in an endless round of repetition, like the whirling monotony of a Dervish dance that dazes one's mind into vacuity. Evidently the name belonged to some candidate for political election. But what an insult to the people, who are supposed to represent the supreme power in their government, openly to apply to them the spell of hypnotism in place of reason, as the medicine man does in the heart of Africa!

The same want of respect for the rational in the popular mind has induced the greed of dollars to open classes for teaching the art of profitable mystification, psychological tricks to help the sale of commodities in spite of the buyers, seductive stratagems of advertisement for the purpose of what amounts to bamboozling. This mentality has its analogy in India where the vast majority of the population, which is non-Brahmin, is allowed a crudely superficial culture and modes of worship that are but a survival of primitive forms of Mesmeric rites. The effect has been a gradual degeneracy of the Brahmins themselves, a vigorously rapid spread of the rank weeds of unreason choking the growth of higher life, creating dark shelters for religious charlatism, and a dense entanglement of bigotry that obstructs progress at every step. We have sadly learnt how the want of confidence in the best in man draws away life's sap from what is best in us, diverting it to what is childish and commonplace.

I am perfectly aware that as a great nation you have your complex personality, full of apparent self-contradictions, which loses its mystery of a living truth directly it is defined in sharp lines, like a fragment of notation whose full musical meaning is not known. For instance, when we say that America is materialistic, we speak of a fact which is too apparent to be completely true. I have had reason to believe that there is a strong current of spiritual idealism flowing beneath the surface soil of the American mind. The unmitigated industrialism in your world, with no other ideal but a breathless multiplication of materials, must of necessity produce a deep longing in your minds for realizing in life the eternal value of the spirit. I have no doubt that this ever and anon finds its outlet in individuals who, though few in number, truly represent the unnumbered generations of your future. Properly to know a people one must know such men who seemingly contradict the supposed nature of the nation, remaining half hidden behind the vast obvious, like the thin wick in the heart of a capacious lamp. As this is not possible for me for want of opportunity, I can only offer you, for what it is worth, a brief description of my own personal experiences which led me to form my opinion about America, and disinclined me to risk any recurrence of the same.

After my visit to Japan in 1916, I crossed over to California, following an invitation to lecture in some of the principal towns of the United States. The subject of my address was *Nationalism* which, when read in the two principal universities of Tokyo, had with an uncomfortable suddenness reduced the temperature of my welcome to freezing point. I believe it was only tolerated in the United States because the American people, in the pride of their own solid common sense, could indulgently excuse extravagant ideas about practical matters from an Oriental dreamer, though they entertained an unaccountable confidence in his knowledge of the occult, in his spiritual prestige that might confer credit in some ever-solvent bank in the Kingdom of Heaven. I remember how, after one of my lectures, I was approached by one who wished to learn from me personal secrets about some other individual whom I had never known. I felt sure that to this person my lecture must have appeared most profoundly incomprehensible, in order to win for me his admiring faith in my supernatural gift. However I have nothing to complain about this lecture of mine, which helped me to earn from your country a small fund for my Institution, and recognition from its readers in continental Europe.

In this essay I discussed how the Western cult of the self-worship of the Nation has gathered its victims from alien continents, exploiting and insulting the greater part of the globe in the blind pride of its physical prowess, while resenting any suspicion of menace from those whom it injured; how it has caused the greatest problem in the world to-day by allowing the explosive passions of hatred and contempt to accumulate in the dark chasm that has been kept open between the two hemispheres.

Meanwhile the great war in Europe ceased, like the frenzied shrieks of a maniac demon exhausted at last into sleep, though the groans of its angry dream still convulsed the weary peace of the night. I strongly felt that, under the continued threat of impending catastrophe likely to involve the whole human world in desolating hostilities, every individual to-day should realize his responsibility for training the mind of the present generation to enable it to see all its important problems in the perspective of universal man. For the most outstanding fact of our age is that the drama of our destiny to-day has the whole world for its stage. Let the politicians mishandle this world situation according to their tradition of nationalistic fanaticism, but the rest of us should have the power to think and act upon a broadly human basis of behaviour.

Having this in mind I started an institution in our country which was to represent our faith in the solidarity of the human races, our aspiration to bridge the widely gaping gulf between the East and West. My idea was that such an institution should be a creation on which the different peoples of the world should leave their individual signature of acceptance. And when I went to the United States in 1921 I was confident that my appeal would find a ready response in a land which in its Eastern and Western outlooks touches the two great seas from whose bosom rises the sun to light the continents of Europe and Asia.

The letter which I wrote to India from New York will explain the mission that occupied by thoughts at that time:

> In every age and in every country facts are given to us in order that we may provide with them some special expression of truth. Facts are like atoms of gases. They fight with or else fly away from one another. But when they are united into a drop of dew they attain beauty and reality. Man must have that creative magic to bring the facts of his time into some unity of creation. The most important of all facts in the present age is that the East and West have met. So long as it remains a mere fact, it will give rise to interminable conflicts. It is the mission of all men of faith to raise this fact into truth. I only wish you had been with me in Europe! You would know at once what is the purpose of the modern age; what is the cry of man, which the politicians never hear. There were politicians too in the courts of the Mughal Emperors. They have left nothing behind them, but ruins. But Kabir and Nanak! They have bequeathed to us their imperishable faith in the unity of Man through God's love.

Though I was sure that the problem with which I meant to deal in my work was not exclusively Indian, that it equally concerned the vital and moral interest of the west, it would have been unreasonable for me not to be reconciled to the rude fact that mine was not the voice that could carry such message to the heart of the American people. It was as futile to complain of some incompatibility between a particular seed and a soil in moral matters, as to make it a grievance if the orchard in New York rejected the mango tree from its hospitality.

This was the first time in my life when I breathed the same privileged air with some of the denizens of the giant world of finance. I felt small, but my welcome to their accommodation proved to be still smaller, almost like that of the needle's eye to a camel. It cannot be said that I made the egregious mistake of thinking that the people's heart was in their bankers' keep; on the contrary, I did try my best to approach it directly with the help of friends; but to my utter dismay I found it barred by an unmerited discourtesy, insulting me with the suspicion that I was a political schemer who was trying to exploit the good-natured credulity of your country.

I was told by some of my best friends there that powerful propaganda seemed to be working against me in consequence of the desperate protest which I had been compelled to make against the Jallianwallabagh atrocities in our own country, shortly before I had left India. If that was the case, it only supports the idea that your country lends herself too easily to all secret spells of insinuation, allowing its crowd psychology to be perpetually handled by clever manipulators.

Such constant churning up of the drifting froth on the surface mind of the nation, leaving its depths ignored, is certainly not the way to train it in truth and wisdom. It pained me when I realized the cheapening of the spiritual value of man in this country through his mind being ceaselessly exploited, in a wholesale manner and with a scientific thoroughness, for the sake of profit and power. Having had this chance to come into personal contact with prosperous America, with the mentality that could produce quickly rotating crops of an enormous harvest of success, I grew afraid of it. The following extract from a letter which I wrote on this occasion to an English friend in India will give you some idea of how I felt:

> Everyday I seem to be growing afraid of the very vision of this success. It has been said in the Upanishad: *Happiness is*

greatness. But ambition points to bigness and calls it greatness, and our track is hopelessly lost. When I look on the picture of Buddha, I cry out for the great peace of inner fulfilment. My longing grows painfully intense as my mind becomes distracted at the stupendous unmeaning of the monstrosity in the things around me. Every morning I sit by my window and say to myself: 'I must not bow my head to this ugly idol worshipped by the West with daily human sacrifice!' I remember that morning at Shelida, when the Vaishnava woman came to me and said: 'When are you coming down from your three-storied building, to meet your love under the shade of the trees?' Just now I am on the top storey of the sky-scraper, to which the tallest of trees dares not send its whisper; but love silently comes to me saying: 'When are you coming down to meet me on the green grass under the rustling leaves, where you have the freedom of the sky and of sunlight and the tender touch of life's simplicity?' I try to say something about money in reply, but it sounds so ludicrous and yet so tragic, that my words grow ashamed of themselves and they stop.

Let me conclude with another extract from a letter of the same period:

When I finish reading your letters from Santiniketan, I wake up from my lyric dream to find myself at the bottom of a prodigious pile of newspaper prose. My surroundings seem to me like the inside of a whale that has swallowed me.

The idea of freedom, which the people in this country have, is the imaginary freedom of a fly shut up in a glass case whose walls are invisible. They are surrounded by an impregnable globe of unreality to which they cling and believe that they are in solid possession of the sky. But I can assure you that you have the right to laugh at these buzzing creatures, with their absurd pride at having made their sky densely substantial. This deludes them with a freedom that is of the eye, while immuring them in a confinement that is of the spirit.

My freedom is unreal, so long as I cherish slavery in my soul. This is a truism, like our idea of death; but opportunity comes when we discover it in our life, and then it discloses to us its ever newness of truth. I seem to pass through a real training for becoming a fakir when I am in this country. Buddha was born to regal surroundings which gave him the fitness to attain the true majesty of beggardom. I wrote a poem when I was in India: *I shall never be an ascetic.* But when I am here, the inspiration comes to me, with a rush of lyrical fervour, to write a hymn to Shiva, the Lord of Ascetics, who has the four quarters of the sky for his mantle.

It may sound to you like a paradox when I say that what oppresses me most in this country is the utter lack of freedom with which the atmosphere is charged. But it is true. I long to draw in the breath of life, but my nostrils get stopped with sand and soot, and then I am choked into acknowledging the truth, that it is not substance which is most important for us, but the modest bareness of it.

Leisure and space are the most precious gifts for us; for we are creators. Our real freedom is in the world of our own creation where our mind can work unhindered and our soul finds its throne from which to govern its own dominion.

1927

The Principle of Literature

In the world of our fairy tales, the son of the Detective, the son of the Merchant and the son of the King set forth in the adventurous quest of the Princess: the Truth, represented by her, is approached from three sides by three different types of mind.

The process which one of them follows is, by analysis, to find in her the secrets of body and mind; but in this region of science, she is of no more value than any other girl,—there is no difference between Princess and scullery-maid. The Detective, be he scientist or philosopher, has nothing to do with feeling, no sense even of utility, all he has is the spirit of Question.

The Princess has another aspect,—that in which she is useful. She spins, weaves and embroiders. The eyes with which the Merchant's son observes her,—turning her spindle, wielding her shuttle, plying her needle,—have in their gaze neither feeling, nor questioning, but only calculation.

The King's son is not physiologist or psychologist, nor has he passed any examination in economics. What he has passed, methinks, is just his twenty-fourth year, and also the impassable heath of the fairy tales. He has crossed difficult paths, not for learning, nor for riches, but for the Princess herself, whose palace is not in the laboratory, nor in the market place, but in that heart's paradise of Eternal Spring where bloom the flowers in the poet's bower of phantasy.

That which is not known by logic, which defies definition, whose value is not in any practical use, but which can only be intimately felt, finds its expression in Literature, is the subject of Aesthetics. No man who has the gift of enjoyment ever nags or pokes any creation of Art with the questions: *Why art thou here? What art thou?*—He exclaims: *It is enough for me that thou art thyself!* This was what the King's son whispered in the ear of the Princess, and it was for the proper utterance of these very words that Shahjahan was compelled to build the Taj Mahal.

We can only define that which can be measured: that which is immeasurable, which eludes all attempts at capture, is not attainable by reason, but by immediate perception. The Upanishad says of the Infinite Being that we can reach Him not with speech nor with the mind, but by our consciousness of delight, wherewith all fear departs from us. Our soul has her hunger for this immediateness of realization, whereby she is enabled also to know herself. The love, the contemplation, the vision that alone can satisfy this hunger finds its place in Literature, in Art.

The space enclosed within walls has been appropriated by my business office, which there buys and sells, pays and charges rent, by the yard. Outside, where is the assembly of stars, undivided space is realized by me through my sense of joy in the boundless. This vastness is superfluous for the purpose of mere physical life, as is proved by the worms that burrow underground. There are in this world also human worms for whom a dearth of sky is no privation; for in them has been killed the mind that cannot live without expanding its wings outside the prison bars of necessity. It was the tyranny of the ghosts of such dead souls that frightened the poet into the prayer:

Doom me not to the futility
Of offering things of joy to the callous!

But the heart of the King's son is fresh and sensitive. He realizes in the Princess that sweep of immensity which is in the sky lighted by the eternal stars; and his response to the sight of her is as befits such realization. The others behave differently. To measure the rhythm of the heart-throbs of the King's daughter, the scientist has no compunction in improvising a tube of tin. The Merchant finds his satisfaction in the tin can wherein he safe-keeps the cream churned by the Princess' own hand. But the King's son does not so much as dream of ordering tin armlets for the Princess,—should he perchance do so it would be for him a veritable nightmare. If, when he wakes, he happens to find gold scarce, he is forthwith impelled to sally forth in search of rose buds for her.

From this can be understood why, in Sanskrit, Rhetoric is called the Grammar of Ornament. Ornament is the symbol of the ultimate. The mother who finds the finality of her joy in her babe, translates this absolute consciousness of hers into the adornments wherewith she decks its body. We view our servant within fixed limits and our return for his service is like-wise limited to a fixed salary. But we view our friend in the unlimited, so ornaments blossom forth in our language and behaviour, in the tone of our voice, our smile, our welcome. In literature we speak of him with decorated words, of which the significance is not in their meaning, but in their feeling the message whereof is brought home by the ring of their melody. The appearances, the thoughts, the dreams which are not made manifest through reasoning,—these are of Literature.

What in English is called *real,* is in our language called *sārthaka* (significant). Common truth is one thing, significant truth quite another. Common truth does not admit of selection; it is the significant that is select. Men of every sort come under the head of common truth, the man of significance is hardly to be found in a million. When, on the impulse of his profound pity, Valmiki was stirred to metrical utterance, it was only with the aid of Rishi Narada that he could find a real man, of a significance worthy of his metre.

Not that significantly real things are rare, but anything that is not significant to me is not real for me. Because the world of reality has more extensive boundaries for the Poet and the Artist, they can bring out the significance of a much larger variety of things. For in Whatsoever we are made aware of some ideal of completeness, that becomes significant to us. A grain of sand is nothing to me, but a lotus flower has for me the full force of certitude. Though at every step the sand may obtrude itself on my attention,—grating on my feet, irritating my eye, setting my teeth on edge,—nevertheless it has not for me any fulness of truth. The lotus does not have to elbow its way into my notice, rather does my mind of its own accord go out to greet and welcome it.

Let me give an example of the sensitive fastidiousness of the mind when choosing the adornments for the object of its adoration. The flower of the *sajinā* is not lacking in beauty, but the poets, when celebrating the enthronement of the King of Seasons, do not by any chance include its name in their songs of acclamation. It has lost prestige with the poets because it happens to figure as an article of diet. For the same reason the flowers of the brinjal or the pumpkin stand with lowered heads outside the gates of poesy,—the kitchen has destroyed their caste. Not alone the poets, but also their sweethearts disdain these flowers as ornaments, though a spray of the delicate *sajinā* flower-clusters in their dark tresses would assuredly not have been ill-becoming. Neither the *kunda* nor *tagar* are gorgeous or scented, yet for them the door to the realm of adornment remains open, for they have not been tainted with the touch of the hunger of the body.

Here pictorial art is at an advantage. The artist's brush need not shrink from painting the superb foliage of the yam, whereas to bring that name, suggestive of a meal, into the description of any verdant scene would tax all the resources of the poet's pen. The sounds of words, moreover, sometimes have undignified associations, by reason of the way they are used in our everyday life, which are liable to give offence in the case of the word picture, for it is not shape or colour, but sound which is of the essence of poetry. I am not usually credited with any squeamish regard for convention, yet have I often to resort to a less usual name, or a round-about phrase, rather than use a word that has a utilitarian significance. I should say here, however, that these considerations do not apply with equal force in the case of the Western poet with whom it is the substance and not the name that dominates.

Be that as it may, it is a common experience that we fail to see in its entirety that which subserves our use, for it is eclipsed by the shadow of our need. The kitchen and pantry are of everyday necessity to the householder but, these are the rooms he fain would keep out of public view. His reception room, which he for himself can do without, is the one on which he lavishes all furniture and adornment, striving to the best of his means, by carpeting it, hanging it with pictures, stocking it with objects of exotic beauty, to give it a touch of the universal; for he would be known to the larger world outside, through this room of his choice, in all the glory of his own personality. In the facts that he eats and stores up food his personality finds no ultimate significance. That he has a special distinction is the tidings which he seeks to communicate through his reception rooms,—wherefore they are decorated.

In the realm of Biology man and beast are not distinct; as there viewed, self-preservation and race preservation are of equal importance in the nature of both. But man's spirit fails to find in these features the true significance of Man. So, however deep-seated or widespread man's desire to dine may be, his literature has but scanty recognition of it. Man's eating propensity may be an insistent, but it is not a significant truth; that is why the satisfaction of his hunger is not one of the joys that have found a place in the paradise of his Art-world.

The sexual relationship of man and woman stands on a higher plane than man's appetite for food, for it has achieved an intimate connection with the relationship of hearts. The sex instinct which, in a basic view of life, has only a secondary place, has risen, in the sex relations of the larger life of man, to a position transcending even the primary; for Love illumines man, within and without, into a supreme intensity of consciousness. That illumination is lacking in the primitive principle of race preservation, which therefore assumes importance only on the plane of science. The union of hearts, as seen by us, is abstracted from the primitive needs of Nature into the glory of its own finality. And hence it has come to occupy so vast a place in Literature and the Arts.

The supreme significance of the union of the sexes is, for man, not in procreation,—*prajanārtham* (for the sake of progeny) as our Lawgiver would have it,—for in that he is merely animal, but in love wherein he is truly man. I do not use the word *animal* with any implication of ethical judgment, but from the viewpoint of the progressive self-realization of man. Owing to their intimately close contact a natural spirit of rivalry prevails between the animal and the spiritual spheres of man's sex-life in their respective claims for the wreath of victory from art and literature. The psycho-analyst has introduced a further complication by asseverating that the animal sex-instinct is also a deep and potent factor in the mental life of man. But whatever practical utility or intellectual value this dictum of science may have, it can have no place in the realm of Literature and Art, which is concerned with the valuation of man's feeling of delight according to his standard of the eternal. The same is the case with considerations of social morality. The problems that have arisen with regard to the place of the sex-relation in Literature cannot be solved from the scientific or moral standpoint, but from that of Aesthetics, which alone can determine which of its two aspects man will adorn and raise on the pedestal of immortality.

We find in every age temporary extraneous circumstances occasionally creating obsessions that penetrate into the field of literature and overshadow for the time its true characteristics. It is not possible, however, for these temporary excitements to find any permanent place in literature, for, being volatile by nature, they soon evaporate. During the great European War, for instance, the war turbulence muddied even the streams of its poetry. When in England the Puritanic age was followed by one of license, its exhalations befogged the radiance of its literature, but even while such period lasted, the presence of this cloud testified not to its own significance, but to that of the light which it could not wholly obscure. In the Middle Ages of Europe the Church attained such power that it tried to throttle science, forgetting that, in its own sphere, science is supreme and owes no allegiance even to religion. Now the opposite phenomenon is at work, and it is science that seeks to establish its sway over every region of man's being: in the pride of its new prestige it has ceased to have misgivings about encroaching beyond its scope.

Science is impersonal. Its very essence is an impartial curiosity about truth. And yet the all-pervading net of this curiosity is gradually enmeshing modern literature within its folds; though of Literature, on the contrary, the essence is its partiality,—its supreme message is the freedom of choice according to the taste of man. It is this freedom which is being assailed by the invasion of science. The sensualism of which

European literature is full to-day owes its origin to this *curiosity*, as its prototype in the Age of the Restoration had its impulse in *lust*. But just as the lust of that age failed to win the laurel which could secure it a permanent place in the Olympus of Literature, neither can the scientific curiosity of this age maintain its keenness for ever.

There was a day in our country when a heat wave of licentiousness passed over our society and stimulated our literature into an outburst of carnalism. It was a temporary aberration of which the modern reader refuses to take any serious notice, not by way of moral censure, but because he has ceased to accord it permanent value.

Of late, it is true, we notice the opposite tendency in some of our modern critics who would rank among the eternal verities the intemperance of the flesh that has been imported into our literature from the Western world. But they forget that the eternal cannot wholly contradict the past. The natural delicacy which has always been a feature of man's aesthetic enjoyment, the aristocracy which has always reigned in the realm of art,—these are eternal. It is only in the rantings of the science-intoxicated democracy of to-day that this modesty, this reticence, is dubbed a weakness, and a rude manifestation of physical hunger is proclaimed to constitute the virility of art.

I have seen an example of this begrimed pugilistic modernism in the form that our *Holi* play has taken amongst the roughs of Chitpore Road. There is no scattering of red powder, no spraying with rose-coloured perfumes, no laughter, no song. Rolling long pieces of wet cloth in the street mud and therewith bespattering one another and the unfortunate passers-by, to the accompaniment of unearthly yells, is the mad form which this old-time Spring Festival has here assumed. Not to tinge but to taint is the object. I do not say that such propensity is foreign to the mentality of man: the psycho-analyst is therefore welcome to revel in a study thereof. My objection to the importation of this common desire to soil into a festival inspired by man's aesthetic sense is not because it is not true, but because it is not appropriate.

Some of those who seek to defend the bringing in of such muddy carousals into the region of our literary enjoyment do so with the question—*But is it not true?* That question, as I say, does not arise. When our drug-befuddled *Bhojpuri* festive party storm the welkin with the unending clang of their intoxicated drums and cymbals, their demonaic shouts of an eternal repetition of the one line of their tuneless song, it is entirely beside the point to ask the suffering neighbours whether or not it is true; the only relevant question can be: *How is it music*? There is admittedly a kind of self-forgetful joy in inebriation; there is undoubtedly great forcefulness in an unrestrained exercise of lung power; and if the ugliness of incivility has to be taken as a sign of virility, then we must needs admire this athletic intoxication also. But what then? This forcefulness still remains of the slums of Chitpore, it cannot aspire to the Elysium of Art.

In conclusion it should be added that, if in the countries ridden by science, an indiscriminate curiosity should, Duhsāsana-like, seek to strip the goddess of Literature of her drapery, they have at least the excuse of science to offer for such conduct. But in our country, where neither within nor without, neither in thought nor in action, has science been permitted an entry, what excuse can serve to cover up the insolence of the spurious, borrowed immodesty that has come to infest its literature? If the question be sent to the other side of the seas: *Why this turmoil of the market-crowd in your literature?* The answer will come: *That is no fault of our literature; the cause lies in the markets that surround us.* When that same question is put on this side, the reply will be: *True, markets we have none; but the noisomeness of the market-place is all there; that is just the glory of our modernism!*

1927

The Function of a Library

Most libraries are possessed with the passion for accumulation. Three-quarters of their books do not come into use,—their overgrown proportion even thrusts into a corner the specially selected few that are meant for being actually used. In our popular parlance, the man of large riches is called a great man. When a millionaire comes into a gathering, they vie to do him honour,—an honour not dependent on what he has to give, but merely on what he has. Much in the same way, the bigness of a library is estimated by the number of its volumes. The facilities offered for their use that should have been its glory, are not deemed necessary for its pride.

The words that are owned by our language have two different repositories,—one is the dictionary, the other is its literature. It is useful to collect all the known words in a comprehensive dictionary, though comparatively but few of them are actually current. On the other hand the range of words found in literature,—which are living and therefore not one of which can be spared,—is ever so much less. And yet it has to be admitted that the value of literature is more than that of the dictionary.

The same truth applies to the library. That part of its contents which is for the purpose of extensive accumulation has its usefulness, but the other part which is for constant and multifarious use, gives it its significance. The average librarian, however, rarely takes thought or trouble to bring the largest number of books to the utmost use, because it is always easier to overwhelm the public mind with the mere display of quantitative abundance.

In order to bring a library into the fullest use, it is necessary that its contents should be clearly and specifically brought to notice, otherwise it is difficult for the ordinary man to find his way about them, and the library is left as a city of vast accommodation that lacks sufficient means of communication.

Those who frequent libraries on some special quest of their own, may manage to make a track for themselves by dint of the urgency of their particular pursuit. But the library itself should recognize its share of responsibility in the matter. Because it has the books, it is incumbent on the library to get them read, for then alone is it justified. It is not enough that it passively permits visitors: its invitation should be active. For, as the Sanskrit proverb tells us: *tannashtam yannadīyaté,* that which is not given is wasted.

The usual thing is for a library to say: *Here is my catalogue, come and select for yourself*. But in the usual catalogue there is no introduction, no invitation, no spirit of welcome. That library alone can be called hospitable, which shows an eagerness to invite readers to the feast at its disposal,—it is such hospitality that makes a library big, not its size. That the readers make the library, is not the whole truth; the library likewise makes the readers.

If this truth is kept in view, we at once realize what a great function is that of the librarian. His duty does not end with the acquisition, classification and care-taking of the volumes in his charge; in other words, it is not exhausted by mere multiplication and division; he must have a proper understanding of his books as well. If a library is too big, it becomes practically impossible for the librarian adequately to acquire such true understanding. That is why I feel that the big library can but function as a storehouse, and only the small one serve as a refectory to furnish the wherewithal for daily sustenance and enjoyment.

My idea of a small library is one that keeps books on every subject, but only select books, not one of which is there merely as an offering of worship to Number, but each one of which stands on its own merits; where the librarian is a true devotee, devoid of ulterior seeking, free from pride in the mere loading of shelves, capable of discriminate rejection. A library, in short, which makes just enough provision that can be placed before its guests for their delectation, with a librarian who has the qualities of a host, not a storekeeper.

Consider, for instance, the case of a library which takes in a number of periodicals, published at home and abroad. If some one on the staff made it his duty regularly to compile a list of the specially interesting articles, and hang it up in a conspicuous place, would that not immensely increase the chances of their being read? As it is, three-fourths of these remain unopened, encumbering space and burdening the shelves as they keep on accumulating. The same is the case with new books. Very few librarians attempt to acquaint themselves, much less their constituents, with the contents. Yet is it not obvious that the wealth they have to offer should be made known as soon as new books come to hand?

Made known to whom? In each case to a special circle of readers. Every library should have as its indispensable limbs such special circles of readers. These alone can give it life. The worth of a librarian I would gauge by his power of attracting and looking after such circles, of acting as the intermediary for an intimacy of relationship between reader and library. That is to say, on him is cast the burden not only of the books, but of their readers as well, and in the maintaining of both is the test of his efficiency, of the proper discharge of his trust.

Even as to the books themselves, the librarian's duty should not be confined to those that he can collect in his own library, but he must also keep himself acquainted with all those others that are published from time to time, subject by subject. For the purposes of our school at Santiniketan, for example, we have to keep ourselves in touch with all the publications intended for children, so as to be able to make our selection. Every library should assist in work of this kind. This they could do by keeping up-to-date lists of books on the different subjects, as they come out and gain reputation. If it became known that a particular library was endeavouring to discharge this duty, I am sure that the publishers would be glad to co-operate by furnishing it with lists of their publications, together with a résumé of their contents.

In conclusion it is my submission to the All India Library Conference that it should consider the question of preparing and circulating such quarterly, half-yearly or at least annual list, from which the main features of the best new books in the English language,—scientific, literary and historical,—may be gathered. If it be the object of this Conference to stimulate the founding and growth of libraries all over the country, then such object can be best promoted by thus affording a guide to the books that should be procured; incidentally also thereby assisting the libraries in what should be their main work—not the mere procuring and keeping of books, but actively acquainting their constituents with and interesting them in their contents.

1929

On Oriental Culture and Japan's Mission

Some years ago I had the real meeting with Japan when a great original mind, from these shores came in our midst. He was our guest for a long time and he had immense inspiration for the young generation of Bengal in those days which immediately preceded a period of a sudden ebullition of national self-assertion in our country. The voice of the East came from him to our young men. That was a significant fact, a memorable one in my own life. And he asked them to make it their mission in life to give some great expression of the human spirit worthy of the East. It is the responsibility which every nation has, to reveal itself before the world. Obscurity should be considered almost as a national crime, it is worse than death and is never forgiven by the history of man. The people must bring out the best in them which belongs to the magnanimity of their soul which is their wealth that exceeds their immediate and exclusive needs and recognizes its responsibility to send cultural and spiritual invitation to the rest of the world. He asked our young men to cherish in their heart a strong faith and a deep pride in their past where they enshrine the vision of the noblest ideals of heroism; of devotion to truth and freedom, devotion to the eternal laws of righteousness. And this, not as a critical scholar, laboriously picking up evidences of actual facts, but as a devotee lovingly conscious of the ideals incarnated in ancient legends, in epics, in mythological creations. He said that if they could maintain a simple attitude of worshipful mind towards a great eternal idea which is the East, they would be able to summon up the strength to suffer martyrdom in their aspiration for a glorious future. He mentioned, as an instance of this truth, the writings of great history of Japan in which has been treasured the inspiration of the best ideals of this country for the coming generations of her children, not a critical history of facts but of truth which is deep in the memory of the people. My friend, of whom I have spoken, was a true Japanese and I am sure that because of this abundant truth in him, he could deeply understand the other Eastern peoples. And a great opportunity it was for us to see with what natural ease he could share the life of our own people, and inspire in their heart an aspiration, not only for the good of their own country but for all humanity. He was one of those who had the gift of sympathetic insight which could discover some abiding human truth from all obscure corners, and detect significant meanings from the most insignificant facts, which are often overlooked. And it was this gift through which he had helped our young generation to know better their own land, to discover the treasure of culture which lies hidden in the national mind of the people, and they had wonderful days of ecstasy and enthusiasm so long as he was in our midst. With an eager love he identified himself with the young men of those days, and they still remember him. The movements to which he gave impetus are still working in our province, and one of those was the art movement in Bengal, which he had helped with his sympathy, understanding, and imagination, his instinct and experience about principle of art. Those young men who sat near him and listened to his words, day after day, are still reaping the benefit of that fruitful opportunity in the morning of their youth. Well, that was a very real meeting which happened in our country—meeting with Japan. And I assure you, my friends, that this meeting had the effect of drawing the heart of our people in Bengal towards your country more than any other fact that has happened since then, or before that time. It was that personal relationship, personal influence, in which he represented the best of Japan. I say best, because it transcended all local and temporary interests of Japan in its love and sympathy; and he worked, worked day and night, among a people whose language he hardly understood, and this very fact was an education for us. I remember when I used to accompany him to some of our village fairs and other places outside the town, what subtle sensitiveness he displayed for things that had some permanent value which was not evident to those who were familiar with them. He would often buy some very cheap things, like simple clay oil-pots that peasants use, with ecstasy of admiration, some things in which we had failed to realize the instinct for beauty which those unsophisticated villagers possessed without their knowing its merit. And then, after over six months in India, he left our country, but his experience, the sentiment which was evoked in his mind, he has given expression to in a very remarkable book, full of suggestive beauty of expression, a part of which is named, 'Ideals of the East'. Then I had the privilege of meeting him once against in America, in Boston, when he was the Curator of the Boston Museum, Oriental Department, and I found what profound admiration he inspired among those cultured Americans of Boston who came into contact with him. On this occasion of our last meeting, he was almost mortally ill and intending to come back to his native soil. He asked me to visit China, promised that he would take me over that country himself personally and show me the real China, which is not quite evident to the shallow curiosity of the ordinary tourist mind. He expressed very profound respect for China. That also revealed his great personality to me. His deep sympathy for India did touch us very greatly, but then I found that it was nothing which was special in its limit; it was only one of the manifestations of his understanding mind, his generous human sympathy. It enhanced my respect for him to know that he had almost a feeling of reverence for the neighbouring country of his, for which very often your people have not their full measure of sympathy and appreciation. He was far above those local and petty prejudices which blind our vision to all that is great in races to which we do not belong ourselves. According to him, China was a great country with endless possibilities; that the genius which her past history revealed, leaving its innumerable memorials scattered everywhere in that land, still lived in the heart of the people. It was his wish that I should know and acknowledge this; and that was another good help which he rendered me. It at once strengthened my interest for the ancient land, my faith in her future, because I could trust him when he expressed his admiration for those people who are to-day living in comparative obscurity, whose lamps of culture are not completely lit up, but who were, according to him, waiting for another opportunity to have the fullness of illumination, shedding fresh glory upon the history of Asia. When I first met him I neither knew Japan nor had I any experience of China. I came to know both of these countries from the personal relationship with this great man whom I had the good fortune to meet and accept as one of my intimate friends. He was followed by three of your most renowned artists, one of whom is still living and I am sure has a universal reputation among his own countrymen, Yokoyama Taikwan; and another young artist, who I believe is no longer living, Hishida, and also another of them. And they worked there, they lived with our students, who were struggling to help their own instincts, find their aspiration from their own traditions and surroundings. Your artists from Japan were intimate with these young spirits of great promise and the memorial of that cooperation is still alive in the modern art movement started in Bengal. I am glad to confess to you at this meeting, that one of the influences which acted towards the awakening of spirit in Bengal flowed from the heart of that great man, Okakura, and I am specially grateful that through this, one of the most fruitful periods of our modern history had its association with Japan. And if this association of culture and sympathy is allowed to grow, then some day will be developed, not merely national culture, national minds, but a continental mind of Asia, greatly needed and long waiting to be revealed.

My friends, you all know what a great force it is in Europe that these Western peoples have such a thing as the continental concert of minds. It is a very real power, this cultural co-operation and bond of intellectual fellowship. It is a very great fact in human history. All the several countries of that continent contribute to a common coffer their individual wealth of mind, and intellectual treasure has been accumulating for centuries in the West. The important fact, which we have to keep in mind, is that they do not all have one language. There was a time in the Middle Age when Latin was the common language of culture but that was not the most glorious period of European civilization. There is no doubt that this classical language was the seed plot in which all the scholars of Europe had done their part of sowing the seeds. But then, when the shoots came up, the transplantation had to be done in different soils of languages that were living, and that was the great opportunity that Europe has had. And now, though the different European countries have different languages and also to some extent, different temperaments, different kinds of gifts, still they have this marvellous illumination of a combined culture which now dominates the whole of the world because of a great power that has been generated with this intellectual and spiritual co-operation of minds. I believe that such good fortune has never occurred to any other continent, never such a great truth of humanity revealed. It proved that when human minds with their respective capacities work together, a very great potent power is generated that has in it immortal life; and this is the highest lesson which we can accept from European civilization. When we talk about European civilization, we use a term which is real in its meaning, it is an undoubted fact. But when they glibly talk of the Oriental mind and culture, they do not realize that we have not yet been able to develop a universal mind, a great background of Oriental cultures. Our cultures are too scattered. They yet have not any possibility of interconnection, and owing to that, they have their provincialism, something which is peculiar to each people with their idiosyncrasy and mannerism that generally has the character of stammering in them.

Peculiarity is not a thing of which we can be proud. Uniqueness of the individuals is great because that uniqueness has in it the essential element of universality. What is peculiar is accidental, is narrow in its range of expression, is exclusive and therefore it does not give us a permanent strength of truth. There are certain qualities in your civilization, the gifts which Japan has, that are unique. They are most admirable, not because they are peculiar to Japan, but because, in their uniqueness, they carry a universal aspect which can be gladly accepted and proudly owned by other people also, if they have the opportunity and wisdom to do so. For instance, it should give us real delight when we find some perfect artistic expression in your soil, finding its way to India and to Europe. It is a narrow mind, void of light, that cannot feel the pride of it, pride for all humanity, to be able to know that these things of eternal value have been produced in the history of man. And we can meet on this ground of culture, which, though unique in each individual race, has its inexhaustible human appeal. Japan has offered her invitation to all time and to all parts of the world in whatever is of immortal value in her work of self-expression in her art, in her traditions that express some sensitive qualities of heart, her courtesy and power of self-control, great dignity of behaviour, which I have daily had the opportunity to admire, and I have deeply wished that our people also could receive inspiration from them without feeling the least sense of humiliation. Men are great borrowers, for when we borrow things of lasting merit from other people, we can claim our birthright to possess them. All real great things belong to all countries, and men of great genius cannot be confined in a classification in any one particular race or country. Such great geniuses have been born in all parts of the world spreading the brotherhood of man. These great hearts, who are like mountain peaks overtowering in their altitude, rise far above the soil that supports them and from that height, which is in the heart of the eternal, they can scan the distant horizons and realize the fundamental unity in all differences around them. You have, I am sure, such great minds in your country, who have their feet on the soil of this land and their minds in the sky—the universal realm of visions—the visions which rise from great souls from all parts of the world and hover and mingle in a translucent atmosphere. I have had the great good fortune to know such individuals in the West and in the East, who have their pride in humanity, who radiate influences round them which are for saving human races from race jealousy and dark suspicions bred of irrational prejudices. Our need is all the greater, in these dark days of dissensions, of cults of lies, for messages from the height that rise above the dust and the mist of the baser passions of man, the voice from the calm of truth, the truth of human unity and the hope of a dawn, when with the advent of light we shall be able to recognize in the faces of each other, the friend, the kindred. My friends, I feel certain that those of you who are listening to me today, know and have met such individuals among yourselves. It may be that they still live in obscurity; it may be that their names will never appear in history, but they are always disseminating light around them and are silently building up the salvation of man. I appeal to you who belong to Japan, who have shown indomitable courage and fortitude in the modern struggle of race, accepted the responsibility of the present age of progress and have taken your honoured place in the comity of nations, I appeal to you, be not content with the exclusive possession of what you have received from the hands of fortune. This is a time for you to be generous in your hospitality, the merit of which virtue is acknowledged by all peoples of the East. Hospitality to distant races should be an expression of patriotism for one's own country. Whenever I come to Japan, I realize this in her atmosphere not only in evident acts and words but in all subtle shades of expression, in all your things of beauty. We that come from outside accept this call with gratitude. And at the same time, I must confess that because I feel almost a personal pride in this building up of your modern history, pride as an Asiatic, therefore, I often feel misgivings at any thing that casts dark shadow upon the course of your progress. I have sometime suffered the pain of such doubts; haven't I seen in the West manifestations of the national pride which gloats on the humiliation of its neighbours and fellow-beings without knowing that such humiliation comes back to itself? I have seen in the West the immense, monstrous pride in some glory that they exclusively claim and want to preserve for their own nation. Unfortunately in the wake of some other evils these germs from the diseased hearts of the nation have come to us floating from the West and our treatment of alien races in the East is beginning to show signs of that supercilious contempt and want of consideration which in the West is justified in the name of patriotism.

A great problem has come to you, my friends of Japan. Now you have something you never had in your history, you have a dependency. You have also a neighbouring nation which is not equal to you in its strength of arms. And you have to deal with these races, these neighbours to whom it is so dangerously easy for you to be unjust with impunity. May I be frank with you and say that when I chance to hear of some instances of ill-treatment to Koreans and to others who are less fortunate than yourselves, it hurts me very deeply causing keen disappointment? I have ever wished that Japan, in behalf of all Eastern peoples, will reveal an aspect of civilization which is generally ignored in other parts of the world. It should be greatly rich in the wealth of human relationship, even in its politics. The generosity in human relationship I claim as something special to the East. We do acknowledge our human responsibilities to our neighbours, to our dependents, to all those who are related to us and this personal element in our civilization is something which we cannot afford to lose. Science is impersonal, and scientific diplomacy and scientific organizations of all kinds are developing this aspect of impersonal dealings with human beings which, even if not always painful, is always humiliating. Certainly it is owing to this that industrial class-wars are now being waged everywhere. The conflict between man and woman, between master and dependent, between neighbours, has become uncontrollable because the bonds of human relationship have snapped or become loose. Everything is ordered with a precision which is perfect, but mechanically perfect, which has callously divested itself of all elements of human sentiment, ignored all injunctions of the codes of honour that ever refused meanly to cling to calculating utility. More than once I have had opportunities to talk to the Koreans who brought their problems to me. I explained to them my views and said that with the changed conditions in the present age no small countries can expect protection in their geographical barriers solely through their own small resources and imperfect training and education. And such helplessness has rendered all the weak spots of the human world danger centres of political storms, like areas of rarified air inevitably inviting a heavier host of wind to a turbulent rush of cyclone. No great nation, for the sake of self-preservation, can allow such weak spots in its neighbourhood to remain out of its control, for that is sure to afford vantage ground to its enemies and neither is it safe for the weaker people themselves to be left alone. And therefore the problem before the Koreans is to cultivate the moral strength which will enable them to establish a mutual relationship honourable for both sides. The moral danger is no less great for the people who unfortunately have the evil opportunity of exercising absolute power upon a weaker race. And for the sake of keeping up a high standard of national character which, after all, is the only source of permanent strength for the people it is imperatively necessary for the ruling nation to allow the subject race to find in themselves enough strength to be able to remind their rulers that they have to be just, honest, sympathetic and respectful. It is meet for the victors to maintain the pride of their righteousness by allowing rights to those who cannot forcibly wrench it away from them and those who, as human beings, have their inalienable claim upon human sympathy. You can establish your lasting kingdom if you can help your subjects to greatness and to self-government by training them up into self-confidence and bringing out into light all their latent power of self-expression. You must know that the day comes when the defeated have their chance for revenge; that peoples have long memories and wrongs rankle deep in their heart; times of trouble are sure to come to all nations when the weak can bring fatal disaster to the stronger. The warnings of providence are often silent, and politicians do not heed to them. They have not the far-sighted vision; they live in the dusky den of the immediate present. And therefore I appeal to you as representatives of your people, win their love whom you can be foolish enough to bully into a sullen subjection, make them trustworthy by trusting them and by respecting them, train them into self-respect which is for your own good. Let the best mission of statesmanship be carried on in an atmosphere of sympathy and understanding, in the grateful heart of a people the best of all backgrounds for the creation of the national genius. And before I leave, let me hope that I have not hurt the susceptibility of my audience when, in a genuine spirit of sympathy, I have offered them my message, thereby offering the best homage that I can render them.

1929

Ideals of Education

The greatest man of modern India, Raja Rammohun Roy was born in Bengal and was the best friend of my grandfather. He had courage to overcome the prohibition against sea-voyage which we had in our country at the time; and he crossed the sea, and came into touch with the great western minds.

My father was fortunate in coming under the influence of Rammohun Roy from his early years which helped him to free himself from the sectarian barriers, from traditions of worldly and social ideas that were very rigid, in many aspects very narrow and not altogether beneficial. My father drew from our ancient scriptures, from the *Upanishads,* truths which had universal significance, and not anything that were exclusive to any particular age or any particular people. We were ostracized by society and this liberated us from the responsibility of conforming to all those conventions that had not the value of truth, that were mere irrational habits bred in the inertia of the racial mind. In my boyhood's dreams I claimed such freedom that we had tasted, for all humanity.

Nations are kept apart not merely by international jealousy but also by their own past, handicapped by the burden of the dead and decaying, the breeding ground of diseases that attack the spiritual man. I could not believe that generations of peoples, century after century, must have their birth chamber in a moral and intellectual coffin which has its restricted space regulation for a body that has lost its movements. Civilization has its inevitable tendency to accumulate dead materials and to make elaborate adjustments for their accommodation, leaving less and less room for life with its claim to grow in freedom. There are signs of that in India, and I know to-day that it is more or less true in all races, for our mind has its inclination to grow lazy as it grows old and to shirk its duty to make changes in the rhythm of the changing times. In the very heart of this rigid rule of the dead, I was brought up in an atmosphere of aspiration, aspiration for the expansion of the human spirit. We in our home sought freedom of power in our language, freedom of imagination in our literature, freedom of soul in our religious creeds and that of mind in our social environment. Such an opportunity has given me confidence in the power of education which is one with life and only which can give us real freedom, the highest that is claimed for man, his freedom of moral communion in the human world. The ghosts of ideals which no longer have a living reality have become the obsession of all nations that carry an overwhelming past behind them perpetually overshadowing their future.

The reign of the ghost has strewn the path of our history lessons with mischief, with prejudices that ever obstruct the mutual understanding of nations, that helps in the cultivation of the thorny crop of national vanity and unscrupulousness in international relationship. From our young days our minds are deliberately trained with the aid of untrue words and unholy symbolism in the name of patriotism, to a collective moral attitude, which we condemn in individuals.

Persons who have no faith in human nature are apt to think that such conditions are eternal in man—that the moral ideals are only for individuals but the race belongs to that primitive nature which is for the animal. And according to them, in the racial life, it is necessary that the animal should have its full scope of training in the cult of suspicion, jealousy, fierce destructiveness, cruel rapacity. They contemptuously brand optimism as sentimental weakness, and yet in spite of that virulent scepticism an enormous change has worked itself out in course of the growth of civilization from the darkest abyss of savagery. I refuse to believe that human society has reached its limit of moral possibility. And we must work all our strength for the seemingly impossible, and must believe that there is a constant urging in the depth of human soul for the attainment of the perfect, the urging which secretly helps us in all our endeavour for the good. This faith has been my only asset in the educational mission which I have made my life's work, and almost unaided and alone, I struggle along my path. I try to assert in my words and works that education has its only meaning and object in freedom—freedom from ignorance about the laws of universe, and freedom from passion and prejudice in our communication with the human world. In my institution I have attempted to create an atmosphere of naturalness in our relationship with strangers, and the spirit of hospitality which is the first virtue in men that made civilization possible.

I invited thinkers and scholars from foreign lands to let our boys know how easy it is to realize our common fellowship, when we deal with those who are great, and that it is the puny who with their petty vanities set up barriers between man and man.

I am glad that I have the opportunity to-day of letting my friends in Japan know something of my life-long cause and to assure them that it is not special to India but it will ever wait for acceptance by other races.

We in India are unfortunate in not having the chance to give expression to the best in us in creating intimate relations with the powerful peoples of the world. The bond between the nations to-day is made of the links of mutual menace, its strength depending upon the force of panic, and leading to an enormous waste of resources in a competition of browbeating and bluff. Some great voice is waiting to be heard which will usher in the sacred light of truth in the dark region of the nightmare of politics. But we in India have not yet had the chance. Yet we have our own human voice which truth demands. Even in the region where we are not invited to act we have our right to judge and to guide the mind of man to a proper point of view, to the vision of ideality in the heart of the real.

The activity represented in human education is a worldwide one, it is a great movement of universal co-operation interlinked by different ages and countries. And India, though defeated in her political destiny, has her responsibility to hold up the cause of truth, even to cry in the wilderness, and offer her lessons to the world in the best gifts which she could produce. The messengers of truth have ever joined their hands across centuries, across the seas, across historical barriers, and they help to form the great continent of human brotherhood. Education in all its different forms and channels has its ultimate purpose in the evolving of a luminous sphere of human mind from the nebula that has been rushing round ages to find in itself an eternal centre of unity. We individuals, however small may be our power and whatever corner of the world we may belong to, have the claim upon us to add to the light of the consciousness that comprehends all humanity. And for this cause I ask your co-operation, not merely because co-operation gives us strength in our work but because co-operation itself is the best aspect of the truth we represent, it is an end and not merely the means.

My friends, you are new converts to western ideals, in other words, the ideals belonging to the scientific view of life and the world. This is great and it is foolish to belittle its importance by wrongly describing it as materialism. For truth is spiritual in itself, and truly materialistic is the mind of the animal which is unscientific and therefore unable to cross the dark screen of appearance, of accidents, and reach the deeper region of universal laws. Science means intellectual probity in our dealings with the material world. This conscientiousness of mind is spiritual, for it never judges its results from the standard of external profits. But in science the oft-used half truth that honesty is the best policy has proved itself to be completely true. Science being mind's honesty in its relation to the physical universe never fails to bring us the best profit for our living. And mischief finds its entry through this backdoor of utility, and Satan has had his ample chance of making use of the divine fruit of knowledge for bringing shame upon humanity. Science as the best policy is tempting the primitive in man bringing out his evil passions through the respectable cover that it has supplied him. And this is why it is all the more needed to-day that we should have faith in ideals that have matured in the spiritual field through ages of human endeavour after perfection, the golden crops that have developed in different forms and in different soils but whose food value for man's spirit has the same composition. These are not for the local markets but for the universal hospitality, for sharing life's treasure with each other and realizing that human civilization is a spiritual feast the invitation to which is open to all, it is never for the ravenous orgies of carnage where the food and the feeders are being torn to pieces.

The legends of nearly all human races carry man's faith in a golden age which appeared as the introductory chapter in human civilization. It shows that man has his instinctive belief in the objectivity of spiritual ideals though this cannot be proved. It seems to him that they have already been given to him and that this gift has to be proved through his history against obstacles. The idea of millennium so often laughed at by the clever is treasured as the best asset by man in his mythology as complete truth realized for ever in some ageless time. Admitting that it is not a scientifical fact we must at the same time know that the instinct cradled and nourished in these primitive stories has its eternal meaning. It is like the instinct of a chick which dimly feels that an infinite world of freedom is already given to it, that it is not a subjective dream but an objective reality, even truer than its life within the egg. If a chick has a rationalistic tendency of mind it ought not to believe in a freedom which is difficult to imagine and contradictory to all its experience, but all the same it cannot help pecking at its shell and ever accepting it as ultimate. The human soul confined in its limitation has also dreamt of a millennium and striven for an emancipation which seems impossible of attainment, and it felt its reverence for some great source of inspiration in which all its experience of the true, good and beautiful finds its reality though it cannot be proved, the reality in which our aspiration for freedom in truth, freedom in love, freedom in the unity of man is ideally realized for ever.

1929

The Philosophy of Leisure

In my country, the cultivation of leisure has been a vital necessity. We may have many other compulsions for work, but hardly one for generating extra heat within our own physical constitution in order to maintain the balance between the outer temperature and the temperature of our body. In consequence, with us, restless activity has not become a pleasure in itself, and our bodily providence has slowed down our physical movements almost below the degree needful for the strenuous purposes of material prosperity.

We should bitterly blame our fate for an utter bankruptcy of civilization, if this strict economy of life were an absolute miserliness which gives up all prospect of profit to avoid the least risk of loss. Forest land is great, crowded with a furiously competing life; but the seemingly empty prairie land has also its own magnanimity, passively waiting to be wooed, yielding exhaustible wealth which has in it the spirit of co-operation, the deeper strength of meekness. The human world also has its prairie land of fertile leisure and forest land of self-assertive life.

Man has his two phases, the one in which he tries to make indefinite additions to the powers of his senses and limbs from the storehouse of cosmic powers; and the other in which he tries to realize through various stages, his oneness with humanity and thus manifest in himself a truth which reveals him much more intimately than the fact of any extension of power.

Man, along with the animal, is born to this earth where he has the materials of his living; and according to the development of his energy and intelligence which helps him in the acquisition and use of these materials, he becomes powerful and wins in the race of life. In this race, the individual competition for success is the main motive force which man has in common with the animal.

This domain of material progress has for its object success which depends upon quickness in time and bigness in quantity for its achievement.

But man, unlike the animal, is born also to his home, his society and his country. These afford him the background, the perspective needed for the expression of his complete being. They belong to the domain of his civilization which urges slow centuries to develop creative ideals through co-operation of minds and endeavours, through magnificent hospitality and love's utmost sacrifice.

This is the realm of great leisure in whose bosom appear the revelations of human spirit which work themselves out from the obscure period of the nebula into the constellation of stars.

The complete human truth is comprehended in the mastery of law that gives power and the realization of harmony which gives perfection, just as in a work of art, the handling of technique and the inspiration of vision are both necessary. Occasionally men lose the sensitiveness of their mind through the rude abrasions of constantly hurried moments. In such a state they become capable only of being aroused by some tortured trick in the technique, by some jerky shock of novelty which is not originality, by even ugliness that coarsely violates our sense of rhythm. These people take pride in proclaiming their disillusionment, after having taken to pieces things that can only have meaning in their wholeness, in this callous world of theirs, Titans have their victory and Gods are defeated. And have we the time to ask ourselves if some of the sights, that overpower us to-day with awe, are not the triumphal towers of the Titans, built with the ruins of our paradise?

The spirit of progress is neither moral nor immoral. With equal indifference it uses its efficiency in inflicting as well as in healing wounds, at the same time, in helping us in a perfect system of robbery and in a perfect organization of charity for those who suffer in consequence. It achieves success through intelligent dealings with Nature's potentialities.

This realm of progress is described in the Upanishads as *Anna Brahma*—the infinite in its aspect of utility. It has its urge in man for realizing the immeasurable in the domain of quantity through an endlessly progressing process of measurement. Directly we lose our faith in it through lethargy or diffidence, we lapse into an animal state in this material universe, and fall passively under the law of natural selection.

The rule of natural selection finds its full sway in a close system of life with rigidly limited resources and restricted possibilities. Man broke the prison wall open, declared his sovereignty and refused to be contented with the small allowance originally allotted to him by Nature, just enough to enable him to carry on a perpetual repetition of a narrow programme of life. He mastered his resources and utilises them for his own indomitable purpose. This working out of one's own purpose through the manipulation of Nature's law is great. It carries in it the proclamation of the right to freedom of the human spirit which refuses to acknowledge limits to its power in the very face of powerful contradictions. The present age is resounding with the declaration of independence for man in the world of nature. This independence is not absolute, but it is a sailing upon a perpetually widening current of emancipation. So long as the movement is maintained, it gives us the taste of the infinite at every point, but directly we stop, we become the captive of the finite and lose the dignity of our soul. There are races of men who have allowed themselves to be stranded upon the sterile sand of their past achievement, like a whale on the seashore, and they remain, to the end of their days, the prey of ravenous evils from all sides. There is a spirit of immortality in the sphere of the material existence which consists in a triumphant movement of realization. It loses its inspiration and becomes a menace to man when we are meanly overcome by the profit it promises and ignore its great meaning—the expansion of power which gives us the divine right to transform this world into a world for Man.

Truth has its other aspect which is described by the Upanishad as *Vigñāna Brahma* or *Ananda Brahma,* the infinite in its aspect of comprehension, aspect of joy. It is the realm of wisdom and love where mere dimension, number and speed have no meaning, where the value of truth is realized by matured mind through patient devotion, self-control and concentration of faculties. It has its atmosphere of infinity in a width of leisure across which come invisible messengers of life and light, bringing their silent voices of creation.

The process of the packing of fruits gains in merit according to the speed it attains by efficient organization of work, by economizing time through mechanical co-ordination of movements. But the fruit gains its quality of perfection, its flavour and mellowness, not by any impatient ignoring of time but by surrendering itself to the subtle caresses of a sun-lit leisure. And thus we see that the idea of time finds its meaning not as a mere duration of the world-process but as a vehicle of creative energy. In the Hindu Pantheon, the deity of time has its other name as the deity of energy, for we find that time not merely measures but it works. We do not know why a certain period of time is necessary for certain changes to happen, why food should not instantaneously be digested, why the mind should at all depend upon time for the assimilation of thoughts. In fact, we never solve the mystery why there should at all be a process of creation which is a process in time.

It is evident that the modern age is riding on a tornado of rapidity. Quickness of speed in an enormity of material production is jealously competing with its own past every moment. We cannot stop its course, and should not, even if we could. Our only anxiety with regard to it is that we may forget that slow productions of leisure are of immense value to man, for these only can give balance to the reckless rush of ambition, give rhythm to the life that misses its happiness by missing the cadence of chastity in its enjoyment; these only can impart meaning to an accumulation which knows how to grow to a hugeness but not to a majesty of expression. As I have said in the beginning, all civilizations are living wealths that have grown on the deep soil of a rich leisure. They are for conferring honour to our personality and giving it its best worth. The perfection of our personality does not principally consist of qualities that generate cleverness or deftness or even accuracy of observation, or the rationality that analyses and forms generalizations. It depends mostly upon our training in truth and love, upon ideals that go to the root of our being. And these require the ministration of quiet time for their adequate recognition and realization in life.

A true gentleman is the product of patient centuries of cultivated leisure that has nourished into preciousness a vision of honour whose value is higher than that of life itself. When I first visited Japan I had the opportunity of observing there the two parts of the human sphere strongly contrasted; one, on which grew up the ancient continent of social ideals, standards of beauty, codes of personal behaviour; and on the other part, the fluid element, the perpetual current that carried wealth to its shores from all parts of the world. In half a century's time Japan has been able to make her own the mighty spirit of progress which suddenly burst upon her one morning in a storm of insult and menace. China also has had her rousing when her self-respect was being knocked to pieces through a series of helpless years, and I am sure she also will master before long the instrument which hurt her to the quick. But the ideals that imparted life and body to Japanese civilization had been nourished in the reverent hopes of countless generations through ages which were not primarily occupied in an incessant hunt for opportunities, which had large tracts of leisure in them necessary for the blossoming of life's beauty and the ripening of her wisdom. These ideals had become one with the nature of the people and therefore these people were often unconscious of their profound value while they were noisily proud of some culture from a foreign market for which they had to pay in cash, because of its utility, and not in sacrifice which is claimed by a truth that has its ultimate value in itself. It is something like being boastful of an expensive pair of high-heeled shoes which has no compunction in insulting the beautiful contour of the living feet that have reached their perfect form in man through ages of evolution.

We have seen the modern factories in Japan, seen numerous mechanical organizations and engines of destruction of the latest type. Along with them we also see some fragile vase, some small pieces of silk, some architecture of sublime simplicity, some perfect lyric of bodily movement. Also we have seen these people's expression of courtesy daily extracting from them a considerable amount of time and trouble, their traditions of behaviour, any deviation from which, however inevitable, so often drove them to suicide. All these have come not from any accurate knowledge of things but from an intense consciousness of the value of reality which takes time for its realization. What Japan reveals in its skilful manipulation of telegraphic wires and railway lines, of machines for manufacturing things and for killing men, is more or less similar to what we see in other countries which have a similar opportunity for training. But in its art of living, its pictures, its code of conduct, the various forms of beauty which its religious and social ideals assume, Japan reveals its own personality which, in order to be of any worth, must be unique. This national personality acquires its richness from its assimilation of some ideal and not from its possession of some trade secret, some up-to-date machinery of efficiency.

What gives us cause for anxiety is the fact that the spirit of progress occupies a great deal more of our mind to-day than the deeper life process of our being which requires depth of leisure for its sustenance. In the present age the larger part of our growth takes place on the outside, and our inner spirit has not the time to accept it and harmonize it into a completeness of creation. In other words, the modern world has not allowed itself time to evolve a religion, a profound principle of reconciliation that can fashion out of all conflicting elements a living work of art—his society. The creative ideals of life, necessary for giving expression to the fulness of humanity, were developed centuries ago. And when to-day these suffer from some misfit as a result of a constant expansion of knowledge and a variety of new experiences, we fail to adjust them into a more comprehensive synthesis than before, and thus not only lose faith in them but in the fundamental principle that they represent. With strenuous efforts, we make stupendous heaps of materials and when the complaint comes that they miss the character of architecture, we contemptuously say that architecture is a superstition and for a democratic age rude piles are more significant than the rhythmic form of a building. Such remarks are easy to make only because we lack leisure truly to know our minds. We are only familiar with the surface of our life which is constantly being soiled and burdened with the sweepings of an enormous traffic. We grow to be fond of a perpetual shabbiness produced by a miscellany of fragments only because the relegation of these to their proper places requires time. And we say time is money, while we forget to say that leisure is wealth, the wealth which is a creation of human spirit whose material may be money.

Invention, construction and organization are spreading fast along the high road of our history, but the creative genius of man which acknowledged its mission to express all that has permanent value in his personality is everyday losing its dignity. It accepts cheap payments from the busy multitude, it is engaged in always keeping irreverent minds amused, it makes faces at things men held sacred and tries to prove that the ideals of social life that had given us grace, the majesty of self-mastery and the heroism of voluntary acceptance of suffering were for the most part unreal, false coins made current by the weak for the pathetic purpose of self-deception. Compressed and crowded time has its use when dealing with material things but living truths must have for their full significance a perspective of wide leisure. The cramped time produces deformities and degeneracy, and the mind constantly pursued by a fury of haste, develops a chronic condition of spiritual dyspepsia. It easily comes to believe that reality is truly represented by nightmare, that nothing but disease is frankly honest in its revelation of the normal, that only the lowest is reliable in its explanation of the highest in a language crudely obscure. Drunkenness may be defined as the habit of enjoyment forced out through a narrowed aperture of sensibility in jets of abnormal sharpness; and all enjoyment takes a drunken character for those who try to snatch it away from fugitive hours that come jumping to them in a staccato style. They become hopelessly addicted to undiluted sensationalism for their brief moments of recreations, and literature demanded by them grows bewilderingly turbulent with psychological perversity and intellectual somersaults. Incessantly handling things that have their market price they lose the judgment of the world of values, the self-luminous truth, the kingdom of personality. They claim explanation from every fact for its truth in a universe of reality while they forget that our personality also needs an adequate explanation in a universal truth.

A particle of sand would be nothing if it did not have its background in the whole physical world.

1929

India and Europe

No report has yet been published which correctly represents my views regarding India and Europe. Almost always the emphasis is put in the wrong place, and so the report becomes one-sided.

The one outstanding visible relationship of Europe with Asia to-day is that of exploitation; in other words its origins are commercial and material. It is physical strength that is most apparent to us in Europe's enormous dominion and commerce, illimitable in its extent and immeasurable in its appetite. Our spirit sickens at it. Everywhere we come against barriers in the way of direct human kinship. The harshness of these external contacts is galling, and therefore the feeling of unrest ever grows more oppressive. There is no people in the whole of Asia to-day which does not look upon Europe with fear and suspicion.

Yet there was a time when we were fascinated by Europe. She had inspired us with a new hope. We believed that her chief mission was to preach the gospel of liberty to the world. We had come then to know only her ideal side through her literature and art. But slowly, Asia and Africa have become the main spheres of Europe's secular activities, where her chief preoccupations have been the earning of dividends, the administration of empires, and the extension of commerce.

Europe's warehouses and business offices, her police outposts and soldiers' barracks, have been multiplied, while her human relationships have declined.

Towards those who are being exploited, there always is wont to grow up a feeling of contempt. For exploitation itself becomes easier, if we can succeed in creating a callousness towards those who are its victims. Just as whenever we go out fishing we are inclined to regard fishes as the least sensitive of all living creatures, so it becomes quite pleasant to loot the Orient, if only we can make our own moral justification easy by relegating coloured races to the lowest groupings of mankind.

Thus modern Europe, scientific and puissant, has portioned out this wide earth into two divisions. Through her filter, whatever is finest in Europe cannot pass through to reach us in the East. In our traffic with her, we have learnt, as the biggest fact of all, that she is efficient, terribly efficient. We may feel astounded by this efficiency; but if, through fear, we bring to it our homage of respect, then we ourselves need to realize that we are fast going down to the very depths of misfortune; for to do such homage is like the crude barbarity of bringing sacrificial offerings to some god which thirsts for blood. It is on account of this fact, and in order to retain her self-respect, that the whole of Asia to-day denies the moral superiority of Europe. At the same time, to withstand her ravages, Asia is preparing to imitate that ruthless aspect which slays, which eats raw flesh, which tries to make the swallowing process easier by putting the blame on the victim.

Personally I do not believe that Europe is occupied only with material things. She may have lost her faith in religion, but not in humanity. Man, in his essential nature, is spiritual and can never remain solely material. If, however, we in the East merely realize Europe in this external aspect, we shall be seriously at fault. For in Europe the ideals of human activity are truly of the soul. They are not paralysed by shackles of scriptural injunctions. Their sanction lies in the heart of man and not in something external to him. This freedom from the changeless, irrational bondage of external regulations, is a very big asset in modern Europe. Man is pouring forth his life for knowledge, for the land of his birth, and for the service of humanity. He acts thus through the urge of his own innate ideals, not because some revered *pundit* has ordained it.

It is this attitude of mind in Europe which is essentially spiritual. For true spirituality always brings freedom with it. The freedom that Europe has achieved to-day in action, in knowledge, in literature and in art, is a freedom from the rigid inanity of matter. The fetters, that we forge in the name of religion, enchain the spiritual man more securely than even worldly ties. The home of freedom is in the spirit of man. That spirit refuses to recognize any limit either to action, or to knowledge. It is courageous enough to cross over the barriers of nature, and the limitations of natural instincts; it never regrets immediate loss that may, or may not, lead to gains in a far distant future.

When the aeroplane goes up in the sky, we may wonder at it as the perfection of material power; but behind this lies the human spirit, strong and alive. It is this spirit of man which has refused to recognize the boundaries of nature as final. Nature has put the fear of death in man's mind to moderate his power within the limits of safety; but man in Europe has snapped his fingers at Death and torn asunder the bonds. Only then did he earn the right to fly—a right of the gods.

But even here the adverse forces—the titans—are alive, who are ready to rain down death from the air. But the titans are not in sole possession. In Europe, there is a constant war between the gods and the titans. Often the titans are victorious; but the victory is sometimes with the gods.

We should not count the result in mere numbers. The calculation should be based on Truth, and on the inner reality of the victory. It is therefore that the Bhagavad Gita says that Truth, even though slight, preserves us from great calamity. The manifestation of the gods is on the positive side of Truth; on the negative side are the titans. So long as we have the least response from the positive side, there need be no fear. The war of the gods and the titans is only possible where the gods are active. There can be no war where both sides are equally feeble.

It is easy enough for us, when someone reviles us for our social evils, to point at worse evils in Europe; but this is negative. The bigger thing to remember is, that in Europe these evils are not stagnant. There, the spiritual force in man is ever trying to come to grips. While, for instance, we find in Europe the evil Giant's fortress of Nationalism, we also find Jack-the-Giant-Killer. For, there is growing up the international mind, this Giant-killer, the international mind—though small in size—is real. In India, even when we are loudest in our denunciation of Europe, it is often her Giant's fortress that we long to build with awe and worship. We insult Jack with ridicule and suspicion. The chief reason for this is, that in India we have ourselves become material-minded. We are wanting in faith and courage. Since in our country the gods are sleeping, therefore, when the titans come, they devour all our sacrificial offerings, —there is never a hint of strife. The germs of disease are everywhere; but man can resist disease only when his vital force is active and powerful.

So, too, even when the worship of the blood-thirsty and false gods of self-seeking are rampant on all sides, man can lift up his head to the skies if his spirit is awake. In Europe, the whole nature of man is awake. Both matter and spirit are active. They alone become entirely materialistic who are only half men, who cripple the native majesty of the spirit before the blind repetition of unintelligent activities; who are niggardly in knowledge and palsied in action; who are ever insulting themselves by setting up a meaningless ritualism in the place of true worship; who have no difficulty whatever in believing that there is special sanctity inherent in particular forms and peculiar rites, even when their significance is neither known, nor knowable. That is why they are night and day afraid of ghosts and ghouls, gods and demons, of the calendar and the stars, of inauspicious days and inauspicious moments. Being themselves weak in spirit, they are enslaved within and enfettered in the outer world.

1929

Wealth and Welfare

The standard of living in modern times has been raised far higher than the average level of our necessity. Where the temptation of high living, normally confined to a negligible small section of the community, becomes widespread, its ever growing burden is sure to prove fatal to civilization. It forces society not only to make provision for the filling of the vessel to the brim, which has its own limit but also for the overflow. This excess, if it is for operative purposes, is a gain, and the expenditure is made true by the profit. But when it is for display and unproductive self-enjoyment then it is an absolute loss which can be suffered with impunity only within certain bounds.

The tendency towards extravagance is natural to man, it is to make manifest his power, his magnanimity. There was a time when it found its play mostly in the surroundings of a king, in the expression of a communal spirit in religion and other collective sentiments. The poorest and the meanest among the citizens found his dignity represented in the public buildings and the pomp and ceremonies of public life. This could never give rise to the personal feeling of envy or fury of insane emulation. Most of the expressions of any great surplus of life and wealth was dedicated to the community. The dark planets merely represent themselves, the radiant star, in its excess of light, represents the constellation: and the wealth reaching that degree of radiance which exceeds the obscure limits of personal necessity once did belong to the illumination of a whole society. This prevented the universal competition in wastefulness which to-day is exhausting human energy and the material resources of the earth.

In former days, in India, public opinion levied heavy taxes upon wealth and most of the public works of the country were voluntarily supported by the rich. Water-supply, medical help, education and amusement were naturally maintained by men of property through a spontaneous adjustment of mutual obligation.

This was made possible, because the limits set to the individual right of self-indulgence were narrow, and the surplus wealth easily followed the channel of social responsibility. In such a society, property was the pillar that supported its civilization, and wealth gave opportunity to the fortunate for self-sacrifice.

There are some who believe that the eradication of the idea of property will give the command spirit its full freedom. But we must know that the urge which has given rise to property, is something fundamental in human nature. If you have the power you may tyrannically do violence to all that constitutes property; but you cannot change the constitution of mind itself.

Property is medium for the expression of our personality. If we look at the negative aspect of this personality, we see in it the limits which separate one person from another. And when, in some men, this sense of separateness takes on an intense emphasis, we call them selfish. But its positive aspect reveals the truth, that it is the only medium through which men can communicate with one another. Most often and for most men, property is the only frame that can give a foundation for the creation of a personal world. It is not merely money, not merely furniture; it does not represent merely acquisitiveness, but is an objective manifestation of our taste, our imagination, our constructive faculties, our desire for self-sacrifice.

Through this creative limitation which is our personality, we receive, we give, we express. Our highest social training is to make our property the richest expression of the best in us, of that which is universal, of our individuality whose greatest illumination is love. As individuals are the units that build the community, so property is the unit of wealth that makes for communal prosperity, when it is alive to its function. Our wisdom lies not in destroying separateness of units, but in maintaining the spirit of unity in its full strength.

When life is simple, wealth does not become too exclusive, and individual property finds no great difficulty in acknowledging its communal responsibility, rather, it becomes its vehicle.

But with the rise of the standard of living, property changes its aspect. It shuts the gate of hospitality, which is the best means of social intercommunication. It displays its wealth in an extravagance which is self-centred. It begets envy and irreconcilable class division. In short, property becomes antisocial. Because, with what is called material progress, property has become intensely individualistic, the method of gaining it has become a matter of science and not of social ethics. It breaks social bonds; it drains the life sap of the community.

There are always insects in our harvest field which, in spite of their robbery, leave a sufficient surplus for the tillers of the soil, and it does not pay to try to exterminate them. But when some pest that has enormous powers of self-multiplication, attacks our food crop, it has to be dealt with as a calamity. In human society, in normal circumstances, there are a number of causes that make for wastage, yet it does not cost us too much to ignore them. But to-day the blight that has fallen on our social life and its resources is disastrous, because it is not restricted to limited regions. It is an epidemic of voracity that has infected the total area of civilization.

We all now-a-days claim our right of freedom to be extravagant in our enjoyment. Not to be able to waste as much upon individual gratification as my rich neighbour does, merely proves a poverty of which I am ashamed, and against which my womenfolk and my parasites are permitted to cherish their grievance. Thus, society, which should be our field of co-operation, has become that of competition, in which, through its tyrannical standard of respectability, all the members are goading one another to spoil themselves to the uttermost limit.

Civilization to-day has turned into a vast catering establishment. It maintains constant feasts for a whole population of gluttons. The intemperance which could safely have been tolerated in a few has spread its contagion to the multitude. The universal greed, produced as a consequence, is the cause of the meanness, cruelty and lies, in politics and commerce that vitiate the whole human atmosphere.

A civilization with such an unnatural appetite must depend for its existence upon numberless victims and these are being sought in those parts of the world where human flesh is cheap.

In Asia and Africa a bartering goes on, whereby the future hope and happiness of entire peoples are sold for the sake of providing fastidious fashion with an endless train of rubbish.

The consequence of such material and moral drain is more evident when one studies the conditions manifested in the fatness of the cities and the physical and mental anaemia of the villages, almost everywhere in the world. For cities have become inevitably important. They represent energy and materials concentrated for the satisfaction of that exaggerated appetite, which is the characteristic symptom of modern civilization. Such an abnormal devouring process cannot be carried on, unless certain parts of the social body conspire and organize to feed upon the whole. This is suicidal; but before its progressive degeneracy ends in death, the disproportionate enlargement of the particular section looks formidably great, and conceals the starved pallor of the entire body—the sacrifice of the large maintaining the small in its enormity, and creating for the time being an illusion of wealth.

The capital needed for the commerce of life accumulates in villages; the city draws upon that for its various functions of civilization. So long as these are productive and creative, it is no loss. But when a disproportionate part of it goes to supply fuel to the fire of an extravagant self-indulgence, precious materials of life are reduced to ash heaps. In a fire-play of recklessness the spendthrift exhausts his future in making a burning rocket of his immediate present, sending it up to the void in a dazzling speed of progress. But it is a brilliant process of dissolution, because by its erratic excesses the food is consumed not for feeding life but for pampering a flame of passion.

1930

The Educational Mission of the Visva-Bharati

I have been asked to speak this evening to my invisible audience about the educational mission to which I have devoted my life and I am thankful for this opportunity.

I am an artist and not a man of science, and therefore my institution necessarily has assumed the aspect of a work of art and not that of a pedagogical laboratory. And this is the reason why I find it difficult to give you a distinct idea of my work which is continually growing for the last thirty years. With it my own mind has grown, and my own ideal of education found freedom to reach its fullness through a vital process so elusive that the picture of its unity cannot be analysed.

Children's minds are sensitive to the influences of the great world to which they have been born. This delicate receptivity of their passive mind helps them, without their feeling any strain, to master language, that most complex instrument of expression full of ideas that are indefinable and symbols that deal with abstractions. Through their natural gift of guessing, children learn the meaning of the words which we cannot explain.

But it is just at this critical period that the child's life is brought into the education factory, lifeless, colourless, dissociated from the context of the universe, with bare white walls staring like eyeballs of the dead. The children have to sit inert whilst lessons are pelted at them like hailstones on flowers.

I believe that children should be surrounded with the things of nature that have their own educational value. Their minds should be allowed to stumble on and be surprised at everything that happens before them in the life of to-day. The new to-morrow will stimulate their attention with new facts of life.

The minds of the adults are crowded; the stream of lessons perpetually flowing from the heart of nature does not fully touch them; they choose those that are useful, rejecting the rest as inadmissible. The children have no such distractions. With them every new fact comes to a mind that is always open, with an abundant hospitality. And through this exuberant, indiscriminate acceptance they learn innumerable facts within a short time, amazing compared to our own slowness. These are the most important lessons of life that are thus learnt in the first few years of our career.

Because, when I was young I underwent the mechanical pressure of a teaching process, one of man's most cruel, and most wasteful mistakes, I felt it my duty to found a school where the children might be free in spite of the school.

At the age of twelve I was first coerced into learning English. Most of you in this country are blissfully unconscious of the mercilessness of your own language. You will admit, however, that neither its spelling, nor its syntax, is perfectly rational. The penalty for this I had to pay, without having done anything to deserve it, with the exception of being born ignorant.

When in the evening my English teacher used to come I was dragged to my daily doom at a most unsympathetic desk and an unprepossessing textbook containing lessons that are followed by rows of separated syllables with accent-marks like soldiers' bayonets.

As for that teacher, I can never forgive him. He was so inordinately conscientious! He insisted on coming every single evening,—there never seemed to be either illness or death in his family. He was so preposterously punctual too. I remember how the fascination for the frightful attracted me every evening to the terrace facing the road; and just at the right moment, his fateful umbrella,—for bad weather never prevented him from coming,—would appear at the bend of our lane.

Remembering the experience of my young days, of the school masters and the classrooms, also knowing something of the natural school which Nature herself supplies to all her creatures, I established my institution in a beautiful spot, far away from the town, where the children had the greatest freedom possible under the shade of ancient trees and the field around open to the verge of horizon.

From the beginning I tried to create an atmosphere which I considered to be more important than the class teaching. The atmosphere of nature's own beauty was there waiting for us from a time immemorial with her varied gifts of colours and dance, flowers and fruits with the joy of her mornings and the peace of her starry nights. I wrote songs to suit the different seasons, to celebrate the coming of Spring and the resonant season of the rains following the pitiless months of summer. When nature herself sends her message we ought to acknowledge its compelling invitation. While the kiss of rain thrills the heart of the surrounding trees if we pay all our dutiful attention to mathematics we are ostracised by the spirit of universe. Our holidays are unexpected like Nature's own. Clouds gather above the rows of the palm trees without any previous notice; we gladly submit to its sudden suggestion and run wildly away from our Sanskrit grammar. To alienate our sympathy from the world of birds and trees is a barbarity which is not allowed in my institution.

I invited renowned artists from the city to live at the school, leaving them free to produce their own work which the boys and girls watch if they feel inclined. It is the same with my own work. I compose my songs and poems, the teachers sit round me and listen. The children are naturally attracted and they peep in and gather, even if they do not fully understand, something fresh from the heart of the composer.

From the commencement of our work we have encouraged our children to be of service to our neighbours from which has grown up a village reconstruction work in our neighbourhood unique in the whole of India. Round our educational work the villages have grouped themselves in which the sympathy for nature and service for man have become one. In such extension of sympathy and service our mind realizes its true freedom.

Along with this has grown an aspiration for even a higher freedom, a freedom from all racial and national prejudice. Children's sympathy is often deliberately made narrow and distorted making them incapable of understanding alien peoples with different languages and cultures. This causes us, when our growing souls demand it, to grope after each other in ignorance, to suffer from the blindness of this age. The worst fetters come when children lose their freedom of heart in love.

We are building up our institution upon the ideal of the spiritual unity of all races. I hope it is going to be a great meeting place for individuals from all countries who believe in the divine humanity, and who wish to make atonement for the cruel disloyalty displayed against her by men. Such idealists I have frequently met in my travels in the West, often unknown persons, of no special reputation, who suffer and struggle for a cause generally ignored by the clever and the powerful. These individuals, I am sure, will alter the outlook for the future. By them will be ushered a new sunrise of truth and love, like that great personality, who had only a small number of disciple from among the insignificant, and who at the end of his career presented a pitiful picture of utter failure. He was reviled by those in power, unknown by the larger world, and suffered an inglorious death, and yet through the symbol of this utmost failure he conquers and lives for ever.

For some time past education has lacked idealism in its mere exercise of an intellect which has no depth of sentiment. The one desire produced in the heart of the students has been an ambition to win success in the world, not to reach some inner standard of perfection, not to obtain self-emancipation.

Let me confess this fact, that I have my faith in higher ideals. At the same time, I have a great feeling of delicacy in giving utterance to them, because of certain modern obstacles. We have now-a-days to be merely commonplace. We have to wait on the reports in the newspapers, representative of the whole machinery which has been growing up all over the world for the making of life superficial. It is difficult to fight through such obstructions and to come to the centre of humanity.

However I have this one satisfaction that I am at least able to put before you the mission to which these last years of my life have been devoted. As a servant of the great cause I must be frank and strong in urging upon you this mission. I represent in my institution an ideal of brotherhood where men of different countries and different languages can come together. I believe in the spiritual unity of man, and therefore I ask you to accept this task from me. Unless you come and say, 'We also recognize this ideal', I shall know that this mission has failed. Do not merely discuss me as a guest, but as one who has come to ask your love, your sympathy and your faith in the following of a great cause.

II

There is no meaning in such words as spiritualising* the machine, we can spiritualise our own being which makes use of the machine, just as there is nothing good or bad in our bodily organs, but the moral qualities are in our mind. When the temptation is small our moral nature easily overcomes it, but when the bribe that is offered to our soul is too big we do not even realize that its dignity is offended. To-day the profit that the machine brings to our door is too big and we do not hesitate to scramble for it even at the cost of our humanity. The shrinking of the man in us is concealed by the augmentation of things outside and we lack the time to grieve over the loss. We can only hope that science herself will help us to bring back sanity to the human world by lessening the opportunity to gamble with our fortune. The means of production constructed by science in her attempts to gain access into nature's storehouse are tremendously complex which only proves her own immaturity just as simplicity is wanting in the movements of a swimmer who is inexpert. It is this cumbersome complexity in the machinery which makes it not only unavailable to the majority of mankind but also compels us to centralise it in monster factories, uprooting the workers' life from its natural soil and creating unhappiness. I do not see any other way to extricate us from these tangled evils except to wait for science to simplify our means of production and thus lessen the enormity of individual greed.

I believe that the social unrest prevalent to-day all over the world is owing to the anarchy of spirit in the modern civilization.

* In reply to the question whether Machines can be spiritualised.

What is called progress is the progress in the mechanical contrivances; it is in fact an indefinite extension of our physical limbs and organs which, owing to the enormous material advantage that it brings to us, has tempted the modern man away from his inner realm of spiritual values. The attainment of perfection in human relationship through the help of religion, and cultivation of our social qualities occupied the most important place in our civilization up till now. But to-day our homes have dissolved into hotels, community life is stifled in the dense and dusty atmosphere of the office, men and women are afraid of love, people clamour for their rights and forget their obligations, and they value comfort more than happiness and the spirit of display more than that of beauty.

Great civilizations in the East as well as in the West, have flourished in the past because they produced food for the spirit of man for all time; they tried to build their life upon the faith in ideals, the faith which is creative. These great civilizations were at last run to death by men of the type of our precocious schoolboys of modern times, smart and superficially critical, worshippers of self, shrewd bargainers in the market of profit and power, efficient in their handling of the ephemeral, who presume to buy human souls with their money and throw them into their dust bins when they have been sucked dry, and who, eventually, driven by suicidal forces of passion, set their neighbours' houses on fire and are themselves enveloped by the flame.

It is some great ideal which creates great societies of men it is some blind passion which breaks them to pieces. They thrive so long as they produce food for life; they perish when they burn up life in insatiate self-gratification. We have been taught by our sages that it is Truth and not things which saves man from annihilation.

The reward of truth is peace, the reward of truth is happiness. The people suffer from the upsetting of equilibrium when power is there and no inner truth to which it is related, like a motor car in motion whose driver is absent.

1930

Meeting of the East and the West

I have felt the meeting of the East and the West in my own individual life. I belong to the latter end of the Nineteenth Century. And to our remote country in Bengal, when I was a boy, there came a voice from across the sea. I listened to it. It would be difficult to imagine what it meant for me in those days. We realized the great heroic ideal which had been held in Ancient Greece and that art which gave expression to its greatness. I was deeply stirred, and felt as if I had discovered a new planet on the horizon.

THE MESSAGE OF THE WEST IN THE 19TH CENTURY

It was the same feeling which I had when I listened to those in my family who recited verses from English literature and from the great poets of those days. Then also I felt as if a new prophet of the human world had been revealed to my mind.

You all know it was the last vanishing twilight of the Romantic West. We had been living in the atmosphere of the lyrical literature of poets like Shelley, Keats, Wordsworth, and we know what inspiration they had within them. And what it was for the rest of the world. There was an upheaval of idealism. In Europe, the French Revolution had not died out, and people were dreaming of freedom, of the brotherhood of man. They still believed in the human ideals that have their permanent value, ultimate value in themselves. And it moved my heart. I cannot express how it did move my soul.

I remember as a boy how a friend who had just read a poem came running to me in the night when I was asleep and awakened me, saying, 'Have you read this?' And he recited the lines to me, and it stirred us deeply. It was that atmosphere, that human aspect of the Western civilization which appealed to us. It was the humanity of the West. It was not anything mechanical;

it did not represent any physical or material quality. Ah, no. It was the message from the heart of the West that touched us deeply.

The West at that time believed in freedom of personality. We heard about Garibaldi, about Mazzini, and it was a new revelation, an aspect of humanity with which we were not quite familiar—the great ideal of the freedom of man, freedom of self-expression for all races and for all countries. And we had great reverence for the people who were dedicated to that dream, through their literature, and also through their practical life.

THE MODERN WEST

I may tell you what I think is the characteristic difference to-day between the East and the West. We, in the East believe in personality. In the West you have your admiration for power.

Whenever our heart is touched with something that is perfect in human nature, in its completeness, in the spiritual aspect of it, we bow our heads before it. We have a feeling of reverence for the divine in man. And I thought that this human aspect of civilization, which I saw and which I realized in the West when I was young, was something permanent that would help to save the whole world.

There are times when some particular people play the part of messengers of humanity. They come to rescue human relations from all kinds of fetters of ignorance or moral degradation and despair and weakness of will. We thought the present age belonged to the West, that they had come to save us, to save the whole world from all forms of weakness and which still remains inexhaustible. All these great revelations of history. We knew what India herself had done in olden times. We knew what Greece had offered to humanity and which still remains inexhaustible. All these great civilizations had the effect of redeeming the minds of men from fetters and narrowness, from sluggishness and stupidity.

It is evident that this modern age can belong to the West. You have the illumination, and we have been waiting for long that it should reach us in the East. And we hoped that you would come to us with a message which was universal, which had nothing provincial or exclusively national in it, and in a language that was not ashamed to have itself surrounded by an atmosphere of beauty,—a beauty that had a universal appeal.

And I say as an individual that the West and the East did meet in India in my younger days. But how short was that twilight of a vanishing age, of chivalry, of idealism higher and greater than one's nationality. That age came to an end, and you know, in what a great clash and conflagration of war and misery all over the world.

THE MENACE OF POWER

And what is the harvest of your civilization? You do not see from the outside. You do not realize what a terrible menace you have become to man. We are afraid of you. And everywhere people are suspicious of each other. All the great countries of the West are preparing for war, for some great work of desolation that will spread poison all over the world. And this poison is within their own selves. They try, and try to find some solution, but they do not succeed, because they have lost their faith in the personality of man.

They do not believe in the wisdom of the soul. Their minds are filled with mutual suspicion and hatred and anger and yet they try to invent some machinery which will solve the difficulties. They ask for disarmament, but it cannot be had from the outside. They have efficiency, but that alone does not help. Why? Because man is human, while machinery is impersonal. Men of power have efficiency in outward things; but the personality of man is lost. You do not feel it, the divine in man, the divinity which is in humanity.

I have felt it, and I have said to myself, I have repeated that song: 'Where shall I find him? Man the Great? The Supreme Man?' Not in the machinery of power and wealth shall I find the humanity of the world. If he is not in the heart of a civilization, where is he? The great man, the harvester, the music-maker, the dreamer of dreams, where is he?

Almost every day I feel my heart go back to my own country, to the personal, the dreamer, the believer in God. I seek Him, and I want to go back to my own country. I have my school there. Do not think that it is an ordinary school. I enjoy the wealth of human relationship there. Those boys and girls, they are my children. There is something that is indescribable in that school. Our relationship is spiritual—and I may not merit it, but I know that they do revere *Man* in my own person; not the schoolmaster, but something higher than that. It is not superstition. In the East we believe in personality which is above all things.

You fight against evil, and that is a great thing. I often think you should come to help us fight all those difficulties, those material evils, from which we suffer. We have been praying for centuries, that the West would really come to us, that their chivalry would help us in our trouble. We are unfortunate. We have much need, for our injuries are great. We had formerly our own system of education—that has vanished. We had our industries to help to eke out the income of those dependent upon agriculture for their livelihood, but all those industries have vanished like the autumn leaves. And we pray that the West would come to us as a member of a common humanity. We claim it from you who have wealth which is overflowing, and we are in the direst and deepest shadow of poverty and distress on our side of the world.

GANDHIJI'S SPIRITUAL POWER

We have been waiting for the Person. Such a personality as we see in Mahatma Gandhi *(applause)*. It is only possible in the East for such a man to become a great personality. He has neither physical nor material power, but through his great influence people who have been in subjection to all kinds of tyrannical power have stood up; and he is the strongest spiritual power in this world today. Not because of his political prudence, but for his spiritual influence the people believe in him, and they are ready to die for their faith. They are ready to suffer. It is a miracle that these people, downtrodden for centuries, are coming out, and without doing any injury to others, they suffer and through suffering, conquer.

And our women,—only the other day they were secluded in their own inner apartments—they have come out to follow this man, this leader. Not an association, not an organization, not a politician, but a Man! And his message goes deep into our veins. He attacks the enemies that are within us. Not like the political machinery which you have that attacks from the outside and that tries to work through the external. But he attacks the inner man. They believe in him, in this man who is not a Brahmin, for he belongs to a class of money-makers who have been despised for centuries.

PERSONALITY IN HUMAN HISTORY

When times were dark, there came a Man in other days to people who were seeking salvation, emancipation from evil. He came to their door. The babe who was born centuries ago brought exaltation to man. Not machinery, not association, not organizations, but a human babe, and people were amazed. And when all the machinery will be rusted, he will live.

I have felt that the civilization of the West to-day has its law and order, but no personality. It has come to the perfection of a mechanical order but what is there to humanize it? It is the Person who is in the heart of all beings. When you follow the atoms, you come to something which has no form, no colour. It is all abstraction; it is reduced to some mathematical formulae. But Personality goes beyond the heart of these atoms. I have seen, I have known it within me, in the depths of my feeling. And I know that only when you come to Him will there be peace.

1930

My Pictures

I

An apology is due from me for my intrusion into the world of pictures and thus offering a perfect instance to the saying that those who do not know that they know not are apt to be rash where angels are timidly careful. I, as an artist, cannot claim any merit for my courage; for it is the unconscious courage of the unsophisticated, like that of one who walks in dream on a perilous path, who is saved only because he is blind to the risk.

The only training which I had from my young days was the training in rhythm in thought, the rhythm in sound. I had come to know that rhythm gives reality to that which is desultory, which is insignificant in itself. And therefore, when the scratches in my manuscript cried, like sinners, for salvation, and assailed my eyes with the ugliness of their irrelevance, I often took more time in rescuing them into merciful finality of rhythm than in carrying on what was my obvious task. In the process of this salvage work I came to discover one fact, that in the universe of forms there is a perpetual activity of natural selection in lines, and only the fittest survives which has in itself the fitness of cadence, and I felt that to solve the unemployment problem of the homeless heterogeneous into interrelated balance of fulfilment is creation itself.

My pictures are my versification, in lines. If by chance they are entitled to claim recognition, it must be primarily for some rhythmic significance of form which is ultimate and not for any interpretation of an idea or representation of a fact.

May 1930

II

When, at the age of five, I was compelled to learn and to repeat the lessons from my textbook, I had the notion that literature had its mysterious manifestation on the printed pages, that it represented some supernatural tyranny of an immaculate perfection. Such a despairing feeling of awe was dissipated from my mind when by chance I discovered in my own person that verse-making was not beyond the range of an untrained mind and tottering handwriting. Since then my sole medium of expression has been words, followed at sixteen by music, which also came to me as a surprise.

In the meanwhile the modern art movement, following the line of the oriental tradition, was started by my nephew Abanindranath. I watched his activities with an envious mood of self-diffidence, being thoroughly convinced that my fate had refused me passport across the strict boundaries of letters.

But one thing which is common to all arts is the principle of rhythm which transforms inert materials into living creations. My instinct for it and my training in its use led me to know that lines and colours in art are no carriers of information; they seek their rhythmic incarnation in pictures. Their ultimate purpose is not to illustrate or to copy some outer fact or inner vision, but to evolve a harmonious wholeness which finds its passage through our eyesight into imagination. It neither questions our mind for meaning nor burdens it with unmeaningness, for it is, above all, meaning. Desultory lines obstruct the freedom of our vision with the inertia of their irrelevance. They do not move with the great march of all things. They have no justification to exist and therefore they rouse up against them their surroundings; they perpetually disturb peace. For this reason the scattered scratches and corrections in my manuscripts cause me annoyance. They represent regrettable mischance, like a gapingly foolish crowd stuck in a wrong place, undecided as to how or where to move on. But if the spirit of a dance is inspired in the heart of the crowd, the unrelated many would find a perfect unity and be relieved of its hesitation between to be and not to be. I try to make my corrections dance, connect them in a rhythmic relationship and transform accumulation into adornment.

This has been my unconscious training in drawing. I find disinterested pleasure in this work of reclamation, often giving to it more time and care than to my immediate duty in literature that has the sole claim upon my attention, often aspiring to a

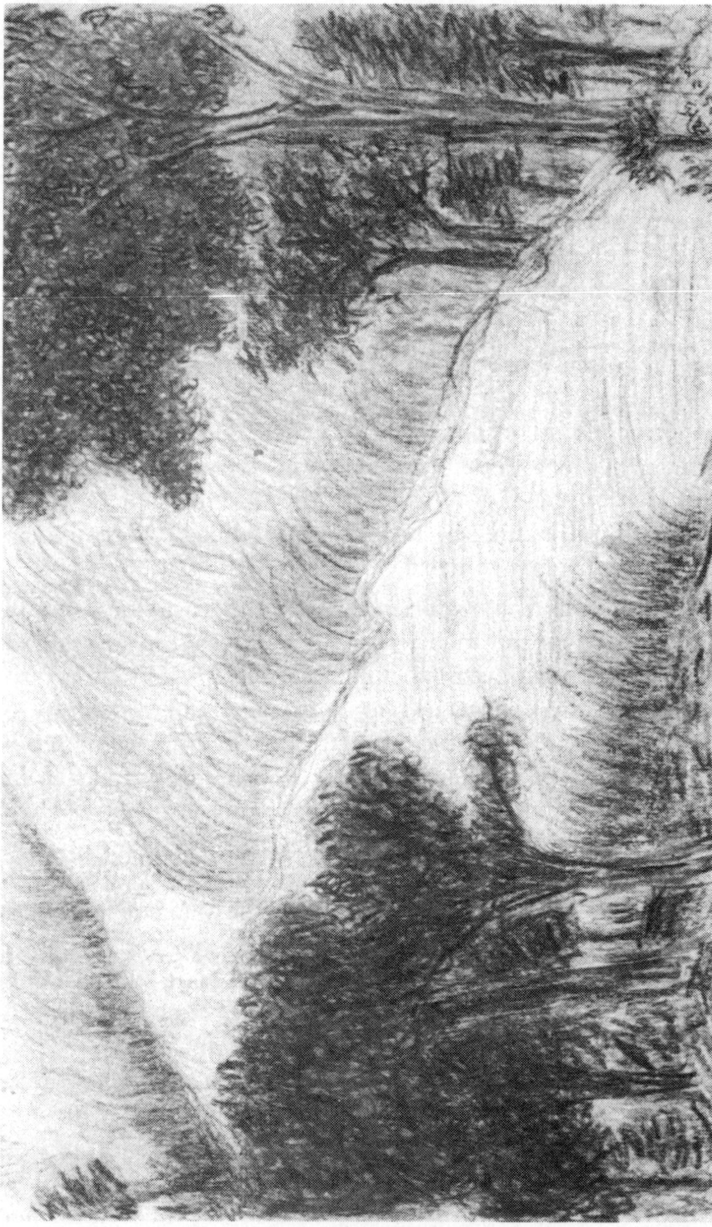

A Painting by Rabindranath Tagore (Courtesy: Rabindra Bhavan, Visva-Bharati)

permanent recognition from the world. It interests me deeply to watch how lines find their life and character, as their connection with each other develops in varied cadences, and how they begin to speak in gesticulations. I can imagine the universe to be a universe of lines which in their movements and combinations pass on their signals of existence along the interminable chain of moments. The rocks and clouds, the trees, the waterfalls, the dance of the fiery orbs, the endless procession of life send up across silent eternity and limitless space a symphony of gestures with which mingles the dumb wail of lines that are widowed gypsies roaming about for a chance union of fulfilment.

In the manuscript of creation there occur erring lines and erasures, solitary incongruities, standing against the world principle of beauty and balance, carrying perpetual condemnation. They offer problems and therefore material to the *Visvakarma,* the Great Artist, for they are the sinners whose obstreperous individualism has to be modulated into a new variation of universal concord.

And this was my experience with the casualties in my manuscripts, when the vagaries of the ostracized mistakes had their conversion into rhythmic inter-relationship, giving birth to unique forms and characters. Some assumed the temperature exaggeration of a probable animal that had unaccountably missed its chance of existence, some a bird that only can soar in our dreams and find its nest in some hospitable lines that we may offer it in our canvas. Some lines showed anger, some placid benevolence, through some lines ran an essential laughter that refused to apply for its credential to the shape of a mouth which is a mere accident. These lines often expressed passions that were abstract, evolved characters that hung upon subtle suggestions. Though I did not know whether such unclassified apparitions of non-deliberate origin could claim their place in decent art, they gave me intense satisfaction and very often made me neglect my important works. In connection with this came to my mind the analogy of music's declaration of independence. There can be no question that originally melody accompanied words, giving interpretation to the sentiments contained in them. But music threw off this bond of subservience and represented moods abstracted from words, and characters that were indefinite. In fact, this liberated music does not acknowledge that feelings which can be expressed in words are essential for its purpose, though they may have their secondary place in musical structure. This right of independence has given music its greatness, and I suspect that evolution of pictorial and plastic art develops on this line, aiming to be freed from an absolute alliance with natural facts or incidents.

However, I need not formulate any doctrine of art but be contented by simply saying that in my case my pictures did not have their origin in trained discipline, in tradition and deliberate attempt at illustration, but in my instinct for rhythm, my pleasure in harmonious combination of lines and colours.

July 1930

III

The world of sound is a tiny bubble in the silence of the infinite. The Universe has its only language of gesture, it talks in the voice of pictures and dance. Every object in this world proclaims in the dumb signal of lines and colours the fact that it is not a mere logical abstraction or a mere thing of use but is unique in itself, it carries the miracle of its existence.

There are countless things which we know but do not recognize their own dignity of truth, independent of the fact that they are injurious or beneficial. It is enough that a flower exists as a flower, but my cigarette has no other claim upon me for its recognition but as being subservient to my smoking habit.

But there are other things which in their dynamic quality of rhythm or character make us insistently acknowledge the fact that they are. In the book of creation they are the sentences that are underlined with coloured pencil and we cannot pass them by. They seem to cry to us, 'See, here I am', and our mind bows its head and never question, 'Why are you?'

In a picture the artist creates the language of undoubted reality, and we are satisfied that we see. It may not be the representation of a beautiful woman but that of a commonplace donkey, or of something that has no external credential of truth in nature but only in its own inner artistic significance.

People often ask me about the meaning of my pictures. I remain silent even as my pictures are. It is for them to express and not to explain. They have nothing ulterior behind their own appearance for the thoughts to explore and words to describe, and if that appearances carries its ultimate worth, then they remain, otherwise they are rejected and forgotten even though they may have some scientific truth or ethical justification.

It is related in the drama of *Shakuntala,* how one busy morning there stood humbly before the maiden of the forest-hermitage a stranger youth who did not give his name. Her soul acknowledged him at once without question. She did know him not but only saw him and for her he was the artist God's masterpiece to which must be offered the full value of love.

Days passed. There came at her gate another guest, a venerable sage who was formidable. And, sure of his claim to a dutiful welcome, proudly he announced. 'I am here!' But she missed his voice, for it did not carry with it an inherent meaning, it needed a commentary of household virtue, pious words of sanction which could assign a sacred value to a guest, the value that was not of the irresponsible art, but of moral responsibility.

Love is kindred to art, it is inexplicable. Duty can be measured by the degree of its benefit, utility by the profit and power it may bring, but art by nothing but itself. There are other factors of life which are visitors that come and go. Art is the guest that comes and remains. The others may be important but art is inevitable.

1930

Self-portrait *(Wax pastel on paper)*

Landscape—Dark Trees against Orange Sky *(Ink and water colour on paper)*

Face of A Woman *(Charcoal on paper)*

Landscape—Dark Trees against Yellow Sky *(Ink and water colour on paper)*

The First and the Last Prophets of Persia

In the beginning of our history when individuals gathered together not as a crowd but as a community, they instinctively realized a mysterious source of power in this meeting. They felt that it was not a mere obvious fact represented by a number, but a truth that could not be measured, counted and analysed. It was an energising force that was creative, and according to the degree of perfection in the solidarity of such gathering, it spontaneously gave rise to a richness of social life, and the beauty and wisdom that found innumerable channels of expression.

This ineffable spirit of unity is the fundamental truth of creation. When in our scientific curiosity to probe the mystery of appearance we snap the bond of relationship, the appearance itself vanishes, and what remains is some abstract mathematical formulae, invisible, intangible, unimaginable. At a certain stage of the analysis of things all that remains is named as protons and electrons, logically proving their unsubstantial existence, but not the existence of what appears in its wholeness as the rock, or flower, you or me. Some great mystery of unity binds these into individual form and character, and relates them to all things far and near; and such immensity of facts held together by an infinite spirit of unity, manifests its creative purpose in various forms and movements.

In the human world the great truth of unity was also at first realized as a power residing in the community, comprehending and transcending all individuals. This mysterious power according to the primitive people was magical, and they symbolized it in their totems and tried to invoke and propitiate it with their magical rites.

This was the first great discovery of man—the mysterious spirit of unity which was beyond the bounds of quantity that can be measured, and this is religion. But as I have already suggested, religion in its first appearance had the aspect of power, which though it gave unity to the tribe itself, created a strong division outside of it. For power is exclusive and the tribe claimed its God as the source of all powers for its own benefit.

So long as God remained as thus divided, religion became cruel and terribly unjust creating more mischief in this world than any passion that is criminal. Even to-day when God is no longer believed to be specially belonging to the tribe, he is fenced in by sectarianism which gives rise to a fierce spirit of dissension and egotistical boastfulness. Truth when tortured and mutilated becomes more heinous than untruth, and therefore when unbelievers bring proofs of the harm that religion has done to man we cannot but remain silent.

It is the mission of all great prophets to see that religion which is to give us spiritual emancipation should not itself be made a fetter to immure our soul in a dungeon of dogma and formalism giving rise to sectarian vanity that obscures our vision of the spiritual unity of man.

The first Prophet whom we know in the history of man was Zoroaster who preached God as the universal truth of unity, the eternal source of goodness and love; and it is significant that in the same soil of Persia which gave birth to him arose the other great Prophet of the modern age, Baha'u'llah, who also preached God as profoundly one, in all races, tribes and sects, the true worship of whom consists in service that has reason for its guide, and goodness and love for its inner motive principle.

We are here to-night to offer our homage to Baha'u'llah. He is the latest Prophet to come out of Asia. His life is certainly a glorious record of unflinching human search after truth; and his message is of great importance for the progress of civilization.

1930

My School

You ought to know one thing that I am by nature a poet. From my very young days, my only vocation was to express my ideas in verses, give shape to my dreams in my poems.

What was it that impelled me to take up this work for which I am not naturally fit?

When I was young, as usual, I was sent to school. Some of you may have read from the translation of my autobiography about the misadventure I had when I began my career as a student in a school. It was a terribly miserable life, which became absolutely intolerable to me. At that time I did not have the capacity to analyse the reason why I suffered, but then when I grew up, it became quite clear to me what it was that hurt me so deeply to be compelled to attend my class in that school where my parents sent me.

I have my natural love for life, for nature, and for my surroundings where I have my dear ones; and to be snatched away from these natural surroundings with which I had all my inner deeper life of relationship, and to send me an exile, to the school, to the class with its bare white walls, its stare of dead eyes, frightened me every day. When I was once inside these walls, I did not feel natural. It was absolutely a fragment torn away from life and this gave me intense misery because I was uprooted from my own world and sent to surroundings which were dead and unsympathetic, disharmonious and monotonously dull.

It could not be possible for the mind of a child to be able to receive anything in those cheerless surroundings, in the environment of dead routine. And the teachers were like living gramophones, repeating the same lessons day by day in a most dull manner. My mind refused to accept anything from my teacher. With all my heart and soul I seem to have repudiated all that was put before me. And then there were some teachers who were utterly unsympathetic and did not understand at all the sensitive soul of a young boy and tried to punish him for the mistakes he made. Such teachers in their stupidity did not know how to teach, how to impart education to a living mind. And because they failed, they punished their victim. And this was how I suffered for thirteen years of my life.

And then I left school when I was thirteen and in spite of all the pressure exerted on me by my elders, I refused to go to my studies in that school.

Since then I have been educating myself and that process is still being carried on. And whatever I have learned, I have learned outside the classes. And I believe that was a fortunate event in my life—that avoiding the schoolmaster when I was still young. And whatever I have done in later life, if I have shown any special gift or originality, I feel certain it was owing to the fact that I was not drilled into a kind of respectable education, which generally all good boys, good students, have to submit to.

And it went on like that. I took to my own work I retired in a solitary place near the Ganges and a great part of my life I lived in a house-boat, writing my poems, stories and plays; dreaming my dreams.

I went on till I gradually became known to my own countrymen and claims were made on me from all parts of my country for writings and for various kinds of help. But I kept to my solitude for the greater part of my days. It is very difficult for me to say what it was, how the call came to me to go out of my isolation of literary life and be among my fellow-beings and share their life and help them in their living.

And it is also a surprise to me how I had the courage to take upon myself to start an educational institution for our children, for I had no experience in this line at all. But I had confidence in myself. I knew that I had very profound sympathy for children, and about my knowledge of their psychology I was very certain. I felt that I could help them more than the ordinary teachers who had the delusion to think that they had proper training for their work.

I selected a beautiful place, far away from the contamination of town life, for I myself, in my young days, was brought up in that town in the heart of India, Calcutta, and all the time I had a sort of homesickness for some distant lane somewhere, where my heart, my soul, could have its true emancipation. Though I had no experience of the outer-world, I had in my heart great longing to go away from my enclosure of those walls and from that huge, stonyhearted step-mother, Calcutta. I knew that the mind has its hunger for the ministrations of nature, mother-nature, and so I selected this spot where the sky is unobstructed to the verge of the horizon. There the mind could have its fearless freedom to create its own dreams and the seasons could come with all their colours and movements and beauty into the very heart of the human dwelling.

And there I got a few children around me and I taught them. I was their companion. I sang to them. I composed some musical pieces, some operas and plays, and they took part in those plays. I recited to them our epics and this was the beginning of this school. I had only about five or six students at that time.

People did not have any confidence in a poet and they had a right to doubt my confidence in bringing up the children and truly educating them in their orthodox fashion. And so I had very few students to begin with.

My idea was that education should be a part of life itself and must not be detached from it and be made into something abstract. And so when I brought these children around me, I allowed them to live a complete life. They held perfect freedom to do what they wished, as much liberty as was possible for me to give them. And in all their activities I tried to put before them something which would be interesting to them. I tried to arouse their interests in all things, in nature's beauty and the surrounding villages and also in literature, through play-acting, through listening to music in a natural manner, not through merely class teaching.

They knew when I was employed in writing some drama and they took an intense interest as it went on and developed, and in the process of their rehearsal they got through a great deal more of reading of literature than they could through grammar and class-teaching. And this was my method. I knew the children's mind. Their subconscious mind is more active than the conscious one, and therefore the important thing is to surround them with all kinds of activities which could stimulate their minds and gradually arouse their interests.

I had musical evenings—not merely music classes, and those boys who at first did not have any special love of music, would, out of curiosity, listen to our songs outside of the room, and gradually they too were drawn into the room and their taste for music developed. I had some of the very great artists of our land and while they went on with their work, the boys could watch them and saw day by day how those works developed.

An atmosphere was created and what was important, this atmosphere had provided the students with a natural impulse to live in harmony with it. In the beginning it was easier to feel this, when I had only a few students; I was then almost their only companion and teacher and it was truly the golden age of our school. I know that the boys who had then the privilege of attending that institution look back on those days with much love and longing. But as the number grew, and it became more and more expensive for me to carry on the school in my own way. In the first place, we in our country have the tradition that it is the teacher who has the responsibility to give education to those who come to him to be taught, and in our country there were students who used to have free tuition, also their lodging free in their teacher's house. It was the teachers who acknowledged their own responsibility. They had the privilege of being educated, and they owed it to society that they should help their students and in return should not claim anything in the shape of fees or remuneration.

And this was our custom from the olden days and I began like that. Free tuition, lodging and boarding and all necessities of life, I supplied to my students out of my own poor resources. But you can imagine with the modern condition of life it was not possible to continue like this, because now you have to get the help of teachers whose salaries are high and there are other expenses which daily seem to increase. I find it impossible now to keep that idea in the heart of this institution that teaching should be a duty of the teacher to impart to the students and that it should not have the atmosphere of a shop where you can buy commodities with money. I was compelled to give up this idea and now gradually it has taken the shape of the ordinary school.

Only I tried my best to have some aspect in the school which they did not have in their orthodox schools. The teachers shared the common life with the boys, it was a community life. In the sports and festivals the teachers and the students fully co-operated with each other. It was not like a cage in which the birds are fed from the outside, but it was like a nest which students themselves co-operated in building up with their own life, with their love, with their daily work and their plays.

I believe that we still have this true to a great extent. It is difficult owing to the fact that my colleagues with whom I have to work are brought up in a different manner, not having the same chance as I had to play truant when they were young and give up their school-days. They have their own ideas about education, and it is difficult wholly to get rid of them. And so something alien to the central ideal does creep into this institution through those who are there to help me. I had in the beginning to struggle very hard with my teachers, not with the students, as very often happens in other schools. But I had to take sides with the boys when they were punished for no fault of their own, but that of their teachers. I had to be firm and defend the boys, which offended my teachers. I remember one day a new teacher came and when he found that some of the boys were doing their lessons up on the tree, he was furious because of this want of discipline on their part. I had then to protect the boys from the schoolmaster. I told him that when these boys grew up to his age they will not have the great privilege of climbing up to the trees to do their lessons. They would become more respectable and keep away from mother-nature.

But I believe that the atmosphere has been created and it is going on. Now it has grown. The number of the students is increasing year by year, which is not always an advantage. But it cannot be helped.

Another aspect which is of later growth is that the number of girls has been increasing. The co-education system is quite a new thing in India. But it has been working perfectly. We have had no cause for complaint. And very often the boys and girls go out together on excursions; the boys help the girls in bringing fuel and fetching water and the girls cook the dinners for the boys and everything is managed by mutual help. That is a great education in itself.

There is another factor which I consider to be important. I always try to get from outside of India, from Europe and from the Far East, lecturers, who come to the school to teach and also to share the simple life of the school with our students. This is another factor creating the atmosphere of this place. Our boys are very natural in their relationship with those foreigners, guests and visitors. My idea is that the mind should find its freedom in every respect, and I am sure that our children have through their early training freedom from the barriers of country and race and creeds and prejudices. And it is always difficult to get rid of those when we grow up and even it is sedulously cultivated in our school-books and also by the people who wish the boys to be proud of their own exploits and running down other countries. And this is really clinging to certain prejudices which are considered nationalistic. And with the help of these visitors I have tried my best to make the minds of our boys more hospitable to the guests who come to us and I think I have been successful.

Then there are other activities. We have in the neighbouring villages some primitive people who need our help and we have started some night-schools and our boys go there and teach them. Then you have the village work in connection with our institutions and those boys who have the opportunity to study the conditions of our village life and to know how to help them efficiently through scientific and up-to-date methods of cultivation and of fighting diseases. To impart not merely academic information, but how to live a complete life is, according to me, the purpose of education.

The only thing I have not been able to provide our boys with is science, owing to the enormous expense it would entail, which in a poor country like ours, is difficult to meet. I have not yet been able to arrange for it. Our students and I hope that some day it will be possible for me to fill up that deficiency.

This is the idea which I have in my mind and in spite of my lack of means, my poor resources, I have done something. Those who have been able to visit our institution can tell you how we have been helping the villages. It is not only for providing needed relief to the villages but also for the educational value of the work itself that children should be trained in the heart of such activities. The villages are the cradles of life and if we cannot give it what is due to it, then we commit suicide. Modern civilization is doing it, depriving the villages of life-stuff and draining away everything from the villages to the pampered towns. Because I believe in this, I have brought my students around this village work which we have started in order to give them the proper training for helping the villagers. I think this is, in short, the idea which I have in mind in my school.

1931

International Goodwill

I wish to thank you for your words of welcome and for your approval of my work. I have been requested to speak a few words about international goodwill, but as this subject is so obviously controversial I hesitate to deal with it. I wish you could have had someone else more competent to deal with it.

One thing which I have realized in the East is that it is rather difficult in the Western Continent to cultivate the international mind. There are certain obstacles in the way which are militating against it. There is the spirit of individualism which has been so much raised by your culture in the West. Then it is apparent also that you have got here politics, and such politics as create differences between nations which are the cause of so much of the spirit of fighting and contention, making peace difficult to attain. We have also the same spirit of egotism in the people in the East, but I believe there is more community of interests there than excessive individualism.

It was during my voyage to America, I suppose, in 1916, that nationalism was first presented to me in its true light. When I came to Japan I had a chance of observing something that deeply hurt my mind. I saw the trophies won from the Chinese people being exhibited there. It was just after China had been humiliated by the Japanese people. It struck me as vulgar and vainglorious that these people should forget everything and show this spirit of bragging. It was almost childish that a self-respecting nation should indulge in such a thing. It came to me very strongly owing to the fact that naturally the Japanese are very courteous and take an immense amount of trouble to make life beautiful and poetical. Because of this intense nationalism in abstract form, humanity is obscured, and that is why the Japanese did not see the shame of indulging in such a display. I feel that this nationalism smothers the higher spirit of man which you often find in the individual.

I am not competent to deal with international relationships between different countries, but, as I have said, your politicians really represent the spirit of aggressiveness which leads towards separateness. I know you are trying to do something to rectify the mischief through the League of Nations, but the nations are not represented by their idealists but only by their politicians. I do not think it is right that the nations should be represented by their politicians in a work which has for its object peace all through Europe. To my mind it is like a band of robbers being asked to organize the police department. (Laughter and applause)

What I have in my own mind is to try to create an atmosphere of mutual sympathy in my own institution. Amongst my own students I have done my best to create that atmosphere. This institution is outside political entanglements, and it is the one institution in which the students are natural to those visitors who come from the West or from other Eastern countries.

I have attempted to create this atmosphere in co-operation with some of the great men from Europe. When travelling through European countries, I sent out my appeal to some of the great scholars. My plan was not merely to teach my scholars, but to work so as to create an atmosphere of cultural co-operation. Many from the West responded to my invitation. I had great scholars from France, from Germany, from Czechoslovakia, from Italy, from Norway and from other countries, and we have had help from Englishmen and Americans.

I have also had great help in my parallel work, which is my village reconstruction work. We have had students from all parts of the world, as well as from other provinces besides Bengal in my own country. This is the kind of practical work which I am trying to do, and even in the midst of this great cyclone of political restlessness in my country I do hope that institutions of this nature will be able to spread their influence to these shores.

It is to counteract this evil of separateness and to have a free channel of communication in a full spirit of sympathy and co-operation that I have dreamed of a day when you in England would come to us, not merely as members of the ruling class, or members of a bureaucracy, but in a detached manner, spreading human love among the people.

1931

Lectures in Iran and Iraq

I. 'SALUTATION TO THE SPIRIT OF PERSIA'

The springtime is hospitable. Her birds in their music, her flowers in their fragrance speak a language which is universal needing no translation to explain them. They make no discrimination in favour of their own land of origin, and their call of beauty which is God's own voice of love comes direct to my heart even though I am a traveller from a far away shore.

The poet also represents the eternal springtime of hospitality. His message is in his music which invokes the harmony of perfection for all humanity, his invitation is to the comradeship in a festival of love's union.

Persia's introduction came to me when I was a boy. It was that of the ideal Persia, the Persia of the poet, the Persia which sends her welcome in songs to strangers across all barriers of geography.

My father was a great scholar. He was intoxicated with Hafiz verses. When I was a boy I often used to listen to his recitation of those poems, and he translated them to me with a fervour of enjoyment that touched my heart.

The vision of Persia was invoked in my imagination by the voice of your own poets, who brought to my mind's sky the breath of your spring breeze with the enchantment of its blossoming roses and nightingales' songs. My arrival in your land today is therefore a continuation of the same enchantment and I am glad to mingle my voice with the rejoicing of life which has broken out in the air of your beautiful country fragrant with the perfume of orange blossoms.

It brings to my mind once again how my father to the end of his days derived deep consolation from your poets' songs assimilating them in his devotional life.

It is fortunate for me that I am able to come to lay my thankful thoughts to the shrines of your great poets. I wish it could have been done on this auspicious occasion in a poet's own manner. But unfortunately I feel like a specimen bird in a museum showcase where the rigid wings are unable to display their dance of a colourful life. My voice is muffled in an alien language, which cannot rhythmically respond to my muse. And therefore the true token of my reverent gratitude I offer in unuttered words to the undying memory of your poets and my salutation to the immortal spirit of Persia in which were cradled and in which still live the spirits of those singers.

17 April 1932

II. 'THESE TWO LANDS SHOULD MEET IN LOVE'

Reply to the Welcome by the Indians of Siraj

It is proper that you should feel just as proud of the country which you have made your home for the present, as for your own land of birth. In your lives these two lands should meet in love and join in a common quest of truth. It rests upon you to justify the fair name of your country, to attract your friends here to whatever is worthy and enduring in India by the example of your personal lives. In China and Japan, the different countries of the world wherever I have met Indians, the same thought of the great responsibility that rests upon them has come to my mind. In China our people have had to act against the interest of their hosts—I cannot tell you how much it pains me to think of this. We must follow the traditions of our olden days when India sent to her neighbouring countries messengers of love. However meagre our individual powers may be, we cannot spare ourselves in contributing to this ideal which our great ancestors have left for us. Be true to India, and true to Iran, serve humanity which comprehends the welfare of both.

19 April 1932

III. TO THE ARMENIANS

Friends,

I thank you from the depths of my heart for your warm welcome. I feel that you are one with me in fellowship and share with me the belief that humanity is one, that differences of race and religion cannot stand in the way of our common pursuit of truth and love.

Friends, I have come here to this great land with that faith in man which is sorely needed in this strife-ridden tired world of today. Risking the strain of a difficult journey, in my old age, I have come here to seek new confirmation of my faith in the linked destiny of man. And I am thrilled by what I have seen and felt in this country which under a great monarch, one of the greatest men of this age, has already achieved. Iran today has not only proved the majesty of its own soul but shed the luster of its glory far and wide inspiring humanity with a new vision of fulfilment. Asia is awake today, she is once more now to offer her spiritual gift to the world, the message of brotherhood, of freedom, of federation in the task of establishing peace and goodwill.

I know that you of the Armenian community too now share the era of freedom and well-being which is in this land and that you feel an urge to contribute to this country the fruits of your own unique culture. Your community has its own particular genius for civilization with which you must enrich the country where you have gained freedom, hospitality and fellowship. Together with your friends, the people of this country of which you form a part, you must joyously set to work in leading this country onward towards perfection. This great land has won my heart as it surely has won yours, and it is a happy occasion for me to share with you the inspiration of creative enthusiasm which fills the atmosphere of this country today.

IV. REPLY TO THE WELCOME BY THE ISPHAHAN MUNICIPALITY

First of all let me express my gratitude for the hearty welcome you have accorded to me and then let me go on and offer you an explanation which I owe to you.

The question may naturally come to your mind as to the object of my visit to your country. I take this opportunity to let you know my secret.

There was a time on olden days when the Emperors of Nations used to invite poets and wise men from other lands. Now that custom is no longer there. The modern statesman at the head of the political machinery has very little concern for culture. His connection with other countries is mostly guided by diplomacy upon which human considerations dare not infringe.

I have had my invitation as a poet and a thinker from different people of Europe and of the Orient. But I could never imagine that such invitation would come to me from those who are at the helm of administration; the kings and rulers of nations. Yet unusual though it is, this rare privilege has come to me. It was a day of great surprise and joy for me when I heard from my friend Dinshaw that an invitation was coming to me from His Imperial Majesty, Reza Shah Pahlevi, King of Persia.

This is in keeping with the tradition of the East when the Emperors represented the humanity of their nation and accepted their duty to establish communication with foreign lands. The revival of this spirit in modern Iran has given me a new hope for Asia, and you can well understand that I accepted with delight the gracious invitation from your monarch.

We, poets, thrive upon the sympathy and approbation of our fellow beings. Let me confess to you that I have no hankering for honour. I consider honour to be fit for the dead, who have done their work and earned their grand memorial stones. Our homage is to their eternal spirit which beckons to us afar. But love is for the living—who need warm fellowship which inspires them to progressive efforts and worthy achievements. My work is to arouse your joy in things of beauty, and I claim your love through which my voice may reach your heart.

We speak with the multitude as one of them, not from the formal aloofness of a preacher or teacher who affords you moral guidance. The altitude of a public platform is not for us poets. I wish I could sit in your midst and open the doors of your heart by the magic of rhythmic utterances. And then I could gather my dues from you in words of love if I have been successful in moving your hearts with my music. We poets manifest through our songs the simple and perennial truths of this life and your confirmation reaches us when you share them with us and are glad.

India's poet has come to Iran with this burden of a joyous song. I sing to the new humanity, today, of the dawn which has appeared in the horizon, and touched the Orient with a golden promise. Through your great King a glorious renewal of your country's life has begun. There is in the atmosphere the stir of joyous activity. I see in your faces the hopes of a magnanimous future. I welcome this renascence in Iran, and carry in my heart the conviction that it will spread all over Asia. Humanity, in the West and the East, suffers acutely from a pessimism born of spiritual apathy. We must break through it and offer once again to the whole world the message of the East, the message of freedom and love which comprehends the welfare of all races and peoples.

Before I leave let me offer to you the love of a wayfaring poet, my grateful appreciation of the delightful days spent in your midst in this city of great beauty. My heart is laden with the memory of your warm friendliness which has made my stay here so happy and fruitful and brought me so near to your heart.

27 April 1932

V. AT TEHRAN

The different races of Asia will no doubt have to solve their own national problems alone according to their own temperament and needs, but the torches held up on their path of progress will send their beckoning lights to each other thus creating a comradeship of culture, a brotherhood of path-seekers. We remain obscure like dark stars when we are inarticulate. When our national genius is active in trimming its lamps and lighting up its surroundings, the illumination it produces spreads a bond of minds far and wide, proving that man is one in spirit.

Before I conclude let me tell you what has been the strongest attraction that has brought me to your country not heeding my physical infirmity and the risks of a difficult journey. In the East we bend our heads before all that is humanly great and not merely what is mechanically perfect. We hail him as great who conquers circumstances because he has conquered himself. In other words we are worshippers of personality. Even in my own corner of India I seemed to have felt the glamour of the greatness of the present ruler of Persia revealing to my mind a vision of a new morning at the verge of a distant skyline. We were sure that a masterful man, a builder of the destiny of a nation has at last appeared in our neighbourhood.

5 May 1932

VI. ADDRESS AT THE TEHRAN LITERARY SOCIETY

Friends,

I thank you for this invitation from the literary club of Tehran. It is natural that I the poet from India should find my place in your midst. Let me hope that you do not expect a regular speech from me, formal and decorous, that you agree with me that it is as absurd to make a poet deliver speeches as to use a flute for a fishing rod or a fencing stick. I am reminded of a similar occasion in China, when the literary people of Peking invited me to a picturesque garden on the hill and after lunch was over asked me to tell them about my ideas on art and literature. I spoke simply sitting in their midst, I was not condemned to be banished to a high platform aloof form my listeners. My place is with you, and not above you, so that I wish today also I could sit with you on the same level in this beautiful garden, and tell you what is in my heart.

It is not at all easy to define fundamental facts of existence such as art is. It is as indefinable as life itself. We only know that the spirit of life that manifests itself in a rose gives a definitely concrete form and character to an impulse which is indefinite and abstract. It has no other ulterior purpose than to fashion a unique form from elements that are amorphous like those of carbon, nitrogen, hydrogen and others having no resemblance whatever to their final result. But this form of a rose is not important in itself, the form which is a limited fact that can be measured and analysed. It is a mysterious dynamic quality imported to it that helps to make the rose transcend all its immediate facts. In this it is not only a thing but it is a thing which has its significance of beauty inexplicable and measureless. A value has been given to it and not merely a substance. This value, this ineffable quality of delight-fulness is maintained by a perpetual rhythm which creates a synchronous rhythm in our own consciousness.

The meaning of art is like that of life itself. Its inner impulse offers its ultimate explanation only in its outer manifestations. That they have come into being like a rose, like a star and have compelled our recognition of them as an inevitable expression of reality is enough. Like life art has its expressions that are dynamic, they constantly give an impetus to our minds and create ripples of various patterns in them which we call emotions. These are artistic emotions, being pure and having no consequence in life beyond their activities in our imagination. Art like life reveals in a rhythmic play of appearances for its own sake.

Before I had come to you, possibly some of you had heard of me, read my writings and admired them. In fact, you had already been acquainted with that aspect of mine which was most significant. Yet when you heard that I was coming to your country an expectation must have been aroused in you which gave you an eagerness of delight. But what is the reason? It must be this that a *knowledge* about myself was not enough but an *image* of me was needed for your complete satisfaction. By that nothing could be added in your mind to all the important factors about myself; only the several ideas about a poet of my name that you already had possessed are going to be focused in a centre and formed into a definite image of reality. This image is not absolutely similar in all your minds and its emotional reactions are also varied according to your temperaments. But its unique definiteness gives satisfaction to your faculty of imagination which seeks to realize its visions in completeness. After the sight of me the picture that is impressed in your mind is an inner work of art, it is a mental image that has a living character.

But of what use is this image of a poet to you? If I were an engineer or a politician you could fix in your memory my figure with an association of some immediate usefulness such as building of bridges or carrying on diplomatic missions. But the image of a poet can have no appeal of utility in your mind.

In fact, all true images that are vivid give us a disinterested satisfaction even if their biographical associations have no importance. The sense of reality which is pure because detached from facts that either compel our recognition for urgent purposes of life or are overlooked because of their apparent insignificance, is delightful. In our storehouse of imagination we have such innumerable images of all that have been significant to us for their own sake, that have added wealth to our consciousness, making our life richer for us, even when they are mingled with the memory of sorrows and sufferings. In fact, these are the materials out of which our life is truly built up—the life of ideal reality. The images which have found their permanence in our minds through the selective process of life, in other words which are most real for us give us our individuality of character. Human art is also busy creating images of ideal reality; our history reveals its character by producing these images and making its choice from them for its treasure of undying worth.

This world is a world of images. The clouds, the skies, the mountains and rivers are part of a common being to which we belong. The trees stand silently around giving us the delight of an intimate companionship, we enjoy the pageantry of leaves and flowers and fruits, the colours and forms in which they abound. We enjoy them because they are not vague, they are real and delightful to us. Because they have some quality of harmony which we call beauty, which makes their reality impressively inevitable and immediate to our minds. We take joy in the springtime blossoming of new life not for any virtue which we know as usefulness but simply because through a fulness of reality it rouses response of reality within us. It delights us by the sheer fact of its existence which is co-extensive with ours.

I had some knowledge of Persia even before my coming. I had read something of your history and geography, and formed some idea of your people and your country. My imagination was aroused through your great poets whose call had come to me even though I had no direct access to them. I used to dream of a Persia where *bulbuls* made love to the roses, where in dreamland gardens poets sat round their wine cups and invoked visions of ineffable meaning. But now that I have come to your country my dream has been formed into a concrete image finding its permanent place in the inner chamber of my experience. It is a definite gain added to the store of all my things of beauty that are joy for ever. I have visited Saadi's tomb; I have sat beside the resting place of Hafiz and intimately felt his touch in the glimmering green of your woodlands, in blossoming roses. The morning sun coming through the iron lattice work wrote its shadow scripts over his tomb; it was the same sun that lighted up the face of his beloved centuries ago. It fell upon my forehead with the memory of an eternal love episode in which we all seemed to have taken part. The past age of Persia lent the old world perfume of its own sunny hours of spring to the morning of that day and the silent voice of your ancient poet filled the silence in the heart of the poet of Modern India. Altogether it was an image which waited for its perfection in my mind since the far-off days when I was a boy and listened from my father to the cadenced music of your great poet.

Every individual has something of a poet within his heart seeking fulfilment through experiences which give a sense of ultimate reality. Man is glad because the sky is blue, because water flows and flowers blossom; not because they are useful and profitable like cheque books and motor cars, but because they are what they are. Our gift of imagination is satisfied through them, they are real to us though we cannot explain them.

God as poet inspires us—the poet within our hearts. In his sunrises and sunsets, green grass and living water he speaks to us as a comrade seeking our response in joy. And I am sure he is glad as a mortal poet is when we enjoy his creations. His great work is to delight our heart, not to convince us of the usefulness of things.

I have always felt that when I do useful work for my fellow beings God praises me, but when I sing to them I win his love. The world of utility we must recognize, its laws we must understand. If we fail to do so we shall be punished. But the world of beauty waits and waits; and even if we pass them heedlessly by the roses will smile, and be beautiful, and wait silently for our auspicious recognition. We are not punished if we callously ignore the ceaseless service of love which is in this universe. Therefore when we enter the heart of existence through love, the Master Poet is happy. He has given us freedom to be apathetic, to accept his creations or to reject them. When the great moment arrives, when our sensitive mind is moved by the fulness of reality, the music which flows from his infinite love reaches us, and our deepest purpose of being is fulfilled.

And then we also come out with our gifts of love, with our creations of beauty which we offer to him for his delight. When I saw your great ruins, Persepolis, your great architecture in Isfahan, your paintings and frescoes I felt that this was the homage of humanity to the Great Poet; the answer of man to God's call of love.

Poets and artists seem to bring their greatest gifts, and ask: 'Art thou satisfied, my Master? Thou hast made us partners in thy joy, pouring thy gifts of love upon us; now we have come to offer thee our best from the depths of our own love for thee.'

And the answer comes from Him to us, from our Master who is also our Friend: 'I have used my power for millions of years in fixing the foundation of this world, burned it in fire, hammered it with earthquakes. After ages of toil came the first flower, the birds sang, life appeared on earth—then was my dream fulfilled. And yet I waited. My joy sought the confirmation of your delight, the answering creations of your love.'

His world of beauty surrounds us, our life is his gift of love. The play of love begins—*lila* as we call it in India—now is to be the union of our human civilization of beauty with God's own world of creation, and be blessed.

My friends, let us not bring discord into this beautiful world, something which is perverse and disharmonious with creation. Roses and nightingales, sunshine and green foliage, they are tuning up the harp of creation—let us join with them.

Let us not be greedy, ugly and destructive, ruled by passions which belie our nature. It has gone on too long, this desecration of our sacred world, which bears the touch of God's own hand. Do you not see how man is creating suffering, tightening the bonds of slavery on weaker nations, exploiting hospitality and kindness for cruel diplomacy? Do these harmonise with starlight, and wide fields, the call of eternity which comes from far horizons? Our deeds are an insult and untold injury to the world fashioned by our Master, and we have to bow our heads in shame for what man has done to man.

God wishes man to manifest his greatness. Science has entered nature's storehouse and is successfully utilising the wealth of its resources. For that we have to be proud. But what have we done to the world of beauty? Have we been equally successful in exploring its inner significance and making accessible to all its endless wealth of delight, fertilising the toil-hardened desert of destitution? No, on the contrary—the more we add to our machines, and our mechanisms of utility, the more we are being alienated from the eternal world of truth and beauty. We lose our heads over our mechanical achievement, we miss our right to be happy. We have learnt to tyrannize and destroy. We have failed to win our freedom by surrendering to love.

This, my friends, is all I have to say to you, I who belong to the brotherhood of a useless tribe called poets. You must use your wisdom in mastering mechanical power, there you have a great field of work. But let me remind you of your responsibility in the human world of love. I claim no right to advise you, to speak from a higher platform, but I claim a corner in your hidden heart where I can talk to you as a friend. If I am fortunate you will receive me there and recognize me as one who seeks to fulfil God's own dream of love.

9 May 1932

VII. MY VISIT TO PERSIA

Persia has been a great inspiration to me. The whole country under the powerful statesmanship of her great King Reza Shah Pahlevi is marching on ahead very fast. Persia is being unified;

her baffling customs and superstitions ruthlessly eliminated; her educational and social foundations are being securely established on a sane healthy nationalism which is in harmony with the modern age. As an Indian it gave me great pleasure to see with my own eyes what a people can achieve under the stress of freedom, how the enthusiasm of nation-building can radically change conditions which are the result of age-long accumulated inertia and dependence on others.

The problem in India is more complicated but what I say to our Government is that they should leave us alone to our destiny and let us solve our own problems in the light of experiment and efforts and necessary suffering. We need the wisdom born of experience and initiative, and must face reality in our own way so that we may exploit the full potentialities of our people.

When others talk of our communal conflicts, linguistic differences and various social disharmonies they conveniently forget that Europe also, even a short time ago, was in no better plight and yet she did not unmanfully accept her limitations as inevitable; she has struggled through her dark periods at immense sufferings and sacrifices which have been worthily rewarded by access to a people's eternal right to self-rule. Spanish Inquisitions, witch-burning, Catholic and Protestant warfares, anti-scientific campaigns and fanaticism—you can go on adding to such unenviable activities of Europe till you come to the Great War when science and modernism only helped to intensify the savagery of fratricidal combat.

Let the people of Asia profit by the lessons which their brothers in the West have to teach us. Truth and freedom are for all, and we shall be proud to accept the gifts of modern Western Science adapting them to the needs of our national genius, our special traditions and circumstances. India is on her path to self-realization; she cannot afford to waste her priceless spiritual and intellectual resources in enforced emulation of ready-made ideals from outside; she must evolve her own civilization unhampered by her dead past or her modern political servitude. My visit to Persia has given me faith in the power of the Eastern peoples to assert themselves and quickly find their way to a united manifestation of their undying heritage in spite of conflict and difficult economic circumstance.

23 May 1932

VIII. REPLY TO THE WELCOME BY THE EMPEROR OF IRAN

I heartily thank your Majesty for the kind invitation to your kingdom and the hospitality graciously offered to me tonight.

Not being a man of any political importance, not having any significant place in the confederacy of nations that are swaying the material destiny of the present-day world I might have considered such an honour as ill-fitted to a person like myself. But I am certain that it is meant for the cause I espouse and the vocation that I claim to be mine own. And therefore I must never shrink from it in false modesty but congratulate one of the modern rulers of me and shapers of history for the recognition he has offered to a member of the fellowship of poets whose mission it is to light lamps along the unending path of human culture. I cannot help rejoicing at the fact that in spite of an insistent preoccupation of utilitarian urgency of this machine-driven age a man of letters finds his welcome in this distracted world for any service he may have rendered to humanity in her all but repressed desire for spiritual self-realization.

In ancient Asia the men whose function was to make human mind fertile with living wealth of beauty and noble aspiration received their highest rewards from the monarchs not merely in a spirit of patronage but that of a high responsibility and cultured appreciation. I am sure that this individual fact of a poet belonging to a distant corner of the earth and speaking a different language finding his seat of welcome at your Majesty's table this evening is not a mere accident but has a deeper historical significance. It is a generous gesture of the national self-respect of a renascent Asia, its expression of the intellectual hospitality to all manifestations that transcend temporal standard and indicate our path to inner perfection. Human civilization has crossed the boundaries of racial and national segregation.

We are today to build the future of man on an honest understanding of our varied racial personality which gives richness to life, on tolerance and sympathy and cooperation in the great task of liberating the human mind from the dark forces of unreason and mutual distrust of homicidal pride of sect and lust of gain. I pray that Iraq may realize this great responsibility of a coming civilization.

Iraq, the land where great historical ages have mingled their glories, lying in the central zone of traffic between West and East may rightly hope to become one of the living links of a coming federation of the peoples of the world. With her vision of far-away beckoning horizons, her glittering atmosphere and the vast voice of her sky, her twin great rivers flowing down through shining centuries of splendour, let her win her right to a boundless freedom in a world of greatness and proclaim under her high-vaulted heavens the majesty of the spirit of man which is the sacred shrine of the spirit of God.

At the conclusion let me read the verse which I have specially written for the occasion and which may be translated thus—

The night has ended.
Put out the light of the lamp
of thine own narrow dark corner
smudged with smoke,
the great Morning which is for all
appears in the East.
Let its light reveal us to each other
who walk on the same path
of pilgrimage.

25 May 1932

IX. ADDRESS TO THE COMMUNITY OF WRITERS

Let me offer my heartiest thanks to His Majesty King Faisal who has graciously invited me to his kingdom enabling me personally to come in touch with the great and ancient civilization of Iraq.

It is a real inspiration to me to be present here at this moment when this old nation is being born anew and the ferment of creative life is shaping its culture towards a glorious fulfilment of freedom rich in the mystery of self-expression. I feel herein the atmosphere of stimulus of youth which stirs the continent of Asia today with the urge of a new age of achievement.

Unfortunately, as you know, my age and health make it difficult for me to cross the barriers of distance and my habits of a sequestered life; and, therefore, it is physically impossible for me to fulfil your expectations, to do much in return of your welcome which is so overwhelming in its kindness.

I am told that this invitation today has been extended to me chiefly on behalf of the literary circles of Baghdad. It is in the fitness of things that the first public reception should be given me by the Community of writers to which I am proud to belong. It fills my heart with delight to know that I am already familiar to you through my works, some of which have been translated into your language, and have won their home in your hearts. This proves, once more, that in the realm of literature there is no distinction of races, that our ideas can freely meet and mingle and build together the vision of a perfection which comprehends the good of the Eternal Man.

Human history has been cruel to man. The greed of the strong has spread its meshes over the weaker races, injuring and exploiting them to feed its own unholy appetite. Humanity is torn by suffering and suspicion, by a disharmony which has wrought havoc in the very depths of our life on earth. It is for us of the Brotherhood of Letters, to rescue humanity from this misery of unnatural relationship, to lift the peoples of different countries to a higher altitude of being. To whichever land we may belong, this must be our common mission on this plane of united effort, to achieve goodwill between man and man, establish a secure foundation of fellowship which will save humanity from suicidal war and the savagery of fanatical superstitions.

We must usher in the age of reason, of co-operation, of a generous reciprocity of cultures which will reveal the richness of our common humanity.

With this fervent desire in my heart, my friends, I have come to your midst. Let me unburden my heart of this secret which has been at the bottom of my present visit to your country.

I have come to appeal to you, my brothers, to join hands with us in fighting the menace of mutual suspicion, of diplomatic double-dealing which tears out the heart of the civic life of humanity today. In the most glorious period of your history, Arabia dominated over half the world, East and West, and even now her sway over India is living in our spiritual and intellectual life through the vast population of Mahomedan we have in our midst. Let your voice reach us once again across the Arabian Sea carrying its majesty of a universal ideal; send us once more your men of faith who will bring together our different communities under the banner of fellowship, of love which admits no difference of race or religion.

In the name of all that is sacred and eternal in Man, in the name of your great Prophet and for the sake of the reputation of your great Religion, I appeal to you to advocate the cause of human fellowship, the tolerance of different creeds and customs and sympathetic neighbourliness necessary for civilized life of co-operation. Our religions have assumed a fratricidal ferocity of barbarism rending the heart of India, poisoning her racial memory and thwarting her progress towards freedom. Let your poets and thinkers, whose words soar above all prejudices and passions bred of dark unreason, help us to bring my unfortunate country to a sober state of life, to sane mentality that knows how to pursue its own path of welfare and save itself from an utter moral devastation. Let me remind you, my brothers, that a mere success in fulfilling the political and economic needs of one's own immediate surroundings is not enough for the responsibility of national self-expression; but your voice must transcend the limits of your own time and country so that your judgment for the moral cause of humanity must find a great utterance when the occasion comes, as has become urgent today in India, where your co-worshippers at the shrine of God are waiting for your guidance.

May 1932

Asia's Response to the Call of the New Age

Man the great appears in the drama of human history from age to age choosing different lands of birth. For many centuries man's creative manifestation had the continent of Asia for its stage, revealing a manifold wealth of civilization. Today the luminous expression of the human personality is in the great continents of the West. Often we try to dwarf its reputation by labelling it as materialistic; but no race can build the heights of greatness on the quicksands of unspirituality. The pure materialist is a pure barbarian drifting in a fortuitous world of chance and circumstance which holds no abiding principles and can yield no permanent foundation. Scientific truths can be won only by those who can give full value to them in ardent faith. This faith is spiritual, this power of unflinching devotion to truth. The Western nations have conquered truth by spiritual endeavour that frees our mind from all intellectual delusions and it is this power which sustains their triumphant position in the world today.

With the diminishing vigour of our physical body its expressions grow more and more mechanical. With the choking up of the channels of her living efforts and aspiration the creative life of Asia languished, dead custom invaded her daily existence, religion and art hardened into unchanging tradition that checked all freedom of thought. This lack of confidence in reason and right relationship with the world of reality is materialistic; it is this which reduces man to slavery and destitution.

On the other hand, the signs of imminent danger which appear today in the Western civilization are due to the same reason. Scientific intelligence and power have made it masterful, rich in certain gifts of truth. But when the relationship between man and truth is contaminated then truth itself comes round and takes revenge. Europe has made science the vehicle of her greed and has hurt the very spirit of science which is disinterested and high above all clamour of profit-hunting. When excess of passion in any form becomes the principal motive power in man's nature then he is wire-pulled by it like a mechanical doll and is powerless to check his blind movements even when urged by reason. Such uncontrollable convulsive spasms of greed or of anger, of jealousy or of suspicion are truly materialistic, however intelligent may be their method and means. The reason of this degradation is not in the use of machinery itself, it lies in spiritual lacunae, in emergence of primitive barbarism in some civilized form. When a free lunatic hurts himself, then it is not the external freedom which is the cause of his hurt but lunacy itself, and if he is a skilful one his danger is all the more fatal.

When I was young, I read with deep pleasure the literature of the West; and my acquaintance with the mind that has the intellectual honesty revealed by the West in her science moved me to profound veneration for its great exponents. Today through this world-wide pursuit of truth in science and other high forms of culture the Eternal Man finds its manifestation. It was to know this great humanity, the ever-awake spirit of Man that one day I took leave of my home for a far away pilgrimage to Europe in the year 1912.

That journey I consider to be auspicious. Because we are Asiatics, a protest against Europe seems to run in our blood. Since the time that its pirates of land and sea have gone out to exploit the weaker continents, from the 17th century onward, the European races have irretrievably damaged their own reputation in the East. But coming to Europe I first discovered that the simple humanity of the peoples and the organized humanity of nations do not belong to the same category. Just as the natural body and the heavily armoured body are different in their attitude and manner; the former expressing the character of life, the latter imitating the machine. I found that there is no difficulty in accepting the natural man as one's own. The humanity that is expressed in him is attractive, is worthy of respect. I loved him, I hailed him in regard and our feelings were reciprocal. It is rare good fortune to be able to know the Eternal Man amongst unknown humanity in a foreign country.

But for that very reason my mind was troubled. It was obvious to me that the peoples' character in the West is being constantly moulded by their passionate political preoccupation and a furious competition of diplomacy with their neighbours; and not only mechanization in their economic world but also in their own inner nature is growing fast. The sole fulfilment of a machine is in achievement of result which in its pursuit of success despises moral compunctions as foolishly out of place. This aspect of the West, darkly designing, is constantly turned towards Asia callously revealing to us its materialism, its tendencies that are mainly for exploitation of victims. I remember, recently in, Iraq a man of eminent position asked me, 'What do you think of the English?' I said, 'The best of them are among the best in humanity.' He smilingly asked, 'What about the next best?' I remained silent. There was a danger of intemperate language if I had tried to answer just then. In Asia the greater part of our business is with this next best. They are large in number, their influence is wide, the memory of their dealings with us lies deep in the minds of multitudes of our people. Their human dealings are not for us and gradually even for their own people they are growing rarer.

I came back home. Soon afterward began the Great War in Europe. Then it was found that the Western people were using science for devastation of the human world. The conflagration set by it has died down, but the embers are still glowing in fierceness. Never in the history of humanity has there been such an appalling orgy of evil. It is this which I call materialism, which gives rise to a moral inertia, that paralyses our will and intelligence even when we are aware of the fatal danger that threatens us.

In the meantime life in Asia has become restless and self-assertive. The reason is, in spite of the unremitting pressure of Europe she has completely lost her true hold upon Asia's mind. Once even when being exploited and beaten Asia acknowledged Europe as in every way superior to herself. Today from one end to the other of Asia there is no longer any feeling of respect for Europe, and even fear in their mutual dealing is fast losing its force. It is impossible for Asia today to lower her prestige before

Europe, because, of the latter's prestige nothing remains but military browbeating. Everywhere with a slight smile she is asking, 'But what of these who are the next best?'

Today we are born at the end of an epoch in the history of humanity. Perhaps in the drama of Europe the scene is being changed for the fifth act of the play. Signs of an awakening in Asia have slowly spread from one end of the horizon to the other. This glow of a new dawn above the eastern mountain ranges of humanity is indeed a great vision—it is a vision of freedom. Freedom, not only from external bondages, but from those of slumberous inaction and disbelief in one's inner power.

What I say is that if Asia is not fully awakened then there is no deliverance for Europe as well. The fatal arrow for Europe lies in the weakness of Asia. The heavy load of suspicion, hostility and hatred, of untruthful diplomacy and spying which Europe carries on her back is due to her grabbing for pieces and portions of the weak Asiatic continent. Rapidly grows the weight of her war armaments; having spread her marts of business far and wide, today at last in an unfathomable sea of wealth, her penury becomes evident.

Once I went out to eastern Asia to welcome there the birth of the new spirit of humanity. Then in the easternmost sky of Asia was fluttering the triumphant banner of Japan, encouraging new hope in the heart of Asia. I experienced joy, yet my mind was deeply disturbed. I realized that though Japan by mastering European science had found her national safety she at the same time had introduced for her future an element of grave danger that is sure to demoralize her international relationship. In Japan's blood has entered the poison of imperialism from the West; and her neighbours are wrought to a state of agonized apprehension. In history the favourable wind does not always blow in one direction. That day is certain to come when the debts due to the weak will have to be paid up to the last penny. Japan in her relation to others has not learnt the art of civilization, which heals and unites, she has trained her hands under Europe in the science that inflicts wounds with efficiency. This fatal cleverness will not spare the hand that wields it when the time comes at last.

The calamity to which I refer is tragic not merely because of its political consequences but for its cruel destruction of human possibilities. If the new age has indeed come to Asia then let Asia give voice to it in her own special idiom of civilization. If instead of that she imitates the roar of Europe, even if it be a lion's roar, yet it will sound pitifully unreal.

However, it cannot be ignored that the East is growing restlessly conscious of her own destiny which she is determined to save from Western encroachment. Just when Turkey was about to collapse there appeared Kemal Pasha. It was a fateful moment. The patched up parts of the Turkish Empire had been rent asunder by the impact of the world war, but this had indeed been a blessing in disguise. Under the guidance of a masterful personality it now became possible to establish securely, on a normal basis and in an efficient modern manner the compact and reduced empire within narrower boundaries. The word 'Empire' means an unnatural expansion of girth gained by tying together with ropes and strings bodies which are not vitally related to each other. When in evil days these bonds get loosened, it becomes difficult indeed to save the units of this unnatural congregation from mutual buffetings. Turkey freed from the burden of bigness became really integrated. England had then planned her downfall by letting loose Greece upon her territory. On the political platform of England sat Lloyd George and Churchill in close conspiracy. In 1921 the European Allies met in conference in England. The proposal that was then made by Bakir Sami, the Turkish representative of Angora, was a willingness to curtail a great part of Turkey's political claims. But Greece doggedly stuck to her own ambitious plans down to the last limit, England supporting her from behind.

In this time of trouble Turkey made alliance with France. With Persia and Afghanistan too she had a good understanding. In the second part of her treaty with Afghanistan we find:

'The contracting parties recognize the emancipation of the nations of the East and confirm the fact of their unrestricted freedom, their right to be independent and to govern themselves in whatever manner they themselves choose.'

In the meantime continued the war between Greece and Turkey. Even now Angora repeatedly sent in vain proposals of peace to end bloodshed. At last all negotiations ended with the defeat of Greece. Under the dictatorship of Kemal Pasha was inaugurated a new era in the development of Turkish civilization with Angora as capital. This new Turkey acceded Europe's lessons in efficiency adjusting them to her own genius of civilization. Kemal Pasha said that Turkey must break through the dark dungeon of unreason belonging to ages that are dead. The Turkish Minister of Justice said, 'Mediaeval principles must give way to secular laws. We are creating a modern, civilized nation, and we desire to meet contemporary needs. We have the will to live, and nobody can prevent us.'

When after his victory in the war Kemal Pasha entered the city of Smyrna he convened a big public meeting and addressing the women, said, 'We have won undoubted victory in the war but that victory will be meaningless if you do not help us. Let the victory of education be yours, then you will be able to accomplish much more than we have done. Everything will be futile if you do not progress with steadfast mind and heart along the path of modern life. Everything will be futile if you do not accept the responsibility that has been placed upon you by scientific habits of living.'

This fact has been acknowledged in eastern Asia by Japan and in Asia's westernmost corner by Turkey: that we must be strictly honest in our relationship with the material world and must organize our life upon a rational basis. This is true, but let us not forget that there are other aspects of the problem for to consider. The sphere of Europe's success has long attracted our attention, but where Europe has failed is in the depths, at the very root, and so this has been kept hidden from us. That greed of Europe which forced opium down China's throat does not die with the death of China; its poison is everyday entering into the vitals of Europe's own life. The supreme method of self-preservation is to establish honest dealings with the human world and not merely with the world of matter. Europe has ignored this truth, thus making all her problems dangerously involved. Japan in her blind imitation of western aggressiveness, has forgotten this eternal principle, but the eternal laws of universe will not forget. History is a record of sudden surprises which have overwhelmed nations too sure of their inviolable superiority to moral laws.

It is good to know clearly how western Asia is responding to the call of this new age. The time has not come yet for mature results on a big canvas of organized endeavour. Here and there signs and symptoms appear which do not compel attention, but the way of truth is to appear in the guise of the small. Asia has not yet swept off the clinging weeds of ancient habit which choke the currents of her national being but through various ferments in her social and economic life her psychology is being rapidly adjusted to a new order of civilization. All over Asia the cry has arisen that sectarian religion cannot be allowed to wreck the natural basis of community life, bringing dissensions where a common economic, social and historical background should preserve an inevitable continuity of co-operation. When during a farewell feast given to an Englishman of high official position in the Government of Palestine he said, 'Palestine is a Muhammadan country, and its government should, therefore, be in the hands of the Muhammadans, on condition that the Jewish and Christian minorities are represented in it,'—then Mufti Haji-el-Husaini of Jerusalem answered, 'For us it is an exclusively Arab, not a Muhammadan, question. During your sojourn in this country you have doubtless observed that here there are no distinctions between Muhammadan and Christian Arabs. We regard the Christians not as a minority, but as Arabs.' I know that unfortunately this catholicity of mind all people, rather, most people, do not possess, but it is a great event that these creative ideas are raising everywhere in Asia their banners of rebellious life.

Observe what is happening in another unknown corner. In Russian Turkestan the Soviet Government in a very short time has imparted new life to the desert-dwelling tribes of Asia. The reason for this rapid success is that at least on the part of the Government there is no obstacle of greed which would deliberately create factions amongst the masses in order to rifle their resources for unholy profiteering. The people have full scope to develop their native gifts and gain inspiration from the modern age. Small nations, disunited and scattered all over this desert area, have each been given the right to establish their own republican government. Moreover, arrangements for spreading education amongst them are rich and various. I have said before in separate context that in the vast empire of the Soviets comprising a large number of nations and races there is nowhere today any fight or discord between the different communities. During the imperialistic government of the Czar this was a matter of daily occurrence. The mental health which makes it possible to maintain the purity of human relationships is a product of education matured in an atmosphere of freedom. Through the benefits of both education and freedom Asia's humanity today is striving to rescue itself from self-humiliation and the tyranny of circumstance. However intense may the pain and suffering of this initial stage of our struggle for freedom nothing can be more glorious than this effort, than this unstinted self-sacrifice for the achievement of human dignity. Through Asia's freedom the freedom of the whole world will be made safe. Let us not forget that imperialistic Europe today is herself entangled in the bondage which she has imposed upon alien peoples who are dragging her down with their weight of wretchedness.

When, in 1912, I went to Europe an English poet asked me, 'What is it that has specially brought you to this country?' I said, 'I have come to know the humanity of Europe.' The lamp of mind has been lighted in Europe as well as the lamp of life, therefore man is not obscured there, his self-revelation is ceaseless and spontaneous. The other day in Persia also I was asked the same question. I said, 'I have come to Persia to know the true Persian.' I could never hope to see him if in that country humanity had lain hidden in intellectual obscurity. I knew that the lamp already lit. Therefore, when the call came from Persia I felt eagerly ready to start on my pilgrimage.

1932

Can Science be Humanized?

There is no meaning in such words as spiritualising the machine; we can spiritualise our own, being which makes use of the machine, just as there is nothing good or bad in our bodily organs, but the moral qualities that are in our mind. When the temptation is small our moral nature easily overcomes it, but when the bribe that is offered to our soul is too big we do not even realize that its dignity is offended. Today the profit that the machine brings to our door is too big and we do not hesitate to scramble for it even at the cost of our humanity. The shrinking of the man in us is concealed by the augmentation of things outside and we lack the time to grieve over the loss. We can only hope that science herself will help us to bring back sanity to the human world by lessening the opportunity to gamble with our fortune. The means that science has produced through which to gain access into Nature's storehouse is tremendously complex which only proves her own immaturity just as simplicity is wanting in the movements of a swimmer who is inexpert. It is this cumbersome complexity in the machinery which makes it not only unavailable to the majority of mankind but also compels us to centralise it in monster factories, uprooting the workers' life from its natural soil creating unhappiness. I do not see any other way to extricate us from these tangled evils except to wait for science to simplify our means of production and thus lessen the enormity of individual greed.

I believe that the social unrest prevalent today all over the world is owing to the anarchy of spirit in the modern civilization. What is called progress is the progress in the mechanical contrivances; it is in fact an indefinite extension of our physical limbs and organs which, owing to the enormous material advantage that it brings to us has tempted the modern man away from his inner realm of spiritual value and thus the balance is lost. The attainment of perfection in human relationship through the help of religion and cultivation of our social qualities occupied the most important place in our civilization up till now. But today our homes have dissolved into hotels, community life is stifled in the dense and dusty atmosphere of the office, man and woman are afraid of love, people clamour for their rights and forget their obligations and they value comfort more than happiness and spirit of display more than that of beauty.

Great civilizations in the East as well as in the West have flourished in the past because they produced food for the spirit of man for all time; they tried to build their life upon their faith in ideals, the faith that is creative. These great civilizations were at last run to death by men of the type of our precocious schoolboys of modern times, smart and superficially critical, worshippers of self, shrewd bargainers in the market of profit and power, efficient in their handling of the ephemeral who presume to buy human souls with their money and throw them into their dustbins when they have been sucked dry, and who, eventually, driven by suicidal forces of passion, set their neighbours' houses on fire and are themselves enveloped by the flame.

It is some great ideal which creates great societies of men; it is some blind passion which breaks them to pieces. They thrive so long as they produce food for life; they perish when they burn up life in insatiate self-gratification. We have been taught by our sages that it is Truth and not things which saves man from annihilation.

The reward of truth is peace, the reward of truth is happiness. People suffer from the upsetting of equilibrium when power is there and no inner truth to which it is related, like a motor car in motion whose driver is absent.

1933

Rammohun Roy

Rammohun Roy inaugurated the modern age in India. He was born at a time when our country, having a lost its link with the inmost truths of its being, struggled under a crushing load of unreason, in abject slavery to circumstance. In social usage, in politics, in the realm of religion and art, we had entered the zone of uncreative habit, of decadent tradition, and ceased to exercise our humanity. In this dark gloom of India's degeneration Rammohun rose up, a luminous star in the firmament of India's history, with prophetic purity of vision, and unconquerable heroism of soul. He shed radiance all over the land; he rescued us from the penury of self-oblivion. Through the dynamic power of his personality, his uncompromising freedom of the spirit, he vitalized our nations being with the urgency of creative endeavour, and launched it into the arduous adventure of realization. He is the great path-maker of this century who has removed ponderous obstacles that impeded our progress at every step, and initiated us into the present era of world-wide cooperation of humanity.

Rammohun belongs to the lineage of India's great seers who age after age have appeared in the arena of our history with the message of Eternal Man. India's special genius has been to acknowledge the divine in human affairs, to offer hospitality to all that is imperishable in human civilization, regardless of racial and national divergence. From the early dawn of our history it has been India's privilege and also its problem, as a host, to harmonize the diverse elements of humanity which have inevitably been brought to our midst, to synthesize contrasting cultures in the light of a comprehensive ideal. The stupendous structure of our social system with its intricate arrangement of caste testifies to the vigorous attempt made at an early stage of human civilization to deal with the complexity of our problem, to relegate to every class of our peoples, however wide the cleavage between their levels of culture, a place in a cosmopolitan scheme of society. Rammohun's predecessors, Kabir, Nanak,

Dadu, and innumerable saints and seers of medieval India, carried on much further India's great attempt to evolve a human adjustment of peoples and races; they broke through barriers of social and religious exclusiveness and brought together India's different communities on the genuine basis of spiritual reality. Now that our out-worn social usages are yielding rapidly to the stress of an urgent call of unity, when rigid enclosures of caste and creed can no more obstruct the freedom of our fellowship, when India's spiritual need of faith and concord between her different peoples has become imperative and seems to have aroused a new stir of consciousness throughout the land, we must not forget that this emancipation of our manhood has been made possible by the indomitable personality of the great unifier, Rammohun Roy. He paved the path for this reassertion of India's inmost truth of being, her belief in the equality of man in the love of the Supreme Person, who ever dwells in the hearts of all men and unites us in the bond of welfare.

Rammohun was the only person in his time, in the whole world of man, to realize completely the significance of the modern age. He knew that the ideal of human civilization does not lie in the isolation of independence, but in the brotherhood of interdependence of individuals as well as of nations in all spheres of thought and activity. He applied this principle of humanity with his extraordinary depth of scholarship and natural gift of intuition, to social, literary and religious affairs, never acknowledging limitations of circumstance, never deviating from his purpose lured by distractions of temporal excitement. His attempt was to establish our peoples on the full consciousness of their own cultural personality, to make them comprehend the reality of all that was unique and indestructible in their civilization, and simultaneously, to make them approach other civilizations in the spirit of sympathetic cooperation. With this view in his mind he tackled an amazingly wide range of social, cultural, and religious problems of our country, and through a long life spent in unflagging service to the cause of India's cultural reassertion, brought back the pure stream of India's philosophy to the futility of our immobile and unproductive national existence. In social ethics he was an uncompromising interpreter of the truths of human relationship, tireless in his crusade against social wrongs and superstition, generous in his cooperation with any reformer, both of this country and of outside, who came to our aid in a genuine spirit of comradeship. Unsparingly he devoted himself to the task of rescuing from the debris of India's decadence the true products of its civilization, and to make our people build on them, as the basis, the superstructure of an international culture. Deeply versed in Sanskrit, he revived classical studies, and while he imbued the Bengali literature and language with the rich atmosphere of our classical period, he opened its doors wide to the spirit of the age, offering access to new words from other languages, and to new ideas. To every sphere of our national existence he brought the sagacity of a comprehensive vision, the spirit of self-manifestation of the unique in the light of the universal.

Let me hope that in celebrating his centenary we shall take upon ourselves the task of revealing to our own and contemporaneous civilizations the multi-sided and perfectly balanced personality of this great man. We in this country, however, owe a special responsibility, not only of bringing to light his varied contributions to the modern age, but of proving our right of kinship with him by justifying his life, his maintaining in every realm of our nation's existence the high standard of truth which he set before us. Great men have been claimed by humanity by its persecution of them and wilful neglect. We evade our responsibility for those who are immeasurably superior to us by repudiating them. Rammohun suffered martyrdom in his time, and paid the price of his greatness. But out of his sufferings, his power of transmuting them to carry on further beneficent activities for the good of humanity, the modern age has gained an undying urge of life. If we fail him again in this day of our nation-building, if we do not observe perfect equity of human relationship offering uncompromising fight to all forms and conventions, however ancient they may be in usage, which separate man and man, we shall be pitiful in our failure, and shamed for ever in the history of man. Our futility will be in the measure of the greatness of Rammohun Roy.

1933

'To the Youth of Hyderabad'

My young friends

I have come to the time of my dismissal from life's workshop barred from further earning. My old age keeps me pensioner to my departed days; I am only allowed to live upon my past achievement. The thoughts that I have thought, the dreams that I have dreamed, gradually matured and came to the season of fruitage, till some of them shrivelled and died and some were ripe for reaping and were garnered.

I began my life of thinking and aspiration when the world in some of its aspects and temperament was different from what it is to-day. It was the fresh period of dew-washed dawn; the horizon radiant with hope, and the young adventurers of truth showed no sign of fatigue or wavering on their path of pilgrimage. We had our faith in what we considered as things of permanent value in human life; we believed in a principle of perfection which has its everlasting truth in a divine personality having an innermost bond of relationship with human spirit. I know that the sceptic age we are passing through is busily digging at the root of all things, developing a belief that the dead soil is the original source and not any mysterious life working within an invisible seed; that the ultimate meaning of man is the animal and spirit is matter. But we must be certain that an age of spiritual nihilism such as the present one, can never be lasting, that it is like the sun under eclipse carrying for the moment a sweeping shadow of doubt across its eternal normalcy of light.

To-day I am here to repeat what I have said before on different occasions, for I believe that by repeating we truly respect the ideas that come to us as precious for our own life and joysome as our gifts to others. We dare to repeat ourselves when we are over seventy, for long before this time we ought to have been able to discover what are those finds of ours that dust has not covered and use has not tarnished. I no longer believe in originality that must pose itself new to justify its name. I hope, if I am worthy of the reputation that fortunately has come to me, that I have spoken some words in my life that will bear repetition to my contemporaries and to listeners who will represent the future.

At the same time keep in your mind that the thoughts that do not become frayed by constant handling that do not tire us to insensitiveness are simple, they are ashamed to play acrobatic feats of cleverness. In other words they are not like the supercilious rockets that dare to make faces at the stars and only contribute ashes to the dust. But they are like our house-lamp with its eternal mystery of beneficent light tenderly watchful, made all the dearer by its daily familiarity.

Though I have confessed that I began my youth in a comparatively remote past from that of yours, do not imagine that I dwell in, a time of dilapidated desolateness, that I am no longer modern. Old age has not its reliable witness in any back number of calendar but in the stagnation of spirit that disclaims its own future. It is cynicism even of the most modern make which is truly senile, for it has lost its vision of the beyond, the deeper meaning of existence. The cleverness which is up to date seems to exult when saying that the doctrine of spirit has grown obsolete and our present-day education only relies upon external forces and material foundations. But I say over and over again that the impertinence of material dominion is extremely old; the revelation of spirit in Man is ever modern though born of an immemorial past. Occasionally it has its time of silence, it disappears from our view, so that its price has to be paid for winning it back. And a poet's mission is to attract the voice which is yet inaudible in the air; to inspire faith in the dream which is unfulfilled; to bring the earliest tidings of the unborn flower to a doubting world.

So many are there to-day who do not believe. They do not know that faith in a great future itself creates that future; that without faith you cannot recognize your opportunities. Prudent men and unbelievers have too often pulled down the shelters of man, but it is the eternal child, the dreamer, the man of simple faith, who has built up civilizations. This creative genius, as you will see in your own past history, had faith which acknowledged no limits and dared danger and death for the sake of immortality.

I have often been asked for messages and it ever troubles me. It is like asking the tree to talk and bird to lecture. As a poet it is for me to maintain only my instinct of happiness even when the gloom is on the sky and the land; the pulsation of light throbs in my own pulse when it vibrates in the unseen depth of the dark. I am here to offer you that unreasoning joy of mine and a hope for life's renewal which thrills in the roots of our being when the spring unloosens the coils of the winter before we come to know it.

Permit me, rather, to share your hope in the stirring of life over this land and I shall join in your rejoicing. I am not a philosopher: therefore keep for me room in your heart, not a seat on the public platform. I want to win your trust and love now that I am close to you, with the faith that is in me of a fruitful future, when your country rises and gives expression to its own spirit, a future in the glory of which we shall all share.

I hope that some profound dreamer will spring from your midst to sing a psalm of life everlasting and all-embracing love, and, therewith overcoming all differences bridge the chasm of passions which has been widening for centuries. Age after age, in Asia great souls have heartened the world with showers of grace and immense assurance, Asia is again waiting for such world spirits to come and carry on the work, not of fighting, not of profit-making, but for interlinking bonds of human relationship.

Intently I hope that the time is at hand when we shall once again be proud to belong to a continent which produces the light that radiates through the storm-clouds of trouble and illuminates life's pilgrim's path.

The organized power of the machine is ready to smite and devour us, from which we must be rescued by that living power of spirit which grows in strength, not through mere addition, but through comprehension. It is right that we should borrow science from the West, her treasure of intellect, which is immense and whose superiority we must acknowledge. But it would be degradation on our part, and an insult to our ancestors, if we forget our own wealth of wisdom, which is of far greater value than a system that produces endless materials and a physical power that is always on the war path.

For the last century and a half, the cultured nations of the earth are rapidly giving up their faith in a spiritual perfection of life. Their doom is upon them, and it is daily growing evident that the terrific glow we see upon the western horizon is not the glow of sunrise, or of a new birth-fire, but is a conflagration of passion. Of that, only those who have lost their mind gazing at the sudden eruption of a flaming success, can be enamoured, as the victim is enamoured of the glittering serpent's eyes.

I say emphatically that we must accept truth when it comes from the West and not hesitate to render it our tribute of admiration. Unless we accept it our civilization will be one sided, it will remain stagnant. Science gives us the power of reason, enabling us to be actively conscious of the worth of our own ideals.

We have been in need of this discovery to lead us out of the obscurity of dead habit, and for that we must turn to the living mind of the West with gratefulness, never encouraging the cultivation of hatred against her. Moreover, the Western people also need our help, for our destinies are now intertwined.

No one nation to-day can progress, if the others are left outside its boundaries. Let us try to win recognition from the West with all that is best and not base in us, and think of her and deal with her, not in revenge or contempt, but with goodwill and understanding, in a spirit of mutual respect.

There was a time when Asia saved the world from barbarism. Then came the night, I do not know how. And when we were aroused from our stupor by the knocking at our gate, we were not prepared to receive Europe who came to us in her pride of strength and intellect. The West came, not to give of its best, or to seek for our best, but heartlessly to exploit us for the sake of material gain. And Europe overcame Asia not through our admiration for her freedom's message and service of humanity but overpowering greed and the racial pride that humiliates. We did Europe injustice because we did not meet her on equal terms. The result was the relationship of the superior and the inferior; and since then we have been imagining that we are destitute. We are still suffering from want of self-confidence. We are not aware of our own treasures.

Let us free ourselves from the meshes of self-abasement, the most deadly of all impositions from the West. Let us prove that we are not beggars. This is our responsibility. Recover from your own homes things that are of undying worth. Then you will be saved and will be able to save all humanity. Some of us, of the East, think that we should ever imitate the West. I do not believe in it. For imitation belongs to the dead mould; life never imitates, it assimilates. What the West has produced is for the West, being native to it. But we of the East cannot borrow the Western mind nor the Western temperament. We want to master the idiom which belongs to our own genius, the river-bed which naturally carries our own thought streams to the ocean of world culture.

You who are young do not need any props of textbook maxims, or I pruning hooks of prohibition, for the guidance of your conscience. Your soul has its natural star, which carries hope for the unborn day of your country's future. I am here to sing the hymn of praise to youth, I who am your poet, the poet of the young.

You know that fairy tale—the eternal story of youth which is current in almost all parts of the world. It is about the beautiful princess taken captive by some cruel giant and the young prince who goes out to free her from the dungeon. Do you not remember when you heard it in your boyhood, how your blood was stirred, how you felt yourselves sitting out in the guise of that prince to rescue her back to freedom. To-day the human soul is lying captive in the dungeon of Giant Machine, and I ask you, my young princes, to light up the fire of enthusiasm in your hearts and rush to rescue the human soul from the tyranny of the relentless greed which keeps it chained.

There are some people, who are proud and wise and practical, who say that it is not in human nature to be generous, that men will always fight one another, that the strong will conquer the weak, and that there can be no real moral foundation for man's civilization. We cannot deny the facts of their assertion: the strong have power in the human world: but I refuse to accept this as a revelation of truth.

I bring to your mind those early days, when nature produced huge monsters. Whoever in those days could dare to believe that they were doomed to perish under their enormity of flesh? Then happened a miracle. All of a sudden, in the midst of that orgy, of bigness and physical strength, appeared Man, without weapons and without protection, naked, small and tender of skin. He discovered the full power of his intellect and stood up against the might of muscle with weapons shaped by his mind, and he held his own and survived.

But the true victory of man's life was not fulfilled even then. For to-day his descendents, half-brute and half-man, have risen up all over the world in terrible form, more devastating even than those pre-historic monsters who, at their worst, were frankly physical. This combination of brute and intellect has given rise to a terror which is stupid in its passion and yet cunning in its weapons; it is blindness made efficient, and, therefore, more destructive than all other forces in the world.

We in the East had once tried our best to muzzle the brute in man and to control its ferocity. But to-day the titanic forces of intellect have overwhelmed our belief in spiritual and moral power. Power in the animals was, at least, in harmony with life, but not so are bombs, poison gases, and murderous aeroplanes, the death dealing weapons supplied by science.

We should know this, that truth—any truth that man acquires, is for all. Money and property to a limited extent belong to individuals, but you must never allow truth to slave for your personal aggrandisement—which means selling God's blessings to make profit. Science also is truth. It has its own place, in the healing of the sick, in the giving of more food, more leisure for life. But when with its help its votaries crush the weak, rob those who are asleep, exploit nature for impious ends, then this sacrilege of theirs will produce punishment and their own weapons will be turned against them as the signs are numerous to-day.

The great human societies are the creation not of profiteers, but of dreamers. It is not Carthage which lives through ages but Athens does. The millionaires who produce their bales of merchandise in outrageous quantities, have never built an alter to the eternal spirit of perfection. To-day it is they who are about to destroy the temples that others have built driving the spiritual man to a ragged vagabondage.

My young friends, I gaze across the distance of age at your young faces, beaming with intelligence and eager interest. I am approaching the shore of the sunset-land. You stand over there with the rising sun. My heart reaches out to your hearts and blesses them.

I envy you. When I was a boy, in the dusk of the waning night, we did not fully know to what a great age we had been born. The meaning of that age has become clear to-day. I believe there are individuals all over the world this moment who have heard its call.

What a delight it may be for you, and what a responsibility, this belonging to a period which is one of the greatest in the whole history of man, when all races have come close to each other. We realize the immense significance of this age dimly, in the light of a glowing fire of pain, and do not even fully know what form it is going to take.

The seed, in which life remains self-contained does not reveal its complete truth. Even when the sheath bursts, it is not known in what shape its life will manifest itself, what fruit the branches will bear.

In human history, the forces of creation oftenest work in the dark, but it is the privilege of man to give them direction, and thus to take part in the unfoldment of his own destiny. The sheath of the present age has burst. It lies in you, in each one of you, to give this new-born life the impulse of growth.

I ask you again what have you got, what out of your own house can you offer in homage to this new age? You must answer this question. Do you know your own mind? Your own culture? What is best and most permanent in your own history? You must at least know that before you can save yourselves from the greatest of insults, the insult of obscurity, of rejection. Bring out your light and add it to this great festival of lamps in world illumination.

I cannot, however, bring myself to believe that any nation in this earth can be great and yet be materialistic. I have a belief that no people in Asia can be wholly given to materialism. There is something in the blue expanse of its sky, in the radiance of its sun, in the silent depth of its night, in the varied wealth of its seasons, which somehow gives to us an understanding of the inner music of existence, and I am sure you are not deaf to it.

To be able to love material things, to clothe them with tender grace, and yet not be grossly attached to them, this is a great achievement. Providence expects that we should make this world our own, and not live in it as though it were a rented tenement. We can only make it our own by some service, and that service is to lend it love and beauty from our soul. From your own experience you can see the difference between the beautiful, the tender, the hospitable; and the mechanically neat and monotonously useful.

Gross utility kills beauty. We have now all over the world a huge production of things, huge organizations, huge administrations of empire, obstructing the path of life. Civilization is waiting for a great consummation, for an expression of its soul in beauty. This must be our contribution to the world.

Deformity has already made its bed in your markets, it is fast encroaching upon the region of your heart, bribing with cheap lures your admiration. If you accept it is your permanent guest, and thus do violence to yourselves, then, indeed, in a generation or two, you will kill this great gift. What will remain? What will you offer humanity in return for your privilege to exist?

You say, 'We must make progress.' Why should there remain forever a gulf between progress and perfection? If you can make them one in beauty, you will reach the ultimate goal of reality.

It is your own mission to prove that love for the earth, and for the things of the earth, is possible without materialism, love without the vulgarity of avarice.

Let us develop the instinct that can grasp the secret of the rhythm of things,—not merely the secret of power which is in science, but the secret of expression. This is the divine secret which is ever taming the wild forces that are mere monstrous facts of the universe having no inner significance of truth.

I am tired and old. This is perhaps my last meeting with you. With all my heart I take this occasion to entreat you not to be turned away by the call of vulgar strength, of stupendous size, by the spirit of storage, by the multiplication of millions, without meaning and without end.

Cherish the ideal of perfection, and to that, relate all your work, all your movements. Then, though you love the material things of earth, they will not hurt you and you will bring heaven to earth and soul into things.

1933

'Women's Place in the World'

The planet which rules my life is a planet of contradictions. I, who began my childhood behind a guarded seclusion of solitude developing a timid shyness in my nature, have always to navigate my career round the world on a surging ocean of crowds. And I who am temperamentally lazy, ever eager to cultivate rhythmic ideas on a rich soil of idleness, am compelled to work harder than most people who would die of boredom if gods in their jesting mood forcibly imposed on them the boon of leisure. At first I try to be true to my original nature and struggle against all contradictory compulsions but my fate is stronger and most often I end by yielding to its conspiracy. The organizers of this Conference will bear witness to the fact that such has been the case with me about my appearance today in this meeting. My timidity and laziness combined all their forces against the invitation till they were routed by my stars which always laugh at my futile recalcitrance. But at the same time there was an undercurrent of strong attraction which helped to bring about this end. For I, as a poet, owe my endless debt to womankind, specially to those who have taken intimate part in shaping my dreams and my destiny. They came to me, as the seasons come to the earth, with varied urgings of flowers and fruitfulness; they brought to my life the inspiration of love and beauty, invocation of the power that lies dormant until touched by womanly grace. I did not have the heart to neglect the occasion like the present one when I would be able to offer my homage to women of my country and tell them that I myself join in the profound expression of recognition given in India to woman in which she is proclaimed as *Shakti,* the living symbol of divine energy whose inner shrine is in the subconscious depth of human nature and outer manifestations in sweetness of service, simplicity of self-dedication and silent heroism of daily sacrifices.

I know that this is the fit occasion when you may wish to hear from me my ideas about women's place in the world and I cannot do better than to quote with a few changes some paragraphs from a paper of mine already published which deals with this subject.

Man having the advantage over woman in a comparative freedom from biological obligations could devote his unhampered leisure in constructing a civilization which naturally followed in a large measure his own temperament and tendencies and woman for ages was constrained to adjust herself to a narrowness of sphere allowed to her. At the present stage of history civilization has become primarily masculine, a civilization of power in which woman from her captivity spends her surplus wealth of emotion in merely decorative purposes of society. Therefore the civilization has lost its balance and is moving by hopping from war to war, trampling helpless life on its path under its drunken tread. Its motive forces are the forces of constant coercions in big scales for the sake of results of absurdly vast dimensions, entailing appalling number of human sacrifices. Today we find this uncadenced civilization crashing at a tremendous speed along a perilous slope, knocking against unforeseen catastrophes, never knowing how to stop. And at last the time has arrived when woman must step in and impart her life-rhythm to this reckless movement of power.

For, woman's function is the patient and passive function of the soil, which not only helps the tree to grow but keeps its growth within the limits of normality. The tree must have life's adventure sending up and spreading out its branches on all sides, but all its deeper bonds of relation are hidden and held firm in the soil. Our civilization must also have its passive foundation, broad and deep and stable. It must not be mere growth but a harmony of growth in which wealth never exceeds the wholesomeness of health.

A man's interest in his fellow-beings becomes real when he finds in them some special form of usefulness or striking gift of powers, but a woman feels interest in her fellow-beings because they are human, not because of some particular purpose which they can serve, uncommon talent which they may possess. Her exuberance of vital interest is spontaneously expressive; it makes her speech, her laughter, her movement, graceful and picturesque: for the note of gracefulness is in this harmony with all our surrounding interests.

Fortunately for us, our everyday world has the subtle and unobtrusive beauty of the commonplace, and we have to depend upon our own sensitive minds to realize its wonders which are modestly reticent. If we can pierce through the exterior, we find that the world in its commonplace aspects is a miracle.

We realize this truth intuitively through our power of love; and women, through this power, discover that the object of their love and sympathy, in spite of its ragged disguise of triviality, has infinite worth for which life itself can be sacrificed.

Wherever there is life's claim which is concretely personal there is woman's world. The domestic world is the world where every individual finds his worth as an individual, therefore his value is not the market value but the inherent value of reality, which is for love to discover, that is to say, the value that God in his infinite mercy has set upon all his creatures.

Woman has her natural power that penetrates through the surface to the heart of things, where in the mystery of life dwells an eternal source of interest; and therefore her love has not necessarily to wait for the excitation of surprising qualities. God has sent woman not merely to explore or exploit but to love the world which is a world of ordinary things and events. She is not in the world of the fairy-tale where the fair woman sleeps for ages till she is touched by the magic wand. In God's world women have their magic wands everywhere, which keep their hearts awake, and these are not the golden wands of wealth nor the iron rods of power.

Of late, with the help of science, civilization has been growing increasingly impersonal in character, so that the full reality of the individual is more and more ignored.

In some societies, infanticide prevailed which ruthlessly kept down the female element of the population as low as possible. The same thing in another form is fast taking place in modern civilization. In its inordinate lust for power and wealth it is daily robbing women of her world of personal relationship, the home is every day being crowded out by the office, and true happiness by sordid claims of utility.

But woman cannot be pushed back for good into the superficial region of the merely decorative by man's aggressive athleticism. For she is not less necessary in civilization than man, but possibly more so. In the geological history of earth the periods of gigantic cataclysms have passed when the earth had not attained that mellowness of maturity which despises all violent exhibition of force. And the civilization of competing commerce and fighting nationalism must also make room for that stage of perfection whose power lies deep in beauty and beneficence.

Therefore although in the present stage of history man is asserting his masculine supremacy and building the tower of his civilization with stone blocks, ignoring the living principle of growth, he cannot altogether crush woman's nature into dust or into his dead building materials. It is not that woman is merely seeking today her freedom of livelihood, struggling against man's monopoly of business, but against man's monopoly of civilization. The monster car of organization is creaking and growling along life's highway, spreading misery and mutilation, for it must have speed and profit before everything else in the world.

Therefore woman must come into the bruised and mained world of the individual; she must claim each one of them as her own, the useless and the insignificant, the lowliest and the lost. She must protect with her care all the beautiful flowers of sentiment from the scorching laughter of the science of proficiency. The world with its insulted individuals has sent its appeal to her. These individuals must find their true value, raise their heads in the sun and renew their faith in god's love through woman's own love.

Let us have no doubt in our minds that those human beings who have been boastful of their arrogant power, and ruthless in their exploitation will be defeated in the next generation of life. It is the same thing that happened in the remote biological age to those great monsters like the mammoths and dinosaurs. They had the gigantic muscles for mighty efforts but at last had to give way to creatures who were physically feebler, taking up smaller space and seeming laughably feminine in their helplessness. And in the future civilization also, the aggressive trespassers of today will have to remove their boundary pillars to make room for the apparently feebler creatures, and the union of man and woman will represent a perfect co-operation in building up of human history on equal terms in every department of life. The future Eve will lure away the future Adam from the wilderness of a masculine dispensation and mingle her talents with those of her partner in a joint creation of a paradise of their own. The rudely elbowing age of relentless rapacity will give way to that of a generous communion of minds and means, when individuals will not be allowed to be terrorised into abject submission by idealistic bullies compelled to lose their own physiognomy in a gigantic mask of a nebulous abstraction.

1933

Reply to the Madras Corporation Address

Mr Mayor and the Members of the Corporation of Madras,

Allow me to offer my thanks for the welcome accorded to me on behalf of the citizens of this great city. There was a time when poets depended upon the favour of the king's court for their recognition. Now that prerogative has descended upon the people and I have had amazing good fortune in winning popular applause in a measure which is too perilously enormous.

However, I have not come to you today as a poet for gathering approbation, but as one possessed of an insistent purpose which like a pod bearing seeds has its only impulse which is for dissemination. The idea that has gained a hold upon my mind and which has given the name Visva-Bharati may be known to you and yet not clearly defined. Therefore I take this opportunity for repeating myself in the hope that my appeal may find some response in some of your minds and make you think.

From the beginning of her history the race problem has been the one great problem with which India has been compelled to deal. Peoples different in colour and culture came into closest contact on her soil which at first gave rise to deadly conflicts till they subsided into a passive mutual tolerance splitting up the multitude into closely guarded compartments. That this has not been the best possible answer to the Sphinx riddle given to us to solve, is amply proved by our history which has borne a continuous series of humiliation upto the present day. The barriers that obstruct the flow of human sympathy to reach all parts of the social system are sure to produce a fatal weakness that easily gives way to all attacks of evil. We can never hope to find our salvation by some artificial means, some apportionment of votes, some political machinery imported from foreign markets. Our minds must be educated truly to realize the deeper bond of human relationship, the lack of which makes us miss our meaning and hinders us in our fulfilment. Visva-Bharati stands for that spiritual attitude of mind which has its faith in the fundamental unity of man, the unity which is not merely a part of a policy but representing an eternal truth.

The problem which appeared before India still claiming its final solution has become today a world problem. The human races have come out of their traditional reservation fence into mutual contact. This sudden change from a life of comparative seclusion to that of mutual proximity will test to the full their moral adaptability. The peculiar qualities which gave special advantage to some of them in former days, may in order to save these very people, have to give place to others of an opposite kind.

It is difficult for us to realize that the sunset clouds of the past, under their golden flourishes and blood-red magnificence conceal approaching doom, and people are still talking in a language which hardly takes count of the impending night. The vastness of the race problem with which we are faced today will either compel us to train ourselves to moral fitness, in place of merely external efficiency, or the complications arising out of it will fetter all our movements and drag us to our death.

Our first meeting has only recognized our differences in language, tradition, and degree of physical strength and in the place of geographical barriers it has thereupon set up the barriers of mutual misunderstanding. Even the religious ministers sent by the West to the East have in their sectarian pride emphasised and exaggerated these differences more than any other body of men. They have produced the psychology which makes it comfortably easy for the military and mercantile powers of their community to carry on their mission of depredation in alien countries helplessly open to their inroads.

This consciousness of difference has poisoned our literature, our history and the education of our children,—it has invaded the frontier line of science where it touches sociology. Like what we have experienced in our own community, the cultivation of intense race egotism is the one thing that has found its fullest scope in this meeting of men. In no period of human history has there been such an epidemic of moral perversity, such a universal churning up of jealousy, greed, hatred and mutual suspicion. Every people, weak or strong, is constantly indulging in a violent dream of rendering itself thoroughly obnoxious to others. In this galloping competition of hurtfulness, on the slope of a bottomless pit, no nation dares to stop or slow down. A scarlet fever with a raging temperature has attacked the entire body of mankind and political passion has taken the place of creative personality in all departments of life.

It is well known that when greed has for its object material gain, then it can have no end. It is like the chasing of the horizon by a lunatic. To go on in a competition of multiplying millions is a steeple-chase of insensate futility, that has obstacles but no goal. It has for its parallel the fight with material weapons, weapons which must be perpetually multiplied, opening up new vistas of destruction and evoking new forms of insanity in the forging of frightfulness. Thus seems to have commenced the last fatal adventure of drunken passion riding on an intellect of prodigious power.

When the condition of the world is so desperate, it will not in the least help us if we in the East, as we already find in Japan, also join in this stampede towards a general annihilation. We must discover our salvation in some other power that has its basis upon sanity, and this power is moral. The ideal of education which Visva-Bharati dreams of realizing in spite of the obstacles of all kinds, is to help in the development of intellectual and moral sympathy for one's fellow-beings, the spirit of service and sacrifice, and the dauntless attitude of refusal towards evil of all kinds in the face of calumny and persecution.

Material force has its power in the physical blows it can inflict and therefore emulation goes on endlessly augmenting the means of dealing such blows. It can only come to a natural stop when man asserts the dignity of his spirit and says: 'I am not afraid.' It is our weakness which maintains a material power dominating us; the power which is spiritual dwells in our strength, in our fearlessness, fortitude and spirit of renunciation.

So long men had been cultivating, almost with a religious fervour, that mentality which is the product of racial isolation; poets sang in a loud pitch of bragging of the exploits of their popular man-slayers; money-makers neither felt pity nor shame in the unscrupulous dexterity of their pocket-picking; and diplomats scattered lies in order to reap concessions from the devastated future of their victims. Man, suckled at the wolfs breast, sheltered in the brute's den, brought up in prowling habit of depredation, suddenly discovers today through a series of cataclysms that his true power lies in yielding up his brute force for the freedom of spirit. The time has come for him to realize that the subtle intricacies of human existence find their perfect unity in the harmony of interdependence, never in the vigorous exercise of elbows in the midst of the mutually pushing multitude, clamouring for a solitary peak of self-assertion.

This spirit of interdependence is the divine spirit of meekness in life which gives it the unseen and inexhaustible strength to inherit the earth, that we find in the green grass whose banner of conquest is humble and yet ever victorious. Therefore I would bring to you the cry of this new Age which is waiting to close the bloodstained pages of its past and to hear the Epic that will voice its hope in a great song of a triumphant humanity.

1934

The Religion of an Artist

I was born in 1861: That is not an important date of history, but it belongs to a great epoch in Bengal, when the currents of three movements had met in the life of our country. One of these, the religious, was introduced by a very greathearted man of gigantic intelligence, Raja Rammohun Roy. It was revolutionary, for he tried to reopen the channel of spiritual life which had been obstructed for many years by the sands and debris of creeds that were formal and materialistic, fixed in external practices lacking spiritual significance. People who cling to an ancient past have their pride in the antiquity of their accumulations, in the sublimity of time-honoured walls around them. They grow nervous and angry when some great spirit, some lover of truth, breaks open their enclosure and floods it with the sunshine of thought and the breath of life. Ideas cause movement and all forward movements they consider to be a menace to their warehouse security.

This was happening about the time I was born. I am proud to say that my father was one of the great leaders of that movement, a movement for whose sake he suffered ostracism and braved social indignities. I was born in this atmosphere of the advent of new ideals, which at the same time were old, older than all the things of which that age was proud.

There was a second movement equally important. Bankimchandra Chatterjee, who though much older than myself, was my contemporary and lived long enough for me to see him, was the first pioneer in the literary revolution which happened in Bengal about that time. Before his arrival our literature had been oppressed by a rigid rhetoric that choked its life and loaded it with ornaments that became its fetters. Bankimchandra was brave enough to go against the orthodoxy which believed in the security of tombstones and in that finality which can only belong to the lifeless. He lifted the dead weight of ponderous forms from our language and with a touch of his magic wand aroused our literature from her age-long sleep. A great promise and a vision of beauty she revealed to us when she awoke in the fulness of her strength and grace.

There was yet another movement started about this time called the National. It was not fully political, but it began to give voice to the mind of our people trying to assert their own personality. It was a voice of impatience at the humiliation constantly heaped upon us by people who were not oriental, and who had, especially at that time, the habit of sharply dividing the human world into the good and the bad according to the hemispheres to which they belong.

This contemptuous spirit of separatedness was perpetually hurting us and causing great damage to our own world of culture. It generated in our young men a distrust of all things that had come to them as an inheritance from their past. The old Indian pictures and other works of art were laughed at by our students in imitation of the laughter of their European schoolmasters of that age of philistinism.

Though later on our teachers themselves had changed their mind, their disciples had hardly yet fully regained confidence in the merit of our art. They have had a long period of encouragement in developing an appetite for third-rate copies of French pictures, for gaudy oleographs abjectly cheap, for the pictures that are products of mechanical accuracy of a stereotyped standard, and they still considered it to be a symptom of superior culture to be able disdainfully to refuse oriental works of creation.

The modern young men of that period nodded their heads and said that true originality lay not in the discovery of the rhythm of the essential in the heart of reality but in the full lips, tinted cheeks and bare breasts of imported pictures. The same spirit of rejection, born of utter ignorance, was cultivated in other departments of our culture. It was the result of the hypnotism exercised upon the minds of the younger generation by people who were loud of voice and strong of arm. The national movement was started to proclaim that we must not be indiscriminate in our rejection of the past. This was not a reactionary movement but a revolutionary one, because it set out with a great courage to deny and to oppose all pride in mere borrowings.

These three movements were on foot and in all three the members of my own family took active part. We were ostracized because of our heterodox opinions about religion and therefore we enjoyed the freedom of the outcast. We had to build our own world with our own thoughts and energy of mind.

I was born and brought up in an atmosphere of the confluence of three movements, all of which were revolutionary. My family had to live its own life, which led me from my young days to seek guidance for my own self-expression in my own inner standard of judgment. The medium of expression doubtless was my mother tongue. But the language which belonged to the people had to be modulated according to the urge which I as an individual had.

No poet should borrow his medium ready-made from some shop of orthodox respectability. He should not only have his own seeds but prepare his own soil. Each poet has his own distinct medium of language—not because the whole language is of his own make, but because his individual use of it, having life's magic touch, transforms it into a special vehicle of his own creation.

The races of man have poetry in their heart and it is necessary for them to give, as far as is possible, a perfect expression to their sentiments. For this they must have a medium, moving and pliant, which can freshly become their very own, age after age. All great languages have undergone and are still undergoing changes. Those languages which resist the spirit of change are doomed and will never produce great harvests of thought and literature. When forms become fixed, the spirit either weakly accepts its imprisonment within them or rebels. All revolutions consist of the fight of the within against invasion by the without.

There was a great chapter in the history of life on this earth when some irresistible inner force in man found its way out into the scheme of things, and sent forth its triumphant mutinous voice, with the cry that it was not going to be overwhelmed from outside by the huge brute beast of a body. How helpless it appeared at the moment, but has it not nearly won? In our social life also revolution breaks out when some power concentrates itself in outside arrangements and threatens to enslave for its own purpose the power which we have within us.

When an organization which is a machine becomes a central force, political, commercial, educational or religious, it obstructs the free flow of inner life of the people and waylays and exploits it for the augmentation of its own power. To-day, such concentration of power is fast multiplying on the outside and the cry of the oppressed spirit of man is in the air which struggles to free itself from the grip of screws and bolts, of unmeaning obsessions.

Revolution must come and men must risk revilement and misunderstanding, especially from those who want to be comfortable, who put their faith in materialism, and who belong truly to the dead past and not to modern times, the past that had its age in distant antiquity when physical flesh and size predominated, and not the mind of man.

Purely physical dominance is mechanical and modern machines are merely exaggerating our bodies, lengthening and multiplying our limbs. The modern mind, in its innate childishness, delights in this enormous bodily bulk, representing an inordinate material power, saying: "Let me have the big toy and no sentiment which can disturb it." It does not realize that in this we are returning to that antediluvian age which revelled in its production of gigantic physical frames, leaving no room for the freedom of the inner spirit.

All great human movements in the world are related to some great ideal. Some of you may say that such a doctrine of spirit has been in its death-throes for over a century and is now moribund; that we have nothing to rely upon but external forces and material foundations. But I say, on my part, that your doctrine was obsolete long ago. It was exploded in the springtime of life, when mere size was swept off the face of the world, and was replaced by man, brought naked into the heart of creation, man with his helpless body, but with his indomitable mind and spirit.

When I began my life as a poet, the writers among our educated community took their guidance from their English textbooks which poured upon them lessons that did not fully saturate their minds. I suppose it was fortunate for me that I never in my life had the kind of academic training which is considered proper for a boy of respectable family. Though I cannot say I was altogether free from the influence that ruled young minds of those days, the course of my writings was nevertheless saved from the groove of imitative forms. In my versification, vocabulary and ideas, I yielded myself to the vagaries of an untutored fancy which brought castigation upon me from critics who were learned, and uproarious laughter from the witty. My ignorance combined with my heresy turned me into a literary outlaw.

When I began my career I was ridiculously young; in fact, I was the youngest of that band who had made themselves articulate. I had neither the protective armour of mature age, nor enough English to command respect. So in my seclusion of contempt and qualified encouragement I had my freedom. Gradually I grew up in years—for which, however, I claim no credit. Steadily I cut my way through derision and occasional patronage into a recognition in which the proportion of praise and blame was very much like that of land and water on our earth.

What gave me boldness when I was young was my early acquaintance with the old Vaishnava poems of Bengal, full of the freedom of metre and courage of expression. I think I was only twelve when these poems first began to be reprinted. I surreptitiously got hold of copies from the desks of my elders. For the edification of the young I must confess that this was not right for a boy of my age. I should have been passing my examinations and not following a path that would lead to loss of marks. I must also admit that the greater part of these lyrics was erotic and not quite suited to a boy just about to reach his teens. But my imagination was fully occupied with the beauty of their forms and the music of their words; and their breath, heavily laden with voluptuousness, passed over my mind without distracting it.

My vagabondage in the path of my literary career had another reason. My father was the leader of a new religious movement, a strict monotheism based upon the teachings of the Upanishads. My countrymen in Bengal thought him almost as bad as a Christian, if not worse. So we were completely ostracized, which probably saved me from another disaster, that of imitating our own past.

Most of the members of my family had some gift—some were artists, some poets, some musicians and the whole atmosphere of our home was permeated with the spirit of creation. I had a deep sense almost from infancy of the beauty of Nature, an intimate feeling of companionship with the trees and the clouds, and felt in tune with the musical touch of the seasons in the air. At the same time, I had a peculiar susceptibility to human kindness. All these craved expression. The very earnestness of my emotions yearned to be true to themselves, though I was too immature to give their expression any perfection of form.

Since then I have gained a reputation in my country, but till very late a strong current of antagonism in a large section of my countrymen persisted. Some said that my poems did not spring from the national heart; some complained that they were incomprehensible; others that they were unwholesome. In fact, I have never had complete acceptance from my own people, and that too has been a blessing; for nothing is so demoralizing as unqualified success.

This is the history of my career. I wish I could reveal it more clearly through the narration of my own work in my own language. I hope that will be possible some day or other. Languages are jealous. They do not give up their best treasures to those who try to deal with them through an intermediary belonging to an alien rival. We have to court them in person and dance attendance on them. Poems are not like market commodities transferable. We cannot receive the smiles and glances of our sweetheart through an attorney, however diligent and dutiful he may be.

I myself have tried to get at the wealth of beauty in the literature of the European languages, long before I gained a full right to their hospitality. When I was young I tried to approach Dante, unfortunately through an English translation. I failed utterly, and felt it my pious duty to desist. Dante remained a closed book to me.

I also wanted to know German literature and, by reading Heine in translation, I thought I had caught a glimpse of the beauty there. Fortunately I met a missionary lady from Germany and asked her help. I worked hard for some months, but being rather quick-witted, which is not a good quality, I was not persevering. I had the dangerous facility which helps one to guess the meaning too easily. My teacher thought I had almost mastered the language, which was not true. I succeeded, however, in getting through Heine, like a man walking in sleep crossing unknown paths with ease, and I found immense pleasure.

Then I tried Goethe. But that was too ambitious. With the help of the little German I had learnt, I did go through *Faust*. I believe I found my entrance to the palace, not like one who has keys for all the doors, but as a casual visitor who is tolerated in some general guest-room, comfortable but not intimate. Properly speaking, I do not know my Goethe, and in the same way many other great luminaries are dusky to me.

This is as it should be. Man cannot reach the shrine if he does not make the pilgrimage. So, one must not hope to find anything true from my own language in translation.

In regard to music, I claim to be something of a musician myself. I have composed many songs which have defied the canons of orthodox propriety and good people are disgusted at the impudence of a man who is audacious only because he is untrained. But I persist, and God forgives me because I do not know what I do. Possibly that is the best way of doing things in the sphere of art. For I find that people blame, but also sing my songs, even if not always correctly.

Please do not think I am vain. I can judge myself objectively and can openly express admiration for my own work, because I am modest. I do not hesitate to say that my songs have found their place in the heart of my land, along with her flowers that are never exhausted, and that the folk of the future, in days of joy or sorrow or festival, will have to sing them. This too is the work of a revolutionist.

If I feel reluctant to speak about my own view of religion, it is because I have not come to my own religion through the portals of passive acceptance of a particular creed owing to some accident of birth. I was born to a family who were pioneers in the revival in our country of a religion based upon the utterance of Indian sages in the Upanishads. But owing to my idiosyncrasy of temperament, it was impossible for me to accept any religious teaching on the only ground that people in my surroundings believed it to be true. I could not persuade myself to imagine that I had religion simply because everybody whom I might trust believed in its value.

My religion is essentially a poet's religion. Its touch comes to me through the same unseen and trackless channels as does the inspiration of my music. My religious life has followed the same mysterious line of growth as has my poetical life. Somehow they are wedded to each other, and though their betrothal had a long period of ceremony, it was kept secret from me. I am not, I hope, boasting when I confess to my gift of poesy, an instrument of expression delicately responsive to the breath that comes from depth of feeling. From my infancy I had the keen sensitiveness which always kept my mind tingling with consciousness of the world around me, natural and human.

I had been blessed with that sense of wonder which gives a child his right of entry into the treasure-house of mystery which is in the heart of existence. I neglected my studies because they rudely summoned me away from the world around me, which was my friend and my companion, and when I was thirteen I freed myself from the clutch of an educational system that tried to keep me imprisoned within the stone-walls of lessons.

I had a vague notion as to who or what it was that touched my heart's chords, like the infant which does not know its mother's name, or who or what she is. The feeling which I always had was a deep satisfaction of personality that flowed into my nature through living channels of communication from all sides.

It was a great thing for me that my consciousness was never dull about the facts of the surrounding world. That the cloud was the cloud, that a flower was a flower, was enough, because they directly spoke to me, because I could not be indifferent to them. I still remember the very moment, one afternoon, when coming back from school I alighted from the carriage and suddenly saw in the sky, behind the upper terrace of our house, an exuberance of deep, dark rain-clouds lavishing rich, cool shadows on the atmosphere. The marvel of it, the very generosity of its presence, gave me a joy which was freedom, the freedom we feel in the love of our dear friend.

There is an illusion I have made use of in another paper, in which I supposed that a stranger from some other planet has paid a visit to our earth and happens to hear the sound of a human voice on the gramophone. All that is obvious to him, and most seemingly active, is the revolving disk; he is unable to discover the personal truth that lies behind, and so might accept the impersonal scientific fact of the disk as final—the fact that could be touched and measured. He would wonder how it could be possible for a machine to speak to the soul. Then if in pursuing the mystery, he should suddenly come to the heart of the music through a meeting with the composer, he would at once understand the meaning of that music as a personal communication.

Mere information of facts, mere discovery of power, belongs to the outside and not to the inner soul of things. Gladness is the one criterion of truth as we know when we have touched Truth by the music it gives, by the joy of the greeting it sends forth to the truth in us. That is the true foundation of all religions; it is not in dogma. As I have said before, it is not as ether waves that we receive light; the morning does not wait for some scientist for its introduction to us. In the same way, we touch the infinite reality immediately within us only when we perceive the pure truth of love or goodness, not through the explanation of theologians, not through the erudite discussion of ethical doctrines.

I have already confessed that my religion is a poet's religion; all that I feel about it is from vision and not from knowledge. I frankly say that I cannot satisfactorily answer questions about the problem of evil, or about what happens after death. And yet I am sure that there have come moments when my soul has touched the infinite and has become intensely conscious of it through the illumination of joy. It has been said in our Upanishads that our mind and our words come away baffled from the supreme Truth, but he who knows That, through the immediate joy of his own soul, is saved from all doubts and fears.

In the night we stumble over things and become acutely conscious of their individual separateness, but the day reveals the great unity which embraces them. And the man, whose inner vision is bathed in an illumination of his consciousness, at once realizes the spiritual unity reigning supreme over all differences of race and his mind no longer awkwardly stumbles over individual facts of separateness in the human world, accepting them as final, he realizes that peace is in the inner harmony which dwells in truth, and not in any outer adjustments; and that beauty carries an eternal assurance of our spiritual relationship to reality, which waits for its perfection in the response of our love.

II

The renowned Vedic commentator, Sāyanāchārya, says:

> यज्ञे हुताशिष्टस्य ओदनस्य सर्वजगतकारणभूता
> ब्रह्माभेदेण स्तुतिः क्रियते ।।

> The food offering which is left over after the completion of sacrificial rites is praised because it is symbolical of *Brahma,* the original source of the universe.

According to this explanation, *Brahma* is boundless in his superfluity which inevitably finds its expression in the eternal world process. Here we have the doctrine of the genesis of creation, and therefore of the origin of art. Of all living creatures in the world, man has his vital and mental energy vastly in excess of his need, which urges him to work in various lines of creation for its own sake. Like *Brahma* himself, he takes joy in productions that are unnecessary to him, and therefore representing his extravagance and not his hand-to-mouth penury. The voice that is just enough can speak and cry to the extent needed for everyday use, but that which is abundant sings, and in it we find our joy. Art reveals man's wealth of life, which seeks its freedom in forms of perfection which are an end in themselves.

All that is inert and inanimate is limited to the bare fact of existence. Life is perpetually creative because it contains in itself that surplus which ever overflows the boundaries of the immediate time and space, restlessly pursuing its adventure of expression in the varied forms of self-realization. Our living body has its vital organs that are important in maintaining its efficiency, but this body is not a mere convenient sack for the purpose of holding stomach, heart, lungs and brains; it is an image—its highest value is in the fact that it communicates its personality. It has colour, shape and movement, most of which belong to the superfluous, that are needed only for self-expression and not for self-preservation.

This living atmosphere of superfluity in man is dominated by his imagination, as the earth's atmosphere by the light. It helps us to integrate desultory facts in a vision of harmony and then to translate it into our activities for the very joy of its perfection, it invokes in us the Universal Man who is the seer and the doer of all times and countries. The immediate consciousness of reality in its purest form, unobscured by the shadow of self-interest, irrespective of moral or utilitarian recommendation, gives us joy as does the self-revealing personality of our own. What in common language we call beauty, which is in harmony of lines, colours, sounds, or in grouping of words or thoughts, delights us only because we cannot help admitting a truth in it that is ultimate. 'Love is enough', the poet has said; it carries its own explanation, the joy of which can only be expressed in a form of art which also has that finality. Love gives evidence to something which is outside us but which intensely exists and thus stimulates the sense of our own existence. It radiantly reveals the reality of its objects, though these may lack qualities that are valuable or brilliant.

The *I am* in me realizes its own extension, its own infinity whenever it truly realizes something else. Unfortunately, owing to our limitations and a thousand and one preoccupations, a great part of our world, though closely surrounding us, is far away from the lamp-post of our attention: it is dim, it passes by us, a caravan of shadows, like the landscape seen in the night from the window of an illuminated railway compartment: the passenger knows that the outside world exists, that it is important, but for the time being the railway carriage for him is far more significant. If among the innumerable objects in this world there be a few that come under the full illumination of our soul and thus assume reality for us, they constantly cry to our creative mind for a permanent representation. They belong to the same domain as the desire of ours which represents the longing for the permanence of our own self.

I do not mean to say that things to which we are bound by the tie of self-interest have the inspiration of reality; on the contrary, these are eclipsed by the shadow of our own self. The servant is not more real to us than the beloved. The narrow emphasis of utility diverts our attention from the complete man to the merely useful man. The thick label of market-price obliterates the ultimate value of reality.

That fact that we exist has its truth in the fact that everything else does exist, and the 'I am' in me crosses its finitude whenever it deeply realizes itself in the 'Thou art'. This crossing of the limit produces joy, the joy that we have in beauty, in love, in greatness. Self-forgetting, and in a higher degree, self-sacrifice, is our acknowledgement of this our experience of the infinite. This is the philosophy which explains our joy in all arts, the arts that in their creations intensify the sense of the unity which is the unity of truth we carry within ourselves. The personality in me is a self-conscious principle of a living unity; it at once comprehends and yet transcends all the details of facts that are individually mine, my knowledge, feeling, wish and will, my memory, my hope, my love, my activities, and all my belongings. This personality which has the sense of the *One* in its nature, realizes it in things, thoughts and facts made into units. The principle of unity which it contains is more or less perfectly satisfied in a beautiful face or a picture, a poem, a song, a character or a harmony of inter-related ideas or facts and then for it these things become intensely real, and therefore joyful. Its standard of reality, the reality that has its perfect revelation in a perfection of harmony, is hurt when there is a consciousness of discord—because discord is against the fundamental unity which is in its centre.

All other facts have come to us through the gradual course of our experience, and our knowledge of them is constantly undergoing contradictory changes through the discovery of new data. We can never be sure that we have come to know the final character of anything that there is. But such a knowledge has come to us immediately with a conviction which needs no arguments to support it. It is this, that all my activities have their sources in this personality of mine which is indefinable and yet about the truth of which I am more certain than anything in this world. Though all the direct evidence that can be weighed and measured support the fact that only my fingers are producing marks on the paper, yet no sane man ever can doubt that it is not these mechanical movements that are the true origin of my writings but some entity that can never be known unless known through sympathy. Thus we have come to realize in our own person the two aspects of activities, one of which is the aspect of law represented in the medium, and the other the aspect of will residing in the personality.

Limitation of the unlimited is personality: God is personal where he creates.

He accepts the limits of his own law and the play goes on, which is this world whose reality is in its relation to the Person. Things are distinct not in their essence but in their appearance; in other words, in their relation to one to whom they appear. This is art, the truth of which is not in substance or logic, but in expression. Abstract truth may belong to science and metaphysics, but the world of reality belongs to Art.

The world as an art is the play of the Supreme Person revelling in image making. Try to find out the ingredients of the image—they elude you, they never reveal to you the eternal secret of appearance. In your effort to capture life as expressed in living tissue, you will find carbon, nitrogen and many other things utterly unlike life, but never life itself. The appearance does not offer any commentary of itself through its material. You may call it *māyā* and pretend to disbelieve it, but the great artist, the *māyāvin,* is not hurt. For art is *māyā*, it has no other explanation but that it seems to be what it is. It never tries to conceal its evasiveness, it mocks even its own definition and plays the game of hide-and-seek through its constant flight in changes.

And thus life, which is an incessant explosion of freedom, finds its metre in a continual falling back in death. Every day is a death, every moment even. If not, there would be amorphous desert of deathlessness eternally dumb and still. So life is *māyā,* as moralists love to say, it *is* and *is not.* All that we find in it is the rhythm through which it shows itself. Are rocks and minerals any better? Has not science shown us the fact that the ultimate difference between one element and another is only that of rhythm? The fundamental distinction of gold from mercury lies merely in the difference of rhythm in their respective atomic constitution, like the distinction of the king from his subject which is not in their different constituents, but in the different metres of their situation and circumstance. There you find behind the scene the Artist, the Magician of rhythm, who imparts an appearance of substance to the unsubstantial.

What is rhythm? It is the movement generated and regulated by harmonious restriction. This is the creative force in the hand of the artist. So long as words remain in uncadenced prose form, they do not give any lasting feeling of reality. The moment they are taken and put into rhythm they vibrate into a radiance. It is the same with the rose. In the pulp of its petals you may find everything that went to make the rose, but the rose which is *māyā,* an image, is lost; its finality which has the touch of the infinite is gone. The rose appears to me to be still, but because of its metre of composition it has a lyric of movement within that stillness, which is the same as the dynamic quality of a picture that has a perfect harmony. It produces a music in our consciousness by giving it a swing of motion synchronous with its own. Had the picture consisted of a disharmonious aggregate of colours and lines, it would be deadly still.

In perfect rhythm, the art-form becomes like the stars which in their seeming stillness are never still, like a motionless flame that is nothing but movement. A great picture is always speaking, but news from a newspaper, even of some tragic happening, is still-born. Some news may be a mere commonplace in the obscurity of a journal; but give it a proper rhythm and it will never cease to shine. That is art. It has the magic wand which gives undying reality to all things it touches, and relates them to the personal being in us. We stand before its productions and say: I know you as I know myself, you are real.

A Chinese friend of mine, while travelling with me through the streets of Peking, suddenly, with great excitement, called my attention to a donkey. Ordinarily a donkey does not have any special force of truth for us, except when it kicks us or when we need its reluctant service. But in such cases, the truth is not emphasized in the donkey but in some purpose or bodily pain exterior to it. The behaviour of my Chinese friend at once reminded me of the Chinese poems in which the delightful sense of reality is so spontaneously felt and so simply expressed.

This sensitiveness to the touch of things, such abundant delight in the recognition of them, is obstructed when insistent purposes become innumerable and intricate in our society, when problems crowd in our path clamouring for attention, and life's movement is impeded with things and thoughts too difficult for a harmonious assimilation.

This has been growing evident every day in the modern age, which gives more time to the acquisition of life's equipment than to the enjoyment of it. In fact, life itself is made secondary to life's materials, even like a garden buried under the bricks gathered for the garden wall. Somehow the mania for bricks and mortar grows, the kingdom of rubbish dominates, the days of spring are made futile and the flowers never come.

Our modern mind, a hasty tourist, in its rush over the miscellaneous, ransacks cheap markets of curios which mostly are delusions. This happens because its natural sensibility for simple aspects of existence is dulled by constant preoccupations that divert it. The literature that it produces seems always to be poking her nose into out-of-the-way places for things and effects that are out of the common. She racks her resources in order to be striking. She elaborates inconstant changes in style, as in modern millinery; and the product suggests more the polish of steel than the bloom of life.

Fashions in literature that rapidly tire of themselves seldom come from the depth. They belong to the frothy rush of the surface, with its boisterous clamours for the recognition of the moment. Such literature, by its very strain, exhausts its inner development and quickly passes through outer changes like autumn leaves—produces with the help of paints and patches an up-to-dateness, shaming its own appearance of the immediately preceding date. Its expressions are often grimaces, like the cactus of the desert which lacks modesty in its distortions and peace in its thorns, in whose attitude an aggressive discourtesy bristles up, suggesting a forced pride of poverty. We often come across its analogy in some of the modern writings which are difficult to ignore because of their prickly surprises and paradoxical gesticulations. Wisdom is not rare in these works, but it is a wisdom that has lost confidence in its serene dignity, afraid of being ignored by crowds which are attracted by the extravagant and the unusual. It is sad to see wisdom struggling to seem clever, a prophet arrayed in caps and bells before an admiring multitude.

But in all great arts, literary or otherwise, man has expressed his feelings that are usual in a form that is unique and yet not abnormal. When Wordsworth described in his poem a life deserted by love, he invoked for his art the *usual* pathos expected by all normal minds in connection with such a subject. But the picture in which he incarnated the sentiment was unexpected and yet every sane reader acknowledges it with joy when the image is held before him of:

... a forsaken bird's nest filled with snow
Mid its own bush of leafless eglantine.

On the other hand, I have read some modern writing in which the coming out of the stars in the evening is described as the sudden eruption of disease in the bloated body of darkness. The writer seems afraid to own the feeling of a cool purity in the star-sprinkled night which is *usual,* lest he should be found out as commonplace. From the point of view of realism the image may not be wholly inappropriate and may be considered as outrageously virile in its unshrinking incivility. But this is not art; this is a jerky shriek, something like the convulsive advertisement of the modern market that exploits mob psychology against its inattention. To be tempted to create an illusion of forcefulness through an over-emphasis of abnormality is a sign of anaesthesia. It is the waning vigour of imagination which employs desperate dexterity in the present-day art for producing shocks in order to poke out into a glare the sensation of the unaccustomed. When we find that the literature of any period is laborious in the pursuit of a spurious novelty in its manner and matter, we must know that it is the symptom of old age, of anaemic sensibility which seeks to stimulate its palsied taste with the pungency of indecency and the tingling touch of intemperance. It has been explained too that these symptoms mostly are the outcome of a reaction against the last-century literature which developed a mannerism too daintily saccharine, unmanly in the luxury of its toilet and over-delicacy of its expressions. It seemed to have reached an extreme limit of refinement which almost codified its conventions, making it easy for the timid talents to reach a comfortable level of literary respectability. This explanation may be true; but unfortunately reactions seldom have the repose of spontaneity, they often represent the obverse side of the mintage which they try to repudiate as false. A reaction against a particular mannerism is liable to produce its own mannerism in a militant fashion, using the toilet preparation of the war paint, deliberately manufactured style of primitive rudeness. Tired of the elaborately planned flower-beds, the gardener proceeds with grim determination to set up everywhere artificial rocks, avoiding natural inspiration of rhythm in deference to a fashion of tyranny which itself is a tyranny of fashion. The same herd instinct is followed in a cult of rebellion as it was in the cult of conformity and the defiance, which is a mere counteraction of obedience, also shows obedience in a defiant fashion. Fanaticism of virility produces a brawny athleticism meant for a circus and not the natural chivalry which is modest but invincible, claiming its sovereign seat of honour in all arts.

It has often been said by its advocates that this show of the rudely loud and cheaply lurid in art has its justification in the unbiased recognition of facts as such; and according to them realism must not be shunned even if it be ragged and evil-smelling. But when it does not concern science but concerns the arts we must draw a distinction between realism and reality. In its own wide perspective of normal environment, disease is a reality which has to be acknowledged in literature. But disease in a hospital is realism fit for the use of science. It is an abstraction which, if allowed to haunt literature, may assume a startling appearance because of its unreality. Such vagrant spectres do not have a proper modulation in a normal surrounding; and they offer a false proportion in their feature because the proportion of their environment is tampered with. Such a curtailment of the essential is not art, but a trick which exploits mutilation in order to assert a false claim to reality. Unfortunately men are not rare who believe that what forcibly startles them allows them to see more than the facts which are balanced and restrained, which they have to woo and win. Very likely, owing to the lack of leisure, such persons are growing in number, and the dark cellars of sex-psychology and drug-stores of moral virulence are burgled to give them the stimulus which they wish to believe to be the stimulus of aesthetic reality.

I know a simple line sung by some primitive folk in our neighbourhood which I translate thus: 'My heart is like a pebble-bed hiding a foolish stream.' The psycho-analyst may classify it as an instance of repressed desire and thus at once degrade it to a mere specimen advertising a supposed fact, as it does a piece of coal suspected of having smuggled within its dark the flaming wine of the sun of a forgotten age. But it is literature; and what might have been the original stimulus that startled this thought into a song, the significant fact about it is that it has taken the shape of an image, a creation of a uniquely personal and yet universal character. The facts of the repression of a desire are numerously common; but this particular expression is singularly uncommon. The listener's mind is touched not because it is a psychological fact, but because it is an individual poem, representing a personal reality, belonging to all time and place in the human world.

But this is not all. This poem no doubt owed its form to the touch of the person who produced it; but at the same time with a gesture of utter detachment, it has transcended its material—the emotional mood of the author. It has gained its freedom from any biographical bondage by taking a rhythmic perfection which is precious in its own exclusive merit. There is a poem which confesses by its title its origin in a mood of dejection. Nobody can say that to a lucid mind the feeling of despondency has anything pleasantly memorable. Yet these verses are not allowed to be forgotten, because directly a poem is fashioned, it is eternally freed from its genesis, it minimizes its history and emphasizes its independence. The sorrow which was solely personal in an emperor was liberated directly it took the form of verses in stone, it became a triumph of lament, an overflow of delight, hiding the black boulder of its suffering source. The same thing is true of all creation. A dewdrop is a perfect integrity that has no filial memory of its parentage.

When I use the word creation, I mean that through it some imponderable abstractions have assumed a concrete unity in its relation to us. Its substance can be analyzed but not this unity which is in its self-introduction. Literature as an art offers us the mystery which is in its unity.

We read the poem:

Never seek to tell thy love
    Love that never told can be;
For the gentle wind does move
    Silently, invisibly.

I told my love, I told my love,
    I told all my heart;
Trembling cold in ghastly fears
    Ah, she did depart.
Soon as she was gone from me
    A traveller came by;
Silently, invisibly,
    He took her with a sigh.

It has its grammar, its vocabulary. When we divide them part by part and try to torture out a confession from them, the poem which is *one* departs like the gentle wind, silently, invisibly. No one knows how it exceeds all its parts, transcends all its laws, and communicates with the person. The significance which is in unity is an eternal wonder.

As for the definite meaning of the poem, we may have our doubts. If it were told in ordinary prose, we might feel impatient and be roused to contradict it. We would certainly have asked for an explanation as to who the traveller was and why he took away love without any reasonable provocation. But in this poem we need not ask for an explanation unless we are hopelessly addicted to meaning-collection which is like the collection mania for dead butterflies. The poem as a creation, which is something more than as an idea, inevitably conquers our attention; and any meaning which we feel in its words is like the feeling in a beautiful face of a smile that is inscrutable, elusive and profoundly satisfactory.

The unity as a poem introduces itself in a rhythmic language in a gesture of character. Rhythm is not merely in some measured blending of words, but in a significant adjustment of ideas, in a music of thought produced by a subtle principle of distribution, which is not primarily logical but evidential. The meaning which the word character contains is difficult to define. It is comprehended in a special grouping of aspects which gives it an irresistible impetus. The combination it represents may be uncouth, may be unfinished, discordant; yet it has a dynamic vigour in its totality which claims recognition, often against our wishes for the assent of our reason. An avalanche has a character, which even a heavier pile of snow has not; its character is in its massive movement, its incalculable possibilities.

It is for the artist to remind the world that with the truth of our expression we grow in truth. When the man-made world is less an expression of man's creative soul than a mechanical device for some purpose of power, then it hardens itself, acquiring proficiency at the cost of the subtle suggestiveness of living growth. In his creative activities man makes Nature instinct with his own life and love. But with his utilitarian energies he fights Nature, banishes her from his world, deforms and defiles her with the ugliness of his ambitions.

This world of man's own manufacture, with its discordant shrieks and swagger, impresses on him the scheme of a universe which has no touch of the person and therefore no ultimate significance. All the great civilizations that have become extinct must have come to their end through such wrong expression of humanity; through parasitism on a gigantic scale bred by wealth, by man's clinging reliance on material resources; through a scoffing spirit of denial, of negation, robbing us of our means of sustenance in the path of truth.

It is for the artist to proclaim his faith in the everlasting yes —to say: 'I believe that there is an ideal hovering over and permeating the earth, an ideal of that Paradise which is not the mere outcome of fancy, but the ultimate reality in which all things dwell and move.'

I believe that the vision of Paradise is to be seen in the sunlight and the green of the earth, in the beauty of the human face and the wealth of human life, even in objects that are seemingly insignificant and unprepossessing. Everywhere in this earth the spirit of Paradise is awake and sending forth its voice. It reaches our inner ear without our knowing it. It tunes our harp of life which sends our aspiration in music beyond the finite, not only in prayers and hopes, but also in temples which are flames of fire in stone, in pictures which are dreams made everlasting, in the dance which is ecstatic meditation in the still centre of movement.

1936

To the Citizens of Delhi

In this busy season when numerous important functions crowd your days, you have against some obvious difficulties, created this opportunity to receive me in behalf of the citizens of Delhi. It is a matter of special gratification to me, because the obstacles have served only to offer emphasis to the sincerity of your love for your poet who by some lucky chance has been able to win recognition for his motherland from some of the proudest people of the world. I can only say in a brief sentence that I thank you from my heart.

On occasions like this the thought has often occurred to me that honour is for the dead and love is for the living. When life's reckoning has been made to the last penny, when all expectations have arrived at an inevitable finality, then only may popular honour come to the man who seems to deserve it; let it come after all deductions have been made and all items of merit survived the scrutiny of time, then let it put a last label to the fortunate name giving it a documentary value of some description. Literary honour is like a tombstone with an authoritative inscription, it solemnly tries to keep fixed with its weight a specified seat for the dead whose movements are stopped forever. But even then how numerous are the cases that have carelessly allowed the stones to crumble and the inscriptions to fade into illegibility in spite of the initial ceremony of a triumphant trumpet blowing.

Once in a far distant time I was young. I remember to have keenly enjoyed in those days any likely prospect of earning reputation from my contemporaries and from others who may gradually fill the auditorium of the future. It takes time for wisdom to ripen and to enable one to realise that in return for any real service rendered, the best gift is not honour but love which is the most precious form of gratitude, which is not a mere repayment of debt but almost a blessing. Honour is burdensome I can assure you but love does not impose any obligations; it is free and therefore it gives freedom. Fortunately in my career as a poet I have often had my reward from my fellow-beings not merely in the shape of loud applause but through a more intimate contact of spiritual nearness. This fact had struck me with a thankful amazement in those great countries of the west where I was necessarily an alien in language and tradition. The only advantage that I possessed was that I did not have to suffer there from the compelling limitations of being nothing better than a mere British subject; whereas I met the people there on the broad platform of common humanity in an unsullied atmosphere of freedom of fellowship. I have felt that they loved me, that I was their comrade, their fellow traveller in the path of life, that they recognized me as their own and they helped me more than themselves by acknowledging my help. During that travel of mine, most memorable in my life, it came to me with the force of a revelation the truth of the fundamental unity of man. I decided to cherish this truth in the heart of Santiniketan and in spite of the painful twisting of our hearts' cords through all the tension of unnatural relationship, we have been able to keep open in our institution the channel of intercommunication of hearts, the hearts separated by differing circumstances, racial and historical. I have constantly been helped in this task by the thought that this is the highest ideal of human truth as preached by India when she said *Atmavat sarva bhuteshu ya pasyati sa pasyati.* It has strengthened my conviction to know that such ideals carrying eternal and universal value have been established in human history by those *Mahatmas,* the great souls, who never bent their knees to political magnates or votaries of wealth but have often risen from the races of ragged fraternity, obscured by utter indigence, stricken by mailed fists and hounded by wielders of kingly sceptre. And they have yet gloriously survived the evanescent glitter of all power and pomp by centuries of civilization. Delhi is the one great city which keeps in her ruins and rubbish heaps this lesson about the vastly different values of facts, one of which is represented in the history of those who have offered us the elixir of life everlasting, and the other of those who have the invincible power to smite us to the dust through all the various mediums of devastation. Today our salutations are for those great saints, Kabir, Nanak and Dadu, who realised God's love in man's love; while the incessant stream of countless salams laving the foot of the thrones, carrying on its glistening waves the abject humiliation of ages has vanished into the void, and those thrones burst like bubbles. Let us know for certain that the record of our own history of Modern India is also being kept in Time's archives and the names that will ever shine in its pages are some that are hushed today in awesome silence and others execrated by the mighty.

My friends, let me conclude this address by requesting you not to burden me with honour, which so often is heavily padded with a great proportion of unreality, but garland your poet with your love. No more hand-clappings but warm hand-clasping; bring the healing balm of sympathy to alleviate the intolerable weariness of the last few miles of my lie's journey. Now when the lonesome toil of nearly forty years of my mature days has approached its end, do not dismiss me off cheaply with promises of memorial meetings when I am no longer amongst you, offer me succour even now when I sorely need it and leave my memorial in my own hands and Time's judgment.

1936

The Communal Award

My friends, considering the gravity of our situation my address today will be brief, because in my age expenditure of breath has to be economised, specially as there is every likelihood of its being wasted.

It is needless for me to say that I have no gift for politics. The subject of this meeting—which is communal awards—carries chiefly a political implication and this for a long while is my first participation in a discussion which deals with politics. In spite of some hesitation I yielded at last to a growing anxiety in my mind for my country; I found it painfully impossible to ignore the sinister threat of a bisecting blade hissing while being sharpened, ready to divide the one vital sensitive cord that is to bind our people into a nation.

Today the shadow of a dark age has fallen upon Europe. She seems boisterously eager to put out the light of ideals which she herself had specially brought to a new age and her newspapers to-day are full of the malevolent measures taken by dictatorial powers against their victims to keep them crippled for good or thrust them completely aside. I shrink from comparing with some of those acts the introduction in our country of a scheme in which there will remain no scruple to wrench off one of the most sensitive roots of our growing national being. The incident will appear too small and be passed over in silent apathy by the larger world, for those who are helplessly affected by it suffer from the cruellest of insults, the insult of insignificance. However, for us the enormity is such that I felt ashamed to claim the privilege of old age and failing health and was drawn out of my accustomed seclusion to cry my warning, even if it be a cry in the wilderness.

The Communal Award, carrying the malediction of a separated political life has been pronounced even upon groups and communities of our country that did not want it. The Indian body-politic is to be divided into eighteen different sections.

Mahatma Gandhi described this process as a vivisection of the body-politic which will emerge as a carcass out of this operation.

And this evil of separate electorate is made worse by the scheme of weightages whereby communities are differently valued to suit the present mood of the Government. For reasons which need not be explained the Hindus are handicapped most in the coming constitution, and Bengali Hindus, instead of receiving any protection, being in the minority, have specially been singled out for a reduction of their representation even below their natural population strength by weightage being cast against them. Though a tacit compliment, it is an open assault employing a novel political arithmetic invidious enough to turn the methods of responsible government into most irresponsible means by which one community is made permanently independent of the co-operation of the other while wielding the right to oppress it, if it so chooses. It is not that we wish to deny our Muslim countrymen the benefit of their numbers, nor that we suspect them of dangerous designs. It is only that we refuse to accept the fate of all future prospect of mutual co-operation blighted by a scheme which puts a premium upon communal allegiance at the expense of national interest—a scheme which engenders suspicion where there should be trust and corrupts both the communities by encouraging fanatics to make political profit out of communal passion. I beg to remind our rulers that even worse than the commercial exploitation of our economic life is this political poisoning of our national blood, worse than punishing subjects on suspicion, without trial for an indefinite period; for it is punishing the future, an eternal damnation for acts of disobedience, real or imaginary proved or unproved.

Ever since the very suggestion of this proposal, the atmosphere in our province has become turbid with passion menacing amenities of civilized life, based upon mutual tolerance and co-operation. Already a spirit of wanton destructiveness seems to be creeping even in the commonwealth of our literature, threatening violence to our language, rapidly creating a situation which could have its analogy if the Scotch people had suddenly revolted with a calvinistic frenzy of bitterness against the English tongue because of its difference from their own traditional speech and thus if they had deliberately attempted to wreck the intellectual communication between them and the rest of the country. This is the first red signal of danger presaging a fatal collision between neighbouring communities whose duty it is to create a comprehensive life of a common welfare. If it is disturbed in an unthinking obduracy of a communal spite, then, not only our political efficiency but economic prosperity also will be involved in ruin. We have been watching on the part of our Government the uneven discrimination in the apportioning of appointments in spite of the risk it runs in lowering the standard of administration. Owing to reasons for which the Hindus are not answerable, our Muslim brethren have suffered for long from inequality of advantages in various lines. With all my heart I should welcome its being gradually brought to a balance. But it is too plain that there is a spirit working behind the arrangement savouring of a purpose not pertinent to the problem, and this has made its process so aggressively unhealthy for our collective good. Offering any encouragement to the clamouring for crumbs of favour at the table of a supreme power not only causes meanness but feebleness of character. It cannot be gainsaid that the Mahomedan own in them virile qualities that are remarkable. There is no doubt that their democratic tendency of mind has given them special fitness for winning in the race of life. Those of them with whom I have had opportunity to come in close relationship I have frankly admired and loved, and their number is not small. I have always intently hoped that all the differences separating us that mostly arise from utter stupidity and primitive spirit of unreason could be removed through nearer personal touch and comradeship. But any biased treatment from any alien source that is not expected to have a natural sympathy and unselfish concern for the country can only emphasize these differences into a mortal mischief. Let us have the far-sighted wisdom to know that concessions acquired through a prudent patronage are always demoralizing, both for those who are fortunate and others who are deprived. They will create complications that will perpetually irritate each other and in the long run will never serve those who have been helped to an easy path of profit. We, who belong to the same soil must, for the sake of a civilized existence and ultimately for the bare self-protection cultivate mutual friendliness, and both the parties should rise above all immediate provocations and allurements, and should distrust the elements, foreign and indigenous, that sow living thorns in their path of fellowship. We, Hindus must not grudge the favoured partners of our destiny the sudden shower of gifts so long as it lasts; the only cause for anxiety lies in the sureness of a reaction that will follow when the saturation point is reached and yet satiety remains distant, when the one-sided game of indulgence crosses the bounds of even autocratic decency. The most ill-omened aspect of the problem which frightens us is when we realize the absurdity of bringing arguments to the present question, being perfectly certain that our rulers long trained in parliamentary ethics, know better than ourselves that communal division in a political organization is fatal to its effectiveness.

And what is the most unfortunate fact about it is, that the vehemence of our wrath is poured upon the Mahomedan who are as much the victims of a disastrous policy as we are ourselves. For it never can be to their best interest this offer of an intoxicant. It will no doubt rudely and constantly disturb our own peace but in the natural course of things one day the other party will have time to sober down and discover in dismay that some very valuable things have been destroyed and possibilities ruined that are not easy to be recovered. However, in the meanwhile, I earnestly ask my Hindu brethren never to lose their temper and aggravate the injury into suicide. As for those who have instituted this policy under various plausible excuses it will be presumptuous for me to warn them for their wrong-headed statesmanship. If they have no compunction to mix some baser alloy in their gift which could have its full value only by its uncorrupted generosity, they will not only miss their dues in thanks which I am sure they cannot afford to despise but—well, they know better.

Those who have studied the modern condition in Europe have surely learnt that for a moment it may become possible to force people reduced to helplessness to swallow injustice but not so to force them to assimilate it. Sooner or later it is ejected in a poisoned mass of contamination. Let us forget for the moment the dominant power that is here to make and mar our future and turn to those of our countrymen who seem to be losing their mental equilibrium through a pathetic illusion of an everlasting good luck and remind them that in this critical period of our history any wrong turn taken in the path of our self-government is sure to lead to a permanent disgrace and calamity. It is not the difference in opportunities which in itself is dangerous but the mental attitude created through it, the attitude of exultation on the one side recklessly pushes its triumph with immediate impunity to ungenerous extremes, and on the other side, the resentment ranking deep seeking to find outlets often in a wrong manner and unreasonable excuses. It encourages both the parties light-heartedly to perpetrate acts that embitter racial memory for all time to come, creating deep-rooted prejudices that attack the foundation of neighbourly good fellowship. It is very much like infusing the air with poison gas to make victory easy using a terribly wasteful method of attaining in iniquitous success that speads its torments far into the heart of an innocent multitude and non-combatant future.

I was born too early for this post-war age of disillusionment. I have had my moral sustenance from the much-maligned Victorian age through its literature and its struggling faith in humanity as it reached us across the sea. Today when we find all through the West the ruthless repression of freedom, and that callously arrogant cynicism which is indifferent to a wide-spread human misery and injustice, I still must almost against all contrary evidence place my confidence in the sensitiveness to the ideals of humanity which I considered as the characteristic trait of the Western mind. And therefore, when I grow aware in our own neighbourhood of some far-reaching and deeply laid diplomatic move which means permanently holding paralysed in its meshes our future for the sake of a tighter grip upon our vitals, I still feel inclined to appeal to the chivalrous humanity of the Englishman representing the best ideals of the Western culture. I believe that if those ideals that show signs of dilapidation were restored once again and somehow brought to bear even upon Indian politics, if the people that determine the fate of this country could win in our hearts the prestige of unswerving fairplay it will not only add to the credit of their civilization but to their worldly benefit in the long run. If those that have called this meeting had no such faith, conscious or unconscious, in this race then this meeting is foolish and devoid of meaning. I am sure, even though they may not clearly define it to themselves, they are certain that the higher stratum of English life does not solely constitute of persons like the late Premier who betrayed his often-pronounced ideals when they concerned India or some Viceroy who cleverly navigated the white paper boat into a stagnant water of inanity, and who must have inwardly chuckled at all our discomfitures and blunders of inexperience. If this pathetic faith which dies hard is an illusion, then let us leave this child's play of meetings and conferences and exclusively concentrate our attention to build our own history in an unaided and dignified aloofness and in patient wisdom. Or even fall back upon the stoic indifference of the oriental mind, the indifference that unconsciously prepares the soil for an unwelcome and unaccustomed cataclysm.

1936

Address at the Parliament of Religions

Friends,

When I was asked to address this distinguished gathering I was naturally reluctant, for I do not know if I can be called religious in the current sense of the term, not claiming as my possession any particular idea of God, authorised by some time-honoured institution. If, in spite of all this, I have accepted this honour, it is only out of respect to the memory of the great saint with whose centenary the present Parliament is associated. I venerate Paramahamsa Dev because he, in an arid age of religious nihilism, proved the truth of our spiritual heritage by realizing it, because the largeness of his spirit could comprehend seemingly antagonistic modes of *sadhana,* and because the simplicity of his soul shames for all time the pomp and pedantry of pontiffs and pundits.

I have nothing new to tell you, no esoteric truth to propound to you. I am a mere poet, a lover of men and of creation. But since love gives a certain insight, I may perhaps claim to have sometimes caught the hushed voice of humanity and felt its suppressed longing for the Infinite. I hope I do not belong to those who, born in a prison-house, never have the good luck to know that it is a prison, who are blissfully unaware that the costliness of their furniture and profuseness of the provisions for their comfort act as invisible walls in a castle of vanity that not only rob them of their freedom but even of the desire for it.

The degree of this freedom is measured according to our realization of the Infinite whether in the outer world, or in the inner life. In a narrow room we may have as much space as is necessary for living and for the exercise of our muscles; the food may be more than sufficient, it may even be sumptuous; yet our inborn craving for what we may call the more, the unattained, if not altogether killed, remains unsatisfied. We are deprived of the Infinite, which is freedom of range, both in the outer world as well as in the ceaseless variety of the world of our experience.

But a more profoundly intimate perception of the Infinite lies in that intensity of our consciousness, which we can only attain when we realize ultimate value in some ideal of perfection, when in the realization of some fact of our life we become aware of an indefinable truth that immensely transcends it. We, in our human nature, have a hunger for *Bhuma*, for immensity, for something a great deal more than what we need immediately for the purposes of life. Men all through their history have been struggling to realize this truth according to the unfolding of their idea of the boundless, and have been gradually changing their methods and plans of existence, constantly meeting failures, but never owning final defeat.

We find that animals have their evolution along the line of the race. They have their individual life which ends with their death. But even in them there is a touch of the Infinite which urges them to outlive their own life in the life of the race, accepting sufferings and making sacrifices for its sake. The spirit of sacrifice in the parents is this touch of the Infinite,—the motive power which makes the race-life possible, which helps to develop those faculties in them that will enable their descendants to find better opportunity for food and shelter.

But in human beings has been further evolved a sense of the Infinite that goes far beyond the struggle for physical life which merely occupies extended time and extended space. Man has realized that the life of perfection is not merely a life of extension, but one which has its selfless enjoyment of the great and the beautiful.

After we have evolved this sense of the beautiful, of the good, of something that we call truth,—which is deeper and larger than any number of facts,—we have come into an altogether different atmosphere from that wherein the animals and trees have their existence. But we have come into this higher realm only very lately.

Ages and ages have passed, dominated by the life of what we call the self, which is intent upon seeking food and shelter, and upon the perpetuation of the race. But there is a mysterious region waiting for its full recognition, which does not entirely acknowledge loyalty to physical claims. Its mystery constantly troubles us and we are not yet fully at ease in this region. We call it *spiritual.* That word is vague, only because we have not yet been able to realize its meaning completely.

We are groping in the dark, not yet clear in our idea of the ultimate meaning at the centre of this world. Nevertheless, through the dim light which reaches us across the barriers of our physical existence, we seem to have a stronger faith in this spiritual life than in the physical. For even those who do not believe in the truth which we cannot define, but call by the name of spirit,—even they are obliged to behave as though they did believe it to be true, or, at any rate, truer than the world which is evident to our senses. And so even they are often willing to accept death,—the termination of this physical life,—for the sake of the true, the good and the beautiful. This fact expresses man's deeper urge for freedom, for the liberation of his self in the realm of the limitless where he realizes his relationship with the truth which relates him to the universe in a disinterested spirit of love.

When Buddha preached *maitri*—the relationship of harmony —not only with human beings but with all creation, did he not have this truth in his mind that our treatment of the world is wrong when we treat it solely as a fact which can be known and used for our own personal needs? Did he not feel that the true meaning of creation can be understood only through love because it is an eternal expression of love which waits for its answer from our soul emancipated from the bondage of self? This emancipation cannot be negative in character, for love can never lead to negation. The perfect freedom is in a perfect harmony of relationship and not in a mere severance of bondage. Freedom has no content, and therefore no meaning, where it has nothing but itself. The soul's emancipation is in the fulfilment of its relation to the central truth of everything that there is, which is impossible to define because it comes at the end of all definitions.

The distinctive feature of materialism is the measurability of its outward expression, which is the same thing as the finiteness of its boundaries. And the disputes, civil and criminal, which have raged in the history of man, have mostly been over these same boundaries. To increase one's own bounds one has necessarily to encroach upon those of others. So, because the pride of Power is the pride of Quantity, pride of the mere number of its recruits and victims, the most powerful telescope, when pointed in the direction of Power, fails to reveal the shore of peace across the sea of blood.

Such is the tragedy that so often besets our history when this love of power, which is really the love of self, domineers over the religious life of man, for then the only means by which man could hope to set his spirit free, itself becomes the worst enemy of that freedom. Of all fetters those that falsely assume spiritual designations are the most difficult to break, and of all dungeons the most terrible are those invisible ones where men's souls are imprisoned in self-delusion bred of vanity. For, the undisguised pursuit of self has safety in its openness, like filth exposed to the sun and air. But the self-magnification, with its consequent thwarting of the best in man, that goes on unashamed when religion deadens into sectarianism is a perverse form of worldliness under the mask of religion; it constricts the heart into narrowness much more effectively than the cult of the world based upon material interests can ever do.

Let me try to answer the question as to what this *Spirit* is, for the winning of which all the great religions were brought into being.

The evening sky is revealed to us in its serene aspect of beauty though we know that from the fiery whirlpools which are the stars, chaotic outbursts clash against one another in a conflict of implacable fury. But *Ishavasyam idam survam,*— over and through it all there is spread a mysterious spirit of harmony, constantly modulating rebellious elements into creative unity, evolving ineffable peace and beauty out of the incoherently battling combatants perpetually struggling to elbow out their neighbours into a turmoil of dissolution.

And this great harmony, this everlasting Yea—this is Truth, that bridges the dark abysms of time and space, reconciles contradictions, imparts perfect balance to the unstable. This all-pervading mystery is what we call spiritual in its essence. It is the human aspect of this truth which all great personalities have made their own in their lives and have offered to their fellow-beings in the name of various religions as means of peace and goodwill,—as vehicles of beauty in behaviour, heroism in character, noble aspiration and achievement in all great civilizations.

But when these very religions travel far from their sacred sources, they lose their original dynamic vigour, and degenerate into the arrogance of piety, into an utter emptiness crammed with irrational habits and mechanical practices, then is their spiritual inspiration befogged in the turbidity of sectarianism, then do they become the most obstinate obstruction that darkens our vision of human unity, piling up out of their accretions and refuse deadweights of unreason across our path of progress,—till at length civilized life is compelled to free its education from the stifling coils of religious creeds, such fratricidal aberrations, in the guise of spiritual excellence, have brought upon the name of God, whom they profess to glorify, uglier discredit than honest and defiant atheism could ever have done.

The reason is, because sectarianism, like some voracious parasite, feeds upon the religion whose colour it assumes, exhausting it so that it knows not when its spirit is sucked dry. It utilises the dead skin for its habitation, as a stronghold for its unholy instinct of fight, its pious vaingloriousness, fiercely contemptuous of its neighbours' articles of faith.

Sectarian votaries of a particular religion, when taken to task for the iniquitous dealings with their brethren which so deeply injure and insult humanity, immediately try to divert attention by glibly quoting noble texts from their own scriptures which preach love, justice, righteousness, and the divinity immanent in Man,—ludicrously unconscious of the fact that those constitute the most damaging incrimination of their usual attitude of mind. In taking up the guardianship of their religion they allow, on the one hand, physical materialism to invade it by falsely giving eternal value to external practices, often of primitive origin, and moral materialism on the other, by invoking sacred sanction for their forms of worship within the rigid enclosure of special privileges founded upon accident of birth, or conformity, irrespective of moral justification. Such debasement does not belong to any particular religion, but more or less to all religions, the records of whose impious activities are written in brothers' blood, and sealed with the indignities heaped upon them.

All through the course of human history it has become tragically evident that religions, whose mission is liberation of soul, have in some form or other ever been instrumental in shackling freedom of mind and even moral rights. The desecration of truth in unworthy hands,—the truth which was meant to raise humanity morally and materially out of the dusky region of animality, is moreover followed by condign punishment, and thus we find that religious perversity is causing more blindness of reason and deadness of moral sensibility than any other deficiency in our education; just as, the truth represented by science, when used for ignoble traffic, threatens us with annihilation. It has been the saddest experience of man to witness such violation of the highest products of civilization, to find the guardians of religion blessing the mailed fist of temporal power in its campaign of wholesale massacre and consolidation of slavery and science joining hands with the same relentless power in its murderous career of exploitation.

When we come to believe that we are in possession of our God because we belong to some particular sect, it gives us a complete sense of comfort to feel that God is no longer needed, except for breaking with the greater unction the skulls of people whose idea of God, fortunately or unfortunately, differs from our own in theoretical details. Having thus made provision for our God in some shadow-land of creed, we feel free to reserve all the space in the world of reality for ourselves,—ridding it of the wonder of the Infinite, making it as trivial as our own household furniture. Such unmitigated vulgarity only becomes possible when we have no doubt in our minds that we believe in God while our life ignores Him.

The pious man of sect is proud because he is confident of his right of possession of God. The man of devotion is meek because he is conscious of God's right of love over his life and soul. The object of our possession needs must become smaller than ourselves and, without acknowledging it in so many words, the bigoted sectarian nurses the implicit belief that God can be kept secured for himself and his fellows in a cage which is of their own make. In a similar manner the primitive races of men believe that their ceremonials have a magic influence upon their deities.

Thus every religion that begins as a liberating agency ends as a vast prison-house. Built on the renunciation of its founder, it becomes a possessive institution in the hands of its priests, and claiming to be universal, becomes an active centre of schism and strife. Like a sluggish stream the spirit of man is choked by rotting weeds and is divided into shallow slimy pools that are active only in releasing deadly mists of stupefaction. This mechanical spirit of tradition is essentially materialistic, it is blindly pious but not spiritual, obsessed by phantoms of unreason that haunt feeble minds with their ghastly mimicry of religion. This happens not only to mediocre individuals who hug the fetters that keep them irresponsible or craving for lurid unrealities, but to generations of insipid races that have lost all emphasis of significance in themselves, having missed their present in their ghostly past!

Great souls, like Ramakrishna Paramahamsa, have a comprehensive vision of Truth, they have the power to grasp the significance of each different form of the Reality that is one in all,—but the masses of believers are unable to reconcile the conflict of codes and commands. Their timid and shrunken imagination, instead of being liberated by the vision of the Infinite in religion, is held captive in bigotry and is tortured and exploited by priests and fanatics for uses hardly anticipated by those who originally received it.

Unfortunately, great teachers most often are surrounded by persons whose minds, lacking transparency of atmosphere, obscure and distort the ideas originating from the higher source. They feel a smug satisfaction when the picture of their master which they offer shows features made somewhat in the pattern of their own personality. Consciously and unconsciously they reshape profound messages of wisdom in the mould of their own tortuous understanding, carefully modifying them into conventional platitudes in which they themselves find comfort, and which satisfy the habit-ridden mentality of their own community. Lacking the sensitiveness of mind which is necessary for the enjoyment of truth in its unadulterated purity they exaggerate it in an attempt at megalomaniac enlargement according to their own insensate standard, which is as absurdly needless for its real appraisement as it is derogatory to the dignity of its original messengers. The history of great men, because of their very greatness, ever runs the risk of being projected on to a wrong background of memory where it gets mixed up with elements that are crudely customary and therefore inertly accepted by the multitude.

I say to you: if you are really lovers of Truth, then dare to seek it in its fullness, in all the infinite beauty of its majesty, but never be content to treasure up its vain symbols in miserly seclusion within the stony walls of conventions. Let us revere the great souls in the sublime simplicity of their spiritual altitude which is common to them all, where they meet in universal aspiration to set the spirit of man free from the bondage of his own individual ego, and of the ego of his race and of his creed; but in that lowland of traditions, where religions challenge and refute each other's claims and dogmas, there a wise man must pass them by in doubt and dismay.

I do not mean to advocate a common church for mankind, a universal pattern to which every act of worship and aspiration must conform. The arrogant spirit of sectarianism which so often uses either active or passive, violent or subtle, methods of persecution, on the least provocation or without any, has to be reminded of the fact that religion, like poetry, is not a mere idea,—it is expression. The self-expression of God is in the variedness of creation; and our attitude towards the Infinite must in its expression also have a variedness of individuality, ceaseless and unending. When a religion develops the ambition of imposing its doctrine on all mankind, it degrades itself into a tyranny and becomes a form of imperialism. That is why we find a ruthless method of fascism in religious matters prevailing in most parts of the world, trampling flat the expansion of the spirit of man under its insensitive heels.

The attempt to make the one religion which is their own, dominate all time and space, comes naturally to men addicted to sectarianism. This makes it offensive to them to be told that God is generous in His distribution of love, and His means of communication with men have not been restricted to a blind lane abruptly stopping at one narrow point of history. If humanity ever happens to be overwhelmed with the universal flood of a bigoted exclusiveness, then God will have to make provision for another Noah's Ark to save His creatures from the catastrophe of spiritual desolation.

What I plead for is a living recognition of the neglected truth that the reality of religion has its basis in the truth of Man's nature in its most intense and universal need and so must constantly be tested by it. Where it frustrates that need, and outrages its reason, it repudiates its own justification.

Let me conclude with a few lines from the great mystic poet of mediaeval India, Kabir, whom I regard as one of the greatest spiritual geniuses of our land:

The jewel is lost in the mud,
    and all are seeking for it;
some look for it in the east, and some in the west;
    some in the water and some amongst stones.
But the servant Kabir has appraised it at its true value,
    and has wrapped it with care
        in a corner of the mantle of his own heart.

1937

China and India

The most memorable fact of human history is that of a path-opening, not for the clearing of a passage for machines or machine guns, but for helping the realization by races of their affinity of minds, their mutual obligation of a common humanity. Such a rare event did happen and the path was built between our people and the Chinese in an age when physical obstruction needed heroic personality to overcome it and the mental barrier a moral power of uncommon magnitude. The two leading races of that age met, not as rivals on the battlefield each claiming the right to be the sole tyrant on earth, but as noble friends, glorying in their exchange of gifts. Then came a slow relapse into isolation, covering up the path with its accumulated dust of indifference. Today our old friends have beckoned to us again, generously helping us to retrace that ancient path obliterated by the inertia of forgetful centuries,—and we rejoice.

This is, indeed, a great day for me, a day long looked for, when I should be able to redeem, on behalf of our people, an ancient pledge implicit in our past, the pledge to maintain the intercourse of culture and friendship between our people and the people of China, an intercourse whose foundations were laid eighteen hundred years back by our ancestors with infinite patience and sacrifice. When I went to China several years ago I felt a touch of that great stream of life that sprang from the heart of India and overflowed across mountain and desert into that distant land, fertilising the heart of its people. I thought of that great pilgrimage, of those noble heroes, who, for the sake of their faith, their ideal of the liberation of self that leads to the perfect love which unites all beings, risked life and accepted banishment from home and all that was familiar to them. Many perished and left no trace behind. A few were spared to tell their story, a story not of adventurers and trespassers whose heroism has proved a mere romantic excuse for careers of unchecked brigandage, but a story of pilgrims who came to offer their gifts of love and wisdom, a story indelibly recorded in the cultural memory of their hosts. I read it when I was received there as a representative of a revered race and felt proud as I traced the deep marks our ancestors had left behind of their achievements. But I also felt the humiliation of our long lasting evil fate that has obscured for us in an atmosphere of inanity the great human value of a noble endeavour, one of the most precious in the history of man.

I told my Chinese hosts on that occasion: 'My friends, I have come to ask you to re-open the channel of communication which I hope is still there; for though overgrown with weeds of oblivion, its lines can still be traced. I have not the same voice that my ancestors had. I have not the wisdom they possessed. My life has not attained that consciousness of fulfilment needed to make this message fruitful. We in India are a defeated race; we have no power, political, military or commercial; we do not know how to help you or injure you materially. But fortunately we can still meet you as your guests, your hosts, your brothers and your friends. Let that happen. I invite you to us as you have invited me. I do not know whether you have heard of the institution I have established in my land. Its one object is to let India welcome the world to its heart. Let what seems a barrier become a path, and let us unite, not in spite of our differences, but through them. For differences can never be wiped away, and life would be so much the poorer without them. Let all human races keep their own personalities, and yet come together, not in a uniformity that is dead, but in a unity that is living.'

That has happened and friends are here from China with their gift of friendship and co-operation. The Hall which is to be opened today will serve both as the nucleus and as a symbol of that larger understanding that is to grow with time. Here students and scholars will come from China and live as part of ourselves, sharing our life and letting us share theirs, and by offering their labours in a common cause, help in slowly re-building that great course of fruitful contact between our peoples, that has been interrupted for ten centuries. For this Visva-Bharati is, and will, I hope, remain a meeting place for individuals from all countries, East or West, who believe in the unity of mankind and are prepared to suffer for their faith. I believe in such individuals even though their efforts may appear to be too insignificant to be recorded in history.

It might be supposed that in a world so closely knit by railways, steamships and airlines, where almost every big city is cosmopolitan, such special invitations for contact are superfluous. But, unfortunately, the contacts that are being made today have done more to estrange and alienate peoples from one another than physical inaccessibility ever did. We are discovering for ourselves the painful truth that nothing divides so much as the wrong kind of nearness. Peoples seem to be coming in each other's way, dodging and trapping one another, without ever coming together. We meet others, either as tourists when we merely slide against the surface of their life, entering hotels only to disappear from their land, or as exploiters in one disguise or another. We are living in a world where nations are divided into two main groups—those who trample on others' freedom, and those who are unable to guard their own; so that while we have too much of intrusion on others' rights, we have hardly any intercourse with their culture. It is a terrorised world, dark with fear and suspicion, where peaceful races in dread of predatory hordes are retreating into isolation for security.

I am reminded of my experience as we were travelling up from Shanghai to Nanking along the great river, Yang Tse. All through the night I kept on coming out of my cabin to watch the beautiful scene on the banks, the sleeping cottages with their solitary lamps, the silence spread over the hills, dim with mist. When morning broke and brought into view fleets of boats coming down the river, their sails stretching high into the air, a picture of life's activity with its perfect grace of freedom, I was deeply moved and felt that my own sail had caught the wind and was carrying me from captivity, from the sleeping past, out into the great world of man. It brought to my mind different stages in the history of man's progress.

In the night each village was self-centred, each cottage stood bound by the chain of unconsciousness. I knew, as I gazed on the scene, that vague dreams were floating about in this atmosphere of sleeping souls, but what struck my mind more forcibly was the fact that when men are asleep they are shut up within the very narrow limits of their own individual lives. The lamps exclusively belonged to the cottages, which in their darkness were in perfect isolation. Perhaps, though I could not see them, some prowling bands of thieves were the only persons awake, ready to exploit the weakness of those who were asleep.

When daylight breaks we are free from the enclosure and the exclusiveness of our individual life. It is then that we see the light which is for all men and for all times. It is then that we come to know each other and come to co-operate in the field of life. This was the message that was brought in the morning by the swiftly moving boats. It was the freedom of life in their outspread sails that spoke to me; and I felt glad. I hoped and prayed that morning had truly come in the human world and that the light had broken forth.

This age to which we belong, does it not still represent night in the human world, a world asleep, whilst individual races are shut up within their own limits, calling themselves nations, which barricade themselves, as these sleeping cottages were barricaded, with shut doors, with bolts and bars, with prohibitions of all kinds? Does not all this represent the dark age of civilization, and have we not begun to realize that it is the robbers who are out and awake?

But I do not despair. As the early bird, even while the dawn is yet dark, sings out and proclaims the rising of the sun, so my heart sings to proclaim the coming of a great future which is already close upon us. We must be ready to welcome this new age. There are some people, who are proud and wise and practical, who say that it is not in human nature to be generous, that men will always fight one another, that the strong will conquer the weak and that there can be no real moral foundation for man's civilization. We cannot deny the facts of their assertion that the strong have their rule in the human world: but I refuse to accept this as a revelation of truth.

It is co-operation and love, mutual trust and mutual aid which make for strength and real merit of civilization. New spiritual and moral power must continually be developed to enable men to assimilate their scientific gains, to control their weapons and machines, or these will dominate and enslave them. I know that many will point to the weakness of China and India and tell us that thrown as we are among other ruthlessly strong and aggressive world peoples, it is necessary to emphasize power and progress in order to avoid destruction. It is indeed true that we are weak and disorganized, at the mercy of every barbaric force, but that is not because of our love of peace but because we no longer pay the price of our faith by dying for it. We must learn to defend our humanity against the insolence of the strong, only taking care that we do not imitate their ways and, by turning ourselves brutal, destroy those very values which alone make our humanity worth defending. For danger is not only of the enemy without but of the treason within us. We had, for over a century, been so successfully hypnotised and dragged by the prosperous West behind its chariot that, though choked by the dust, deafened by the noise, humbled by our helplessness, overwhelmed by speed, we yet agreed to acknowledge that this chariot-drive was progress, and that progress was civilization. If we ever ventured to ask, however humbly: 'Progress towards what, and progress for whom?'—it was considered to be peculiarly and ridiculously oriental to entertain such doubts about the absoluteness of progress. It is only of late that a voice has been heeded by us, bidding us take account not only of the scientific perfection of the chariot, but of the depth of ditches lying across its path. Today we are emboldened to ask: what is the value of progress if it make a desert of this beautiful world of man? And though we speak as members of a nation that is humiliated and oppressed and lies bleeding in the dust, we must never acknowledge the defeat, the last insult, the utter ruin of our spirit being conquered, of our faith being sold. We need to hear again and again, and never more than in this modern world of head-hunting and cannibalism in disguise that:—By the help of unrighteousness men do prosper, men do gain victories over their enemies, men do attain what they desire; but they perish at the root.

It is to this privilege of preserving, not the mere body of our customs and conventions, but the moral force which has given quality to our civilization and made it worthy of being honoured, that I invite the co-operation of the people of China, recalling the profound words of their sage, Lao-tze: Those who have virtue attend to their obligations; those who have no virtue attend to their claims. Progress which is not related to an inner ideal, but to an attraction which is external, seeks to satisfy endless claims. But civilization, which is an ideal, gives us power and joy to fulfil our obligations.

Let us therefore abide by our obligation to maintain and nourish distinctive merit of our respective cultures and not be misled into believing that what is ancient is necessarily outworn and what is modern is indispensable. When we class things as modern or old we make a great mistake in following our calendar of dates. We know that the flowers of Spring are old, that they represent the dawn of life on earth,—but are they therefore symbol of the dead and discarded? Would we rather replace them with artificial flowers made of rags, because they were made 'yesterday'? It is not what is old or what is modern that we should love and cherish but what has truly a permanent human value. And can anything be more worthy of being cherished than the beautiful spirit of the Chinese culture that has made the people love material things without the strain of greed, that has made them love the things of this earth, clothe them with tender grace without turning them materialistic? They have instinctively grasped the secret of the rhythm of things,—not the secret of power that is in science, but the secret of expression. This is a great gift, for God alone knows this secret. I envy them this gift and wish our people could share it with them.

I do not know what distinctive merit we have which our Chinese friends and others may wish to share. Once indeed our sages dedicated themselves to the ideal of perfect sympathy and intellect, in order to win absolute freedom through wisdom and absolute love through pity. Today we cannot boast of either such wisdom or such magnanimity of heart. But I hope we are not yet reduced to such absolute penury of both as not to be able to offer at least a genuine atmosphere of hospitality, of an earnestness to cross over our limitations and move nearer to the hearts of other peoples and understand somewhat of the significance of the endless variety of man's creative effort.

1937

To Subhas Chandra Bose

As Bengal's poet I invite you on Bengal's behalf to accept the leadership of our country. God the Preserver, says the Gita, incarnates Himself whenever need arises to protect the meek and chastise the wicked. Enmeshed in the evils of misfortune, out of the very throes of the body-politic is the leader born. Trodden down under the heel of foreign domination, her energies dissipated by internal divisions, Bengal's destiny is today darkened by ever deepening clouds.

Divided against ourselves we are weak at home while the adverse forces mobilise outside Bengal's frontiers. Our economy, our method of work, our moral tone are woefully inadequate. Our politics is like a boat in which the oars do not keep time with the helm. When the mind is ridden by an evil fate it acts like virus in a worn-out body. That is how we become divided against ourselves, we throw out our well-wishers, make strangers of friends, insult those who are worthy of respect, and, in this way weaken our own ranks from the rear.

Just at the moment when it devolves upon each one of us to raise by dint of our own worth the lofty pinnacle of our national glory and place it high before the eyes of the whole world, some malicious self-seekers there are, who in their suicidal stupidity dig holes of calumny into the very foundation of the structure. Maligning one another, they serve only to strengthen the insolence of the enemy.

When there is a wound from outside, the festering sore rouses all the venom that lie dormant inside the body and precipitates a sepsis. Worn out by this conspiracy of between the forces of disease inside and outside the body, our mind becomes inert and cannot fully exert itself for its immunity. At such times of crisis what we need most is the protecting right arm of self-reliant strong men, who can, with impunity, overside the obstacle of an adverse fate that may lie on the road of our triumphant march.

Subhas Chandra, I have watched you from afar when you first began your penance for the country. In that dawn of your *sadhana,* in the uncertain twilight, I was assailed by misgivings about you. I have felt hesitant to place my full faith in you. Your blunders, your weaknesses have caused me pain. Today you are revealed in the clear light of the midday sun—there is no room for doubt to darken the sky. In your lifetime you have absorbed many an experience. Your adherence to duty is a positive proof of your vitality and strength. Incarceration, banishment, incurable disease—all these have sorely tested this strength. They were powerless to overcome you. Rather have they broadened your mind and you have emerged out of these trials with a vision that reaches beyond the bounds of the country and encompasses—the extensive grounds of world history. You have made allies out of your troubles and obstacles have proved to be so many steps in the ladder of your success. That you could do so, was owing to your refusal to accept defeat. We, in Bengal, need to emulate this strength of character more than anything else.

For various reasons Bengal has been denied of many opportunities by her own people and by those who are strangers to the land. We desire that by her own courage and initiative Bengal should forge blessings out of this course of fate. Let her determination not to accept apparent defeat, lead Bengal to her triumph.

As I look around, I see the hands of a cruel fate working in every walk of life in Bengal. In the face of this unkind destiny, we should bravely affirm that we have within our own character that ingredient wherewith to build our fort of resistance. We can save ourselves if only we can break open the lock and deliver this source of strength that lies within. Astride the ferocious shark of evil times we shall have to cross the sea of nightmare. It is with the hope that you will uphold our courage that I now call upon you to lead us in the path of this dare-devil adventure. Howsoever difficult be the goal, if we but persevere in our united effort, we shall reach the end.

It is here that the crux of the problem lies. But why should we use that conditional if, why should we give way to misgivings? Unite we must if the nation is to survive. It is up to you to rouse the determination, throughout the length and breadth of the country, that Bengal will not die humiliated by fate, that Bengal will raise its proud head above the buffetings of misfortune. You are the spirit of tireless youth, you have in your nature that unflinching courage which can uphold hope in the face of an impending crisis. In the faith that you will implant in the soil of Bengal that banner of death-triumphing hope, that flag of fearless freedom, I welcome you to be the leader of the country.

Let Bengal's millions speak in one voice, in firm and clear accents that the seat of leadership is ready for you. May you resolve the spirit of mutual mistrust in the Bengalee, may his diffidence be over. May your example put meanness and niggardly conduct to ignominy and shame. Let Bengal, through upholding and maintaining her self-respect in victory and again in defeat, uphold and maintain the prestige of her accredited leader.

The Bengalee is a logician born. He delights in hairsplitting arguments. Right from the commencement of a project to its very end, he finds a peculiar pleasure in sitting in opposition and refuting the other man's viewpoint in the pride of his sterile intellect. He is more interested in picking holes and finding faults than in taking a comprehensive view of things. He forgets that his controversies lead nowhere, that they are the unproductive luxuriance of an idle mind. The need of the day is not arguments but a spontaneous will to do things. Let the composite will of the nation that appoints you to the leader mould you to the great responsibility that devolves upon such leadership. May the whole nation find its self-expression in your person.

I have seen during the Bengal partition movement how that will expressed itself in its resistance to ward off the impending blow of the scimitar which sought to sever the body-politic of Bengal. Bengal rose like one man against the mighty power of the Crown. Her people did not then sit idle and deliberate in the fashion of wiseacres as to whether it was possible to oppose and defeat (circumvent) the design of the foreign power. What she did then was to will with all her heart.

In the years that followed I have seen that very desire burning strong and bright in the heart of the younger generation. They were born with the fire. But alas! the fire that should have lit the lamps and given us light was the fire used to burn and destroy. They paid dearly for the mistake. They themselves were consumed by the flames and after the conflagration was over, there remained no light to guide the benighted. But misguided though it was, the heroism that they showed even in the tragic futility of their blunder, was something which I did not see anywhere in India at that time. The series of sacrifices that they made, the way they braved misfortunes one after another, the precious lives that they lay down at the altar of the country—these have all been burnt into the ashes of futility. But, they have, nevertheless, despite the immediate results, proved for all time to come that invincible will-power of Bengal.

The agents of law and order might well try to darken these chapters of history punctuated by the heart-rending blunders of the restless youth. But, try as they may, they can never black out the radiance inherent in the spirit of youth.

True, we have seen many signs of weakness of our country. Our hope lies deep in the recesses of her being where her sources of secret strength awaits the future hour. It is up to you to see that this hope materialises and comes to fruition. All that is best in Bengalee character—his pleasant and affectionate nature, his imagination, his penetrating vision, his talent in creative arts, the power he has of absorbing the gifts of an alien culture—all these should no longer be allowed to remain abstractions, but should be harnessed for actual work. It is for you to create a new springtime of sprouting hopes. You are to deliver the country from all that is worn out and old, all that is steeped in darkness.

You may say that the work of such magnitude is not for one man to undertake single-handed. That is true. It is also a fact that this work cannot be done by men working in separate units. Nothing will be impossible to achieve if the whole country could come together drawn by the centripetal force of a towering personality. Those who are real and natural leaders of the country, never stand by themselves. They belong to all men of all times. They stand on the crest of the present and are the very first to bow in obeisance to the first purple rays that usher the dawning future. Keeping that in mind I invite you and through you the whole nation to give a lead to the country.

Let no one misapprehend that in my provincial pride I want to separate Bengal from the rest of India or that I want to place anybody on a seat of rivalry with the Mahatma who has brought in a new age in the realm of politics and has thus made India's name famous in the comity of nations. My appeal is being made today because I want Bengal fully and substantially to co-operate with India and because I want this valuable co-operation to bear real fruit. I do not wish that a powerless and weak Bengal should lag behind empty-handed while the other provinces bring their own offerings to the Motherland. Through your *sadhana* let Bengal's self-dedication be true and noble, let her lamps of offering shine with her own true light.

Many years ago while addressing another meeting I had the occasion to convey my message of welcome to the leader of Bengal, yet to be. After so many years I take the occasion to welcome him in the very person. I am no longer capable, nor do I have the strength necessary to co-operate, body and soul, with the leader in doing actual field work. As one of the very last duties left to me I may only invoke the will of the country and may pray that that will might actuate and strengthen your will. And then I shall bless you and take your leave to go, knowing full well that you have made your country's sorrows your own and that the deliverance of the country comes apace carrying along with it your ultimate reward and recognition.

1939

Convocation Address at Gurukula Kangri

I regret that my feeble body and a distressing malady do not allow me the pleasure of being present at this great gathering when the *Snatakas* of this University will be bidding farewell to their Alma Mater and go out boldly into the wide world fortified with the knowledge they have gathered at the feet of their masters. I wish them all success in their endeavours of the future and I bless them with all my heart.

That aspect of our education which has drawn my attention very considerably ever since I took to the arduous task of being a teacher I would like to emphasize once more before you. I am aware that I shall be repeating myself but that is inevitable for one at my age.

As a people we must be fully conscious of what we are. It is a truism to say that the consciousness of the unity of a people implies the knowledge of its parts as well of its whole. But, most of us not only have no such knowledge of India, they do not even have an eager desire to cultivate it.

By asserting our national unity with vehemence in our political propaganda, we assure ourselves that we possess it, and thus continue to live in a make-believe world of political day-dreams.

The fact is, we have a feeble human interest in our own country. We love to talk about politics and economics; we are ready to soar into the thin air of academic abstractions, or roam in the dusk of pedantic wildernesses; but we never care to cross our social boundaries and come to the door of our neighbouring communities, personally to enquire how they think and feel and express themselves, and how they fashion their lives.

The love of man has its own hunger for knowing. Even if we lack this concerning our fellow beings in India, except in our political protestations, at least love of knowledge for its own sake could have brought us close to each other. But there also we have failed and suffered. For weakness of knowledge is the foundation of weakness of power. Until India becomes fully distinct in our mind, we can never gain her in truth; and where truth is imperfect, love can never have its full sway. The best function of our Education Centres is to help us to know ourselves; and then along with it, her other mission will be fulfilled which is to inspire us to give ourselves.

What has given such enormous intellectual power to Europe is her coordination of minds. She has evolved a means by which all countries of that continent can think together. Such a great concert of ideas, by its own pressure of movement, naturally wears away all her individual aberrations of thought and extravagances of unreason. It keeps her flights of fancy close to the limits of reticence. All her different thought rays have been focussed in one common culture, which finds its complete expression in all the European universities.

The mind of India, on the other hand, is divided and scattered; there is no one common pathway along which we can reach it. We cannot but look with regret at the feebleness of stimulation in our academic training for the forming of our mind which in co-operation of knowledge and sympathy may comprehend the larger mind of the country. The most important object of our educational institutions is to help each student to realize his personality, as an individual representing his people, in such a broad spirit, that he may know how it is the most important fact of his life for him to have been born to the great world of man.

We in India are unfortunate in not having the chance to give expression to the best in us in creating intimate relations with the powerful peoples of the world. The bond between the nations today is made of the links of mutual menace, its strength depending upon the force of panic, and leading to an enormous waste of resources in a competition of browbeating and bluff. Some great voice is waiting to be heard which will usher in the sacred light of truth in the dark region of the nightmare of politics. But we in India have not yet had the chance. Yet we have our own human voice which truth demands. Even in the region where we are not invited to act we have our right to judge and to guide the mind of man to a proper point of view, to the vision of ideality in the heart of the real.

1941

Crisis in Civilization

Today I complete eighty years of my life. As I look back on the vast stretch of years that lie behind me and see in clear perspective the history of my early development, I am struck by the change that has taken place both in my own attitude and in the psychology of my countrymen—a change that carries within it a cause of profound tragedy.

Our direct contact with the larger world of men was linked up with the contemporary history of the English people whom we came to know in those earlier days. It was mainly through their mighty literature that we formed our ideas with regard to these newcomers to our Indian shores. In those days the type of learning that was served out to us was neither plentiful nor diverse, nor was the spirit of scientific enquiry very much in evidence. Thus their scope being strictly limited, the educated of those days had recourse to English language and literature. Their days and nights were eloquent with the stately declamations of Burke, with Macaulay's long-rolling sentences; discussions centred upon Shakespeare's drama and Byron's poetry and above all upon the large-hearted liberalism of the nineteenth-century English politics.

At the time though tentative attempts were being made to gain our national independence, at heart we had not lost faith in the generosity of the English race. This belief was so firmly rooted in the sentiments of our leaders as to lead them to hope that the victor would of his own grace pave the path of freedom for the vanquished. This belief was based upon the fact that England at the time provided a shelter to all those who had to flee from persecution in their own country. Political martyrs who had suffered for the honour of their people were accorded unreserved welcome at the hands of the English. I was impressed by this evidence of liberal humanity in the character of the English and thus I was led to set them on the pedestal of my highest respect. This generosity in their national character had not yet been vitiated by Imperialist pride. About this time, as a boy in England, I had the opportunity of listening to the speeches of John Bright, both in and outside Parliament. The large-hearted, radical liberalism of those speeches, overflowing all narrow national bounds, had made so deep an impression on my mind that something of it lingers even today, even in these days of graceless disillusionment.

Certainly that spirit of abject dependence upon the charity of our rulers was no matter for pride. What was remarkable, however, was the wholehearted way in which we gave our recognition to human greatness even when it revealed itself in the foreigner. The best and noblest gifts of humanity cannot be the monopoly of a particular race or country; its scope may not be limited nor may it be regarded as the miser's hoard buried underground. That is why English literature which nourished our minds in the past, does even now convey its deep resonance to the recesses of our heart.

It is difficult to find a suitable Bengali equivalent for the English word 'civilization'. That phase of civilization with which we were familiar in this country has been called by Manu '*Sadachar*' (*lit.* proper conduct), that is, the conduct prescribed by the tradition of the race. Narrow in themselves these time-honoured social conventions originated and held good in a circumscribed geographical area, in that strip of land, Brahmavarta by name, bound on either side by the rivers Saraswati and Drisadvati. That is how a pharisaic formalism gradually got the upper hand of free thought and the ideal of 'proper conduct' which Manu found established in Brahmavarta steadily degenerated into socialized tyranny.

During my boyhood days the attitude of the cultured and educated section of Bengal, nurtured on English learning, was charged with a feeling of revolt against these rigid regulations of society. A perusal of what Rajnarain Bose has written describing the ways of the educated gentry of those days will amply bear out what I have said just now. In place of these set codes of conduct we accepted the ideal of 'civilization' as represented by the English term.

In our own family this change of spirit was welcomed for the sake of its sheer rational and moral force and its influence was felt in every sphere of our life. Born in that atmosphere, which was moreover coloured by our intuitive bias for literature, I naturally set the English on the throne of my heart. Thus passed the first chapters of my life. Then came the parting of ways accompanied with a painful feeling of disillusion when I began increasingly to discover how easily those who accepted the highest truths of civilization disowned them with impunity whenever questions of national self-interest were involved.

There came a time when perforce I had to snatch myself away from the mere appreciation of literature. As I emerged into the stark light of bare facts, the sight of the dire poverty of the Indian masses rent my heart. Rudely shaken out of my dreams, I began to realize that perhaps in no other modern state was there such hopeless dearth of the most elementary needs of existence. And yet it was this country whose resources had fed for so long the wealth and magnificence of the British people. While I was lost in the contemplation of the great world of civilization, I could never have remotely imagined that the great ideals of humanity would end in such ruthless travesty. But today a glaring example of it stares me in the face in the utter and contemptuous indifference of a so-called civilized race to the well-being of crores of Indian people.

That mastery over the machine, by which the British have consolidated their sovereignty over their vast Empire, has been kept a sealed book, to which due access has been denied to this helpless country. And all the time before our very eyes Japan has been transforming herself into a mighty and prosperous nation. I have seen with my own eyes the admirable use to which Japan has put in her own country the fruits of this progress. I have also been privileged to witness, while in Moscow, the unsparing energy with which Russia has tried to fight disease and illiteracy, and has succeeded in steadily liquidating ignorance and poverty, wiping off the humiliation from the face of a vast continent. Her civilization is free from all invidious distinction between one class and another, between one sect and another. The rapid and astounding progress achieved by her made me happy and jealous at the same time. One aspect of the Soviet administration which particularly pleased me was that it provided no scope for unseemly conflict of religious difference nor set one community against another by unbalanced distribution of political favours. That I consider a truly civilized administration which impartially serves the common interests of the people.

While other imperialist powers sacrifice the welfare of the subject races to their own national greed, in the USSR I found a genuine attempt being made to harmonise the interests of the various nationalities that are scattered over its vast area. I saw peoples and tribes, who, only the other day, were nomadic savages being encouraged and indeed trained, to avail themselves freely of the benefits of civilization. Enormous sums are being spent on their education to expedite the process. When I see elsewhere some two hundred nationalities—which only a few years ago were at vastly different stages of development—marching ahead in peaceful progress and amity, and when I look about my own country and see a very highly evolved and intellectual people drifting into the disorder of barbarism, I cannot help contrasting the two systems of governments, one based on co-operation, the other on exploitation, which have made such contrary conditions possible.

I have also seen Iran, newly awakened to a sense of national self-sufficiency, attempting to fulfil her own destiny freed from the deadly grinding-stones of two European powers. During my recent visit to that country I discovered to my delight that Zoroastrians who once suffered from the fanatical hatred of the major community and whose rights had been curtailed by the ruling power were now free from this age-long repression, and that civilized life had established itself in the happy land. It is significant that Iran's good fortune dates from the day when she finally disentangled herself from the meshes of European diplomacy. With all my heart I wish Iran well.

Turning to the neighbouring kingdom of Afghanistan I find that though there is much room for improvement in the field of education and social development, yet she is fortunate in that she can look forward to unending progress; for none of the

European powers, boastful of their civilization, has yet succeeded in overwhelming and crushing her possibilities.

Thus while these other countries were marching ahead, India, smothered under the dead weight of British administration, lay static in her utter helplessness. Another great and ancient civilization for whose recent tragic history the British cannot disclaim responsibility, is China. To serve their own national profit the British first doped her people with opium and then appropriated a portion of her territory. As the world was about to forget the memory of this outrage, we were painfully surprised by another event. While Japan was quietly devouring North China, her act of wanton aggression was ignored as a minor incident by the veterans of British diplomacy. We have also witnessed from this distance how actively the British statesmen acquiesced in the destruction of the Spanish Republic.

On the other hand, we also noted with admiration how a band of valiant Englishmen laid down their lives for Spain. Even though the English had not aroused themselves sufficiently to their sense of responsibility towards China in the Far East, in their own immediate neighbourhood they did not hesitate to sacrifice themselves to the cause of freedom. Such acts of heroism reminded me over again of the true English spirit to which in those early days I had given my full faith, and made me wonder how imperialist greed could bring about so ugly a transformation in the character of so great a race.

Such is the tragic tale of the gradual loss of my faith in the claims of the European nations to civilization. In India the misfortune of being governed by a foreign race is daily brought home to us not only in the callous neglect of such minimum necessities of life as adequate provision for food, clothing, educational and medical facilities for the people, but in an even unhappier form in the way the people have been divided among themselves. The pity of it is that the blame is laid at the door of our own society. So frightful a culmination of the history of our people would never have been possible, but for the encouragement it has received from secret influences emanating from high places.

One cannot believe that Indians are in any way inferior to the Japanese in intellectual capacity. The most effective difference between these two eastern peoples is that whereas India lies at the mercy of the British, Japan has been spared the shadow of alien domination. We know what we have been deprived of. That which was truly best in their own civilizations the upholding of the dignity of human relationship, has no place in the British administration of this country. If in its place they have established, with baton in hand, a reign of 'law and order', in other words a policeman's rule, such mockery of civilization can claim no respect from us. It is the mission of civilization to bring unity among people and establish peace and harmony. But in unfortunate India the social fabric is being rent into shreds by unseemly outbursts of hooliganism daily growing in intensity, right under the very aegis of 'law and order'. In India, so long as no personal injury is inflicted upon any member of the ruling race, this barbarism seems to be assured of perpetuity, making us ashamed to live under such an administration.

And yet my good fortune has often brought me into close contact with really large-hearted Englishmen. Without the slightest hesitation I may say that the nobility of their character was without parallel—in no country or community have I come across such greatness of soul. Such examples would not allow me wholly to lose faith in the race which produced them. I had the rare blessing of having Andrews—a real Englishman, a real Christian and a true man—for a very close friend. To-day in the perspective of death his unselfish and courageous magnanimity shines all the brighter. The whole of India remains indebted to him for innumerable acts of love and devotion. But personally speaking, I am especially beholden to him because he helped me to retain in my old age that feeling of respect for the English race with which in the past I was inspired by their literature and which I was about to lose completely. I count such Englishmen as Andrews not only as my personal and intimate friends but as friends of the whole human race. To have known them has been to me a treasured privilege. It is my belief that such Englishmen will save British honour from shipwreck. At any rate if I had not known them, my despair at the prospect of western civilization would be unrelieved.

In the meanwhile the demon of barbarity has given up all pretence and has emerged with unconcealed fangs, ready to tear up humanity in an orgy of devastation. From one end of the world to the other the poisonous fumes of hatred darken the atmosphere. The spirit of violence which perhaps lay dormant in the psychology of the West, has at last roused itself and desecrates the spirit of Man.

The wheels of Fate will some day compel the English to give up their Indian empire. But what kind of India will they leave behind, what stark misery? When the stream of their centuries' administration runs dry at last, what a waste of mud and filth they will leave behind them! I had at one time believed that the springs of civilization would issue out of the heart of Europe. But today when I am about to quit the world that faith has gone bankrupt altogether.

As I look around I see the crumbling ruins of a proud civilization strewn like a vast heap of futility. And yet I shall not commit the grievous sin of losing faith in Man. I would rather look forward to the opening of a new chapter in his history after the cataclysm is over and the atmosphere rendered clean with the spirit of service and sacrifice. Perhaps that dawn will come from this horizon, from the East where the sun rises. A day will come when unvanquished Man will retrace his path of conquest, despite all barriers, to win back his lost human heritage.

Today we witness the perils which attend on the insolence of might; one day shall be borne out the full truth of what the sages have proclaimed:

'By unrighteousness man prospers, gains what appears desirable, conquers enemies, but perishes at the root.'

1941